陕西师范大学
SHAANXI NORMAL UNIVERSITY

U0634965

萧正洪◎主编

中国西部研究

第四辑

WESTERN
CHINA STUDIES
Vol.4

天津出版传媒集团
天津人民出版社

图书在版编目(CIP)数据

中国西部研究 = Western China Studies. 第四辑 /
萧正洪主编. -- 天津 : 天津人民出版社, 2024. 10.
ISBN 978-7-201-20632-5

Ⅰ. C53

中国国家版本馆CIP数据核字第2024AA7952号

Western China Studies Vol.4
中国西部研究 第四辑
ZHONGGUO XIBU YANJIU DI SI JI

出　　版　天津人民出版社
出 版 人　刘锦泉
地　　址　天津市和平区西康路35号康岳大厦
邮政编码　300051
邮购电话　(022)23332469
电子信箱　reader@tjrmcbs.com

责任编辑　李佩俊
封面设计　明轩文化 ·王　烨
　　　　　 TEL:23674746

印　　刷　天津海顺印业包装有限公司
经　　销　新华书店
开　　本　787毫米×1092毫米　1/16
印　　张　12
字　　数　360千字
版次印次　2024年10月第1版　　2024年10月第1次印刷
定　　价　98.00元

编辑委员会

Preface

Regarding the current development of China, the Western regions still face significant challenges. It is widely recognized that understanding and interpreting the origins and evolution of China's excellent traditional culture and explaining the historical inevitability of the formation and development of the Chinese national community necessitates considering Western China. It is impossible to accurately understand and interpret China as a whole without understanding and interpreting Western China. However, the development of Western China, whether in terms of its economic and social foundations or the types and nature of the difficulties it faces, differs from other regions, especially China's central and eastern regions. The development of education and security in Western China is currently of outstanding importance and urgency.

Therefore, in this issue, we have selected several articles on education development in Western China. These include studies on higher education based on survey data and discussions on issues such as social and educational rights. Furthermore, as we have consistently emphasized, the development of the culture of Western China is also an important part of Chinese wisdom. The new historical era provides us with opportunities and experiential materials for theoretical and practical innovation. Accordingly, this issue also publishes several papers related to national language capabilities and dissemination, the history of the ancient capital, and other topics. We hope that the rigorous analysis and in-depth discussions reflected in these papers promote academic progress in related fields and provide useful references for the international community to understand contemporary China.

Western China Studies, an English journal sponsored by Shaanxi Normal University, is committed to scientific and rational analysis and evaluation of the historical traditions, social foundations, resource endowments, environmental conditions, institutional constraints, and strategic choices of related issues based on the actual development of Western China. We strive to present well-supported arguments and detailed information. All discussions aim to address pressing local issues while maintaining a significant international perspective.

On the occasion of this new issue, we especially look forward to scholars at home and abroad contributing different opinions on relevant topics. We encourage discussion through the various columns of our journal, continually deepening our understanding of the experience of Western China, that is indispensable to Chinese wisdom.

Contents

Study on Endogenous Development of Western China Higher Education: Problem, Influencing Factors, and Improvement[*]

Li Ying, Hu Zhanshuo[**]

Abstract: This study examines the current state, challenges, and underlying causes of higher education development in western China, proposing an endogenous development path. When existing external support falls short of achieving high-quality development, higher education in western China should fully leverage internal motivation. This approach involves accumulating physical capital, enhancing human capital, and constructing disciplinary platforms to improve various aspects of quality and contribute to the sector's overall strength.

Keywords: western China; higher education development; endogenous development

1.Introduction

As a "late-developing" higher education nation, China's regional higher education systems differ in terms of their inception, pace, development efficiency, quality, strength, and vitality. The higher education system in western China is a crucial stronghold that the nation must maintain to protect its sovereignty and integrity. Due to its large ethnic minority population and abundant resources, China's western region, which accounts for more than half of its land area, has emerged as an important strategic area with distinct development characteristics. Under the guidance of national macro-strategy, higher education in western China has begun to progress in a positive direction: the practical implementation of counterpart support policies, provincial-ministerial co-construction, and revitalization efforts have made its development trajectory increasingly clear, and the overall trend is improving. In the new era, the national government recognizes that the dream of becoming a strong higher education nation will be difficult without modernizing

---

* Date Received: January 5, 2023; Date Revised: May 17, 2024.

** Li Ying(李莹), Ph.D., Postdoctoral Researcher of Faculty of Education, Shaanxi Normal University. Corresponding Author: Hu Zhanshuo(胡展硕), Ph.D., Postdoctoral Researcher of Faculty of Education, Shaanxi Normal University.

higher education in western China.

However, significant differences exist between higher education systems in western and eastern China due to the unequal distribution of regional resources. In the first round of China's "Double First-Class" assessment of colleges and universities, only 51 institutions from western China were shortlisted for "first-class disciplines", compared to a much larger proportion of institutions from eastern China. A study indicates that by 2020, eight provinces in western China—Guangxi, Yunnan, Guizhou, Qinghai, Xizang, Gansu, Xinjiang, and Ningxia—would still be unable to achieve higher education popularization, creating a "C-shaped lagging zone"[1] on China's map. Furthermore, the gross enrollment rate in higher education in the 12 western provinces lags behind the eastern provinces by an average of 13%.

National policy support has been insufficient to completely halt the quality development challenges facing higher education in western China. Higher education in western China must urgently overcome its constraints and become fully aware of the critical internal factors necessary to stimulate the endogenous momentum of high-quality development. Therefore, this study focuses on the endogenous development of higher education in western China, using statistical and literature research methods and policy analysis to examine the status of higher education among the population, funding, and faculty in western China's colleges and universities, as well as the state's policies on higher education in the region. It identifies the development problems facing higher education in western China and explores and analyzes the factors influencing its endogenous development. Based on these findings, the study proposes strategies for promoting the endogenous development of colleges and universities in western China.

2. The Problem of Western Higher Education

In the 1950s, the development and improvement of higher education in western China followed institutional adjustments. To some extent, the "inward migration" and "westward migration" from the eastern coast helped to close the gap between the development of colleges and universities in eastern and western China. However, following the reform and opening up, the focus of higher education policy shifted to the eastern region. This shift, coupled with the unequal distribution of regional resources and the imbalance of economic development between regions, constrained higher education in the west and thus widened the gap with higher education in the East.

---

[1] The data acquired from a speech by Prof. Li Shuohao of Lanzhou University at the Summit Forum on the Development and Reform of China's Higher Education in the New Era held by the Ministry of Education in 2020.

2.1 Insufficient investment in total funding for western higher education

In 1985, the development focus of central and local universities shifted; central universities aimed to impact world-class standards, while provincial universities worked to support local economic and social development.

Firstly, higher education in western China receives insufficient funding. The annual budgets of colleges and universities directly under the Ministry of Education in the eastern and western regions reveal two aspects.

First, the "rich-poor gap" is enormous among colleges and universities directly under the Ministry of Education. The 2020 and 2021 budgets for the top ten colleges and universities directly under the Ministry of Education reached 164.069 billion yuan and 177 billion yuan, respectively. In contrast, the total budgets of the 12 colleges and universities directly under the Ministry of Education in the western region amounted to only 65.38 billion yuan and 69.036 billion yuan over the same two years. In 2021, 13 colleges and universities directly under the Ministry of Education had budgets exceeding 10 billion yuan, a threefold increase over the previous year. In the western region, only two colleges and universities (Xi'an Jiaotong University and Sichuan University) had comparable budgets to similar institutions in the eastern region. Overall, Eastern China's colleges and universities have significantly larger funding budgets than those in western China.

Second, local colleges and universities in western China receive significantly less funding than those in Eastern China. Provincial budget data for local colleges and universities show that 98 institutions from 12 western provinces have a total budget of 84.08 billion yuan, roughly equivalent to 2.7 times the annual budget of Tsinghua University. The top ten colleges and universities are concentrated in Guangxi, Sichuan, and Chongqing.

Secondly, the funding sources for higher education in western China are poorly structured. Local governments categorize their financial inputs into production-constructive projects and social livelihood projects. The former prioritizes short-term economic growth, whereas the latter focuses on ensuring social stability over a longer period. Due to factors such as the local economic development cycle, economic development focus, local GDP ranking, public service levels, local officials' political cycles, and performance appraisals, and the tendency of graduates to seek employment in more developed eastern cities, local governments in western China often invest more in infrastructure construction while reducing financial input to higher education. This limits talent development in local universities and undermines western China's human capital levels.

In addition to state funding and tuition fees, local higher education funding sources are significant; however, private schools and other educational funding sources should also alleviate the pressure on local financial investment in higher education, but the current situation is not encouraging. Except for Sichuan, Chongqing, Yunnan, and Shaanxi, the proportion of private school organizers in 2020 was lower than the national average of 0.32%. In Xizang, Gansu, Qinghai, Ningxia, and Xinjiang, the proportion was even lower. For example, Gansu, Qinghai, and Ningxia accounted for only 0.26%.

Regarding donated income in the 12 provinces of western China, the proportion was lower than the international average of 0.26%. In terms of other education funding, only Chongqing and Guizhou had levels higher than the national average of 4.67%; the rest fell short of the national average.

Thirdly, the utilization of higher education funds in western China is inefficient. Local universities, as primary contributors to local economic and social development, are tasked with providing scientific research services to local governments, enterprises, institutions, and social organizations. They also participate in national projects to secure research funding or income from the transfer of scientific and technological services. Scientific research funding constitutes a significant portion of local universities' special funds, and universities are required to monitor and evaluate the utilization of this funding to ensure maximum benefits for contributors, project undertakings, and their respective units.

Local colleges and universities prioritize the quantity of scientific research projects and funds over the completion of scientific research projects for auditing purposes. Due to a shortage of professional project budgeting personnel, project leaders typically rely on estimated completion plans drafted by project budgeters. Errors in scientific research project costing lead to incomplete financial performance verification despite project completion. Additionally, the fluctuating number of scientific research projects at all levels makes it challenging to monitor the funding efficiency of such projects, resulting in the inefficient utilization of project funds.

Moreover, some individuals fail to complete scientific research tasks on time, resulting in the recovery of projects by the initiating unit. For instance, from 2018 to 2021, the National Leading Group Office of Educational Science Planning withdrew overdue projects from 2012 to 2016 and ordered the recovery of allocated funds. Over this five-year period, there were 179 overdue projects, with 38 in western colleges and universities, negatively impacting local college and university funding. This inefficiency adversely affects the rational operation and utilization efficiency of funds in local universities.

2.2 Weak level of discipline building in western higher education

The "Double First-Class" construction program aims to utilize top-tier disciplines to propel the advancement of top-tier universities. A university's technical core lies in teaching and scientific research, with majors and courses serving as its outputs. Disciplines play a crucial role in the continuous advancement of education and scientific research. "Discipline is not only a scientific concept and knowledge system but also an academic system and the construction of disciplines aims to cultivate competitive professionals with high -level expertise." The development of disciplines in western universities is foundational, and its caliber directly influences the overall standard of university education and the institution's reputation. To a significant extent, the establishment of disciplines in local universities shapes the trajectory of optimizing and upgrading the regional industrial structure, while the quality of discipline construction in western universities profoundly impacts the vitality of economic development.

Firstly, universities in the western region generally rank lower than those in the eastern region. According to the most recent ranking statistics,[①] the number of colleges and universities in the western region listed in the World University Rankings accounts for only 16.47% of the national total. Similarly, colleges and universities in the western region listed in China's domestic university rankings represent only 20.92% of the national total. According to the 2020 national university list, western China is home to 734 colleges and universities, comprising 26.79% of the nation's total. These figures indicate a significant disparity in the comprehensive ranking of the western region.

Secondly, the overall level of discipline construction in the western region is lower than that in the colleges and universities in the eastern region. The internal logic of discipline development is propelled by discipline-specific factors, while external factors such as social demand also influence it. The changing times impact both discipline development and social demand. Since the implementation of the national "Double First-Class" construction initiative, universities across all regions and at all levels have prioritized the development of their disciplines. Some institutions have opted to elevate their existing advantageous disciplines, while others have chosen to consolidate resources to focus on specific disciplines or a select few. Among the disciplines listed, 447 colleges and universities rank within the top 30%, constituting 15.15% of the total number of disciplines listed. However, only 107 colleges and universities rank within the top 10%,

---

[①] The data on colleges and universities acquired from the national list of colleges and universities published annually by the Ministry of Education.

accounting for 11.13% of the total number of disciplines listed.[①]

2.3 Insufficient pool of high—level talent for western higher education

If colleges and universities are to achieve significant success, the quality of their faculty, particularly the ratio of high-level talents to full-time teachers, is crucial. For colleges and universities in western regions, reasonable talent mobility becomes a realistic necessity in constructing "Double First-Class" institutions to stimulate teacher motivation. Teacher mobility not only enhances teachers' competitive spirit but also consistently improves the quality of education and teaching in these institutions. However, due to the "syphon effect" of the "Double First-Class" construction, talent flow in western colleges and universities is disorderly, leading to irrational loss of high-level talent.

On one hand, there has been a recent increase in the number of full-time teachers at provincial and local colleges and universities, with improvements and optimizations observed in academic structure, title levels, and other aspects. However, these improvements are contingent upon factors such as the welfare offered by local colleges and universities, their geographical location, subject platforms, and limitations on teacher mobility, including the recruitment of talent. High-level teachers continue to gravitate towards key colleges and universities, accelerating the development of the teaching force's structure. Simultaneously, teachers from local urban colleges and universities are increasingly relocating to colleges and universities in provincial capital cities. The development of provincial capital colleges and universities contributes to economic growth in the provincial capital, thereby widening the gap between the development of local cities. Over time, the "Matthew effect" has become evident in the inter-school mobility of high-level teachers in colleges and universities.

On the flip side, high-level talent possesses a distinct academic self-awareness, making it challenging to align their talent training and discipline team building with their unique academic insights. Colleges and universities wield a certain level of influence in the academic market, rendering them the "top choice" for talent. However, universities in developed countries emerge as the "preferred" destination for talent due to their unparalleled strength and competitiveness in the academic arena. With attractive incentives such as high salaries and prestigious positions, coupled with favorable geographic conditions that facilitate access to colleges and universities, developed area universities naturally draw talent away from western colleges and universities towards the

---

① The data obtained from the statistics released by the Soften Chinese Universities Ranking.

eastern region. Similarly, inland colleges and universities see a talent flow towards coastal areas, drawn by the superior scientific research environment, working conditions, and logistical support available there.

3. Influencing Factors of Higher Education Development in Western China

Western higher education must enhance the flow of endogenous development and elucidate how factors such as physical capital, disciplinary platforms, human capital, and other endogenous development-related elements contribute to this process.

3.1 Educational funding investment

In the knowledge economy, local higher education plays a crucial role in generating, disseminating, and innovating knowledge. The accumulation of knowledge contributes significantly to the advancement of both the economy and society. Consequently, higher education serves as a cornerstone for supporting regional economic development, leading to more robust and sustainable political, cultural, and social progress. As a pivotal sector within China's tertiary industry, higher education continues to enhance the quality of regional social development. Globally, higher education is recognized as a vital industry due to its extensive demand potential, substantial return on investment, and strategic significance in societal advancement. As regional economies continue to evolve, the importance of higher education in fostering talent development, technological innovation, and other critical areas will only grow. Higher education stands to benefit greatly from and make substantial contributions to the improvement and diversification of the regional economy's industrial structure.

On one hand, the level of regional economic development significantly influences the funding allocated to higher education. Economic growth serves as the bedrock of development, driving the demand for skilled individuals within society. The scale of regional higher education development largely hinges on the pace of economic growth, with market forces stimulating the expansion of higher education institutions in the region. Moreover, heightened economic development enhances individuals' cognitive abilities, fostering a greater desire for and pursuit of higher education opportunities, thus laying the groundwork for the growth of higher education operations within the region.

The development index of higher education encompasses various factors such as scale, quality, structure, and efficiency. Quantity expansion, indicative of higher education's scale growth, is the most immediate metric reflecting its development. Higher education serves as a conduit for knowledge dissemination and the cultivation of human capital crucial for societal progress, ultimately driving economic growth and elevating labor force remuneration. Consequently, the scale of higher education significantly influences its developmental trajectory.

In 2020, Sichuan, Shaanxi, and Chongqing boasted notably higher GDP levels compared to other western provinces, with Sichuan ranking sixth nationwide (following Guangdong, Jiangsu, Shandong, Zhejiang, and Henan). These three provinces also exhibit some of the most developed higher education systems in the western region. Notably, Sichuan and Chongqing play strategic roles in bolstering the "Chengdu-Chongqing Economic Circle" and the "Yangtze River Economic Belt," leveraging their combined economic strengths to enhance social services and advance regional higher education development. Conversely, regions like Xizang, Qinghai, and Ningxia, characterized by lower GDP levels, experience constraints in higher education growth due to their relatively underdeveloped local economies, resulting in suboptimal development.

While the central government extends economic aid and talent support to bolster higher education development in various regions through policies like counterpart assistance, the inherent challenges posed by the level of local economic development hinder the activation of regional higher education's endogenous potential, creating bottlenecks in its advancement and impending breakthroughs.

On the flip side, western higher education institutions are poised to play a pivotal role in driving economic and social progress. There exists a symbiotic relationship between higher education and robust regional economies. Higher education serves as a catalyst for regional economic advancement through the accumulation and dissemination of knowledge, thereby functioning as a key agent in knowledge production and distribution.

Drawing insights from advanced models of regional higher education development observed in developed nations worldwide, such as the "Wisconsin Idea" or the "Silicon Valley Type", as well as initiatives like Japan's "Plan for Reorganization of Higher Education", which advocates for the establishment of universities in metropolitan areas to ensure a more equitable distribution of regional higher education resources, it becomes evident that higher education makes an indispensable contribution to local economic and social progress.

Notably, Shaanxi and Sichuan emerge as prominent higher education hubs within the western region, boasting a substantial number of universities and high-quality educational institutions ranking among the top 12 nationwide. The higher education sectors in Sichuan and Shaanxi significantly contribute to the regional economy, accounting for 2.51% and 3.56%, respectively, underscoring the pivotal role of higher education in driving economic growth and social development within the region.

3.2 Academic platforms

Primarily, technology will underpin teaching methodologies, fostering innovative advancements in information technology education. Historically, the limited understanding of technological evolution and the prevailing local economic constraints have constrained western colleges and universities, compelling them to adhere to traditional teaching approaches such as oral dissemination and chalkboard presentations. Instructors predominantly rely on textbooks as instructional aids, with technology utilization confined to conventional slide presentations and classroom resources.

Secondly, in western China, the principles of science and technology intertwine with those of talent development. Western colleges and universities shoulder the responsibility of nurturing talents to serve local social and economic advancement. They prioritize students from minority and remote areas, differing significantly from those in the more developed eastern coastal regions, where awareness of technology is more prevalent. These students from the "old, young, border, and poor" regions are poised to become integral contributors to local economic and social rejuvenation.

Furthermore, science and technology will spearhead the modernization of talent development strategies in Western colleges and universities. Leveraging modern technology, particularly information technology, to optimize the distribution of educational resources and facilitate the sharing of teaching materials represents a novel approach to fostering equity in higher education. Given that education modernization is synonymous with human advancement, cultivating these individuals into innovative talents is imperative in the information age.

3.3 Human capital sustainability

First and foremost, human capital profoundly influences the advancement of Western higher education institutions. These institutions rely on human resources and must attract a diverse student body. According to statistics, the average number of individuals per 100,000 population with university, high school, junior high, and elementary school education in China stands at 15,467, 15,088, 34,507, and 24,767, respectively. In contrast, in western provinces, the corresponding averages are 14,450, 12,508, 29,663, and 29,260, respectively, with lower numbers of individuals with all levels of education per 100,000 than the national average (Table 1). Inner Mongolia, Shaanxi, Ningxia, Xinjiang, and Chongqing exceed the national average in the number of individuals with university degrees per 100,000 population (Table 1). In 2020, individuals aged 15 and above in the western region had an average of 9.26 years of education, slightly below the national average of 9.91 years (Table 3). Inner Mongolia, Shaanxi, and Xinjiang boast the highest

9

average years of education among individuals aged 15 and above in the western region (Table 4). The educational attainment level required for the development of western higher education institutions already lags behind the national average, and the significant phenomenon of "brain drain to the southeast" exacerbates the shortage of human capital in these institutions.

Table 1[①]   Number of people with each type of educational attainment per 100,000 population by region

Unit: People/100,000

Region	University	High School	Middle School	Primary School
National	15467	15088	34507	24767
Eastern Region	19904	16041	35227	20578
Middle Region	13670	15894	35934	24531
Western Region	14450	12508	29563	29260

Table 2   Number of people with various types of educational attainment per 100,000 population in the western provinces

Unit: People/100,000

Region	University	High School	Middle School	Primary School
Inner Mongolia	18688	14814	33861	23627
Guangxi	10806	12962	36388	27855
Chongqing	15412	15956	30582	29894
Sichuan	13267	13301	31443	31317
Guizhou	10952	9951	30464	31921
Yunnan	11601	10338	29241	35667
Xizang	11019	7051	15757	32108
Shaanxi	18397	15581	33979	21686
Gansu	14506	12937	27423	29808
Qinghai	14880	10568	24344	32725
Ningxia	17340	13432	29717	26111
Xinjiang	16536	13208	31559	28405

---

① The data in Tables 1 to 7 are obtained from the *China Education Statistical Yearbook* and the *China Education Expenditure Statistical Yearbook* of past years.

Table 3　Average years of schooling for the population aged 15 and over by region

Unit: Year

Region	2020	2010
National	9.91	9.08
Eastern Region	10.45	9.64
Middle Region	9.87	8.99
Western Region	9.26	8.27

Table 4　Average number of years of schooling for the population aged 15 and above in the western provinces

Unit: Year

Region	2020	2010
Inner Mongolia	10.08	9.22
Guangxi	9.54	8.76
Chongqing	9.80	8.75
Sichuan	9.24	8.35
Guizhou	8.75	7.65
Yunnan	8.82	7.76
Xizang	6.75	5.25
Shaanxi	10.26	9.36
Gansu	9.13	8.19
Qinghai	8.85	7.85
Ningxia	9.81	8.82
Xinjiang	10.11	9.27

Secondly, full-time teachers play a crucial role in the functioning and performance of western universities. In 2020 (Table 5), China's higher education teaching force comprised 1,833,000 full-time teachers, with 453,000 higher education teachers in the western region, accounting for only 24.7% of the total number of full-time teachers across all universities. Nationwide, 43.30% of teachers hold associate or higher titles, compared to 40.68% in the Western region. From 2016 to 2020 (Tables 6 and 7), the total number of full-time teachers increased by over 230,000 nationwide, while the number in Western colleges and universities increased by more than 60,000. During the same period, the proportion of teachers with associate senior titles or higher and teachers with doctoral degrees in the Western region increased by 1.02% and 4.99%, respectively, compared to national increases of 1.1% and 5.13%. Despite the yearly increase in the number and proportion of teachers with higher titles and doctoral degrees in Western colleges and universities, there remains a significant disparity between the overall national level and the growth of corresponding indicators in Eastern China's regions.

Table 5   National higher education teachers titles and qualifications by region (2020)

Region	Number of full-time teachers	Number of teachers with full senior title	Number of teachers with associate senior titles	Percentage of deputy senior title or above	Number of Ph.D. degree teachers	Percentage of teachers with doctoral degrees	Number of teachers with master's degrees	Percentage of teachers with master's degree
National	1832982	242951	550705	43.30%	513062	27.99%	681535	37.18%
Eastern Region	902785	142395	285614	47.41%	312770	34.65%	314958	34.89%
Middle Region	476233	47535	133850	38.09%	101667	21.35%	185572	38.97%
Western Region	452964	53021	131241	40.68%	98625	21.77%	181005	39.96%

Table 6   National higher education faculty titles and qualifications (2016-2020)

Year	Region	Number of full-time teachers	Number of teachers with full senior title	Number of teachers with associate senior titles	Percentage of deputy senior title or above	Number of Ph.D. degree teachers	Percentage of teachers with doctoral degrees	Number of teachers with master's degrees
2016		1601968	202154	473801	42.20%	366289	22.86%	581615	36.31%
2017		1633248	208917	490184	42.80%	397974	24.37%	596302	36.51%
2018		1672753	217874	504719	43.20%	433807	25.93%	612308	36.60%
2019		1740145	229157	525371	43.36%	475787	27.34%	639922	36.77%
2020		1832982	242951	550705	43.30%	513062	27.99%	681535	37.18%

Table 7   Teacher titles and qualifications in education in the Western Region (2016-2020)

Year	Region	Number of full-time teachers	Number of teachers with full senior title	Number of teachers with associate senior titles	Percentage of deputy senior title or above	Number of Ph.D. degree teachers	Percentage of teachers with doctoral degrees	Number of teachers with master's degrees
2016		392507	43283	112403	39.66%	65854	16.78%	152050	38.74%
2017		401010	44930	116374	40.22%	73023	18.21%	156726	39.08%
2018		412124	47015	119886	40.50%	80674	19.58%	162578	39.45%
2019		428370	49801	125203	40.85%	90904	21.22%	169659	39.61%
2020		452964	53021	131241	40.68%	98625	21.77%	181005	39.96%

4. Enhancement Strategies for the Development of Western Higher Education

Western higher education institutions should capitalize on the inherent advantages of national policy support, leveraging the region's geographical benefits to expedite the enhancement of educational funding. This can be achieved through mechanisms such as the "input-use" mechanism, the establishment of sustainable development mechanisms for education IT, and the implementation of talent attraction and training initiatives. These efforts will contribute to the high-quality growth of Western higher education.

4.1 Broadening funding channels and improving utilization

On one hand, there is an active promotion of the performance-based appropriation system in local universities within western provinces. However, to stabilize local higher education and its significance for local economic and social development, there must be an increase in annual investment, particularly in China's western region. Given the region's extensive and narrow national border, it is imperative to nurture outstanding higher education institutions in the west. To optimize the utilization of limited funds, aside from regular basic funding for local colleges and universities, a "merit-based funding" system has been implemented. This system establishes a competitive funding framework for similar local institutions across the province. Moreover, a "merit system" has been introduced to facilitate competition among similar colleges and universities within the province for grants. This system quantifies key factors influencing the endogenous development of western institutions, such as national talents, the construction of national experimental teaching platforms, the development of national key disciplines, and the establishment of national first-class undergraduate majors. It also refines the weighting of various factors affecting grants. Consequently, special grants can be allocated to local institutions with genuine development potential and strength, thereby fostering discipline advancement, stimulating institutional vitality, and promoting the sustainable growth of western colleges and universities. An exemplary model of this approach is the Perkins Act, implemented during the Obama administration in vocational education, which revamped the original competitive funding system, reinforcing its constructive impact. The benefits of this merit-based funding initiative undoubtedly highlight the elements of an enhanced vocational education system, fostering comprehensive reform across the vocational education spectrum in the United States.

On the contrary, local governments in western regions should actively coordinate the efficiency of regional higher education funding. Insufficient investment by local governments remains the primary cause of funding shortages in higher education in the west, and the inefficiency of existing funding further exacerbates this challenge. Firstly, local governments in the west must proactively adapt their governmental functions to address both current and long-term needs, encompassing all aspects of the province's local universities. Improving expenditure systems necessitates not only scrutinizing the haphazard expansion of local colleges and universities but also actively planning their future development and budget allocations. Secondly, western local governments must rectify instances of excessive or misplaced spending while also preventing underspending, taking proactive measures to allocate financial resources for higher education effectively. Ensuring the efficient use of funds in local universities entails adhering to the philosophy of "one piece of higher education in the entire province." This approach involves establishing comprehensive budgeting processes, monitoring and evaluating fund utilization, and applying funds judiciously. Thirdly, western local governments should enhance their project expenditure systems. Provincial governments must maintain a clear focus on higher education development within the province, allocating education funds to support strategic national disciplines, regional development disciplines, and foundational disciplines. Tailored expenditure project systems should be created to align with the unique characteristics of each discipline and institution. Moreover, enhancing the allocation of funds for teaching-oriented colleges and universities is crucial to bolstering teaching reform initiatives. Funds should be distributed based on discipline levels, institutional operational characteristics, and collaborative innovation efforts. Implementing a dynamic fund management system for colleges and universities will guide active participation in fundraising for institutional operations, thus mitigating homogeneous development across the province's higher education landscape.

4.2 Empowering talent cultivation through academic platforms

Western higher education institutions, serving as the primary hubs for talent development, play dual roles as catalysts for social change and drivers of economic growth in the region. The symbiotic relationship between colleges and universities and their surrounding areas significantly influences the caliber of talent nurtured by western higher education institutions, particularly in the realm of science and technology, thereby fostering new paradigms of higher education in the knowledge economy era. Nonetheless, the impact of technology on both educators and learners is nuanced. To swiftly acclimate to the evolving landscape of scientific education, students at western colleges and universities must cultivate a mindset that prioritizes learning through a technological lens. Although UNESCO introduced the concept of lifelong learning as early as the 1960s, its practical implementation remains uncertain due to inadequate learning resources available in many regions and countries, including various higher education institutions across China. Insufficient access to learning resources poses a significant challenge, underscoring the crucial role of scientific and technological platforms as vital conduits for delivering learning resources to learners.

On one hand, western colleges and universities ought to harness modern science and technology more effectively to extract and integrate resource data. This approach can address the deficiencies of existing educational and teaching methods, as well as management practices. By developing a new platform for knowledge acquisition based on software learning and leveraging the reach of new media networks, institutions can broaden students' learning resources and deepen their understanding of various subjects.

On the other hand, nurturing innovative talent is imperative to bolster the endogenous development capabilities of western higher education institutions and enhance their modernization. Given the urgent need for innovative talent in the economic and social development of the western region, colleges and universities must conduct a thorough assessment of their strengths and weaknesses. They should leverage information technology to establish conducive environments for talent development and devise innovative training systems. Embracing this critical historical responsibility, western higher education institutions should strive to enhance fundamental methodologies, align with national strategies, and provide vital intellectual support to the region. Concurrently, the advancement of information technology elevates the development status of higher education in the western region, contributing substantially to the realization of a robust higher education system nationally.

4.3 Attracting and cultivating local high−level talents

On one hand, there is a need to enhance the higher education evaluation system by integrating a high-level talent policy tailored to the specific characteristics of western China. Policy evaluation involves assessing the effectiveness of policy implementation. Evaluating the policy on high-level talents in western higher education institutions focuses on gauging its impact and effectiveness. Initially, the objective of attracting high-level talents to the western region was to retain and draw in such individuals. In recent years, local governments have implemented various talent attraction policies, complemented by territorial universities' initiatives. These policies have become more diverse and refined over time, addressing issues such as household registration, providing ample material support, resolving employment and educational concerns for talent families, and ensuring a conducive living environment. Therefore, governments and universities in the western regions must establish an evaluation system to assess policy effectiveness and promptly disclose the results. This transparency enables potential talents considering relocation to the west to understand the local policies pragmatically and gauge their implementation's efficacy openly.

To adopt a forward-thinking approach in talent evaluation, there is a necessity to enhance the assessment of high-level talents post-relocation. This entails creating an evaluation system that incorporates not only their qualifications and credentials but also their performance, abilities, potential, and contributions post-relocation.

On the other hand, the introduction of high-level talents should consider their efficiency and performance assessment upon arrival, providing a practical basis for optimizing talent introduction policies further. This approach ensures that talent recruitment strategies align with the region's needs and priorities, fostering sustainable development and growth.

On the contrary, educators in western universities need to actively cultivate their intrinsic drive for professional development. Teaching and research in universities should be viewed as interconnected components rather than separate endeavors, with each reinforcing the other. In western higher education institutions, especially local ones, the student body primarily consists of individuals from the region. However, due to historical limitations, some students may have been confined to textbook knowledge, hindering their ability to engage with new ideas and foster innovative thinking. As purveyors of fundamental knowledge, educators in western universities must foster a culture of knowledge innovation in their classrooms to stimulate students' creativity.

Enhancements in teachers' research endeavors not only serve to enrich their knowledge base but also facilitate the transmission of cutting-edge insights to their students. Faced with the unique and diverse student body of western universities, educators must tailor their approach to accommodate students' abilities. They should embrace the dual responsibility of teaching and research, understanding the crucial role of integrating both to cultivate talent for the region's development.

Teachers in western universities should continuously update their teaching and research methodologies, integrating the region's social and economic characteristics into their practices. By doing so, they can remain at the forefront of professional development in the western region, equipping students with the skills and knowledge necessary to contribute effectively to regional progress.

References

Gao, X.(高兴武). Public Policy Evaluation: System and Process(公共政策评估:体系与过程). *Chinese Public Administration*(中国行政管理), 2008(2): 58-62.

Li, Q. (黎庆兴) & Li, D.(李德显). Talent Mobility Dilemma of Colleges and

Universities Under the Perspective of Push and Pull Theory and Its Path(推拉理论视域下高校人才流动困境及其治理路径). *Jiangsu Higher Education*(江苏高教), 2021 (10): 46-52.

Liu, X.(刘献君). On the Construction of Disciplines in Colleges and Universities(论高校学科建设). *Journal of Higher Education*(高等教育研究), 2000(5):16-20.

Liu, X.(刘献君). *Thinking of the University and the Governance of the University*(大学之思与大学之治). Wuhan: Huazhong University of Science and Technology Press(武汉:华中科技大学出版社), 2000: 17-27.

Liu, Y. (刘彦伟) & Hu, X.(胡晓阳). Changes in the Structure of Funding Sources for General Higher Education in China in the Mid to Late 1990s(20世纪90年代中后期我国普通高等教育经费来源结构的变动). *Journal of Higher Education*(高等教育研究), 2005(6): 34-39.

Zhang, X.(张晓旭). Research on the Construction and Optimization of Faculty in Local Colleges and Universities(地方高校师资队伍建设与优化研究). *Journal of National Academy of Education Administration*(国家教育行政学院学报), 2014 (4): 38-42.

Zhou, G. (周光礼). Academic Breakthrough in the Construction of"Double First-class"—On the Integrated Construction of University Disciplines, Specialties and Courses ("双一流"建设中的学术突破——论大学学科、专业、课程一体化建设). *Educational Research*(教育研究), 2016, 37(5): 72-76.

The Historical Evolution and Balancing Adjustment of the Relationship between National Educational Rights and the Right to Education[*]

Zhan Zhongle, Liang Zhicheng[**]

Abstract: The relationship between national educational authority and the right to education is a foundational issue in educational jurisprudence. Article 46 of our country's Constitution stipulates that citizens have the right and the obligation to receive an education, underlying which is the legal relationship between the state's authority over education and the individual's right to education. This provision governs the legal system of education, and exploring its origins and institutional significance helps to observe the interplay between power and rights, as well as to regulate the exercise of national educational authority. At the inception of the current constitution, an education philosophy centered around labor was implemented, treating the citizen's access to education as both a right and an obligation. This included the obligations to receive compulsory education, pre-employment education, and education aimed at workers. This provided a regulatory foundation for the expansion of national educational authority. In 1985, the evolution of educational objectives towards talent cultivation led to a regulatory contraction of the obligation to receive education, and the exercise of national educational authority gradually became more standardized. On this basis, a fundamental framework for the balance and adjustment between power and rights can be constructed: the intervention of national educational authority in the right to education needs to meet the normative

* This article was originally published in *Journal of Shaanxi Normal University* (*Philosophy and Social Sciences Edition*), Vol.52, No.5. Original Title: 国家教育权与受教育权关系的历史嬗变及其平衡调适.

Translators: Li Yutong(李雨桐),Editor, Editorial Department of Journal of Shaanxi Normal University. Her research focuses on English Editing and Publishing of Academic Journal. Gong Nan(宫图), Postgraduate of Faculty of Education, Shaanxi Normal University. Her research focuses on Vocational Education. Qi Zhanyong(祁占勇), Professor of Faculty of Education, Shaanxi Normal University. His research focuses on Education Policy and Law.

** Zhan Zhongle(湛中乐), Ph.D. in Law, Professor of Law School, Peking University. Liang Zhicheng(梁芷澄), Ph.D. Candidate, Law School, Peking University.

requirements of the scope and intensity of the right to education, legal reservation, and substantive reasoning, thereby ensuring the internal balance of the educational regulatory system.

Keywords：Constitution; Education Law; state educational authority; right to education; obligation to education

The development of modern education is inseparable from state safeguards. State intervention in educational activities provides institutional and organizational guarantees for the realization of the right to education, such as the establishment of public schools offering educational opportunities. At the same time, there is an inherent tension between the compulsory demands of state educational authority on educational activities and the autonomous nature of the right to education. Specifically, the right to education means that citizens have the capacity to freely choose the content and form of education they receive. State intervention in educational activities can influence the autonomy of learners within educational activities. Practically speaking, controversies such as the state's implementation of the "Double Reduction Policy" to regulate educational activities (The State Council of the People's Republic of China, 2021), whether the state can include "sex education" in the compulsory education curriculum (Chen, 2022), and whether the state has the right to require schools in minority ethnic regions to use the common language for instruction(The National People's Congress of the People's Republic of China, 2021), all pertain to the relationship between the state's educational authority and the right to education. Therefore, the questions this article attempts to answer are: To what extent can the state limit the exercise of citizens' right to education? Where are the normative boundaries of state educational authority? How can the state ensure the realization of the autonomy of the right to education while regulating educational activities?

The legalization of education means that the state's regulation of educational activities through its educational authority must comply with normative requirements. Therefore, to answer the aforementioned questions, we must revisit Article 46 of our Constitution, which states, "Citizens of the People's Republic of China shall have the right and the obligation to receive education." (General Office of the Standing Committee of the National People's Congress, 2018) This provision is the foundational norm for understanding the state's educational authority and the right to education. On the one hand, the Constitution grants citizens the right to education, acknowledging their capacity to autonomously engage in educational activities; on the other hand, it imposes an obligation to education, providing justification for state intervention in educational activities and thus allowing for state-imposed limitations on the right to education. It can be said that Article 46 of the Constitution establishes the basic structure of the relationship between the state's educational authority and the right to education in our country. As for the extent to which the state can restrict the right to education, there is still no definitive interpretation.[①] The ambiguity of Article 46 of the Constitution presents obstacles to resolving current disputes.[②] To understand this clause, we need to return to the historical context of the "1982 Constitution," retrace the evolution of the relationship between power and rights underlying it, and uncover the logic behind its creation to define the normative boundaries of the state's educational authority. Moreover, "to insist on legislating by law, the most fundamental is to insist on legislating by the constitution, resolutely implementing the Constitution's provisions, principles, and spirit into legislation, and reflecting them in various laws and regulations." (Xi, 2022) Article 46 of the Constitution is a principled requirement of the legal system of education, and understanding the relationship between power and rights therein helps to enhance the systematization, integrity, and coordination of the legal system of education. Thus, this article attempts to start from the historical changes of Article 46 of the current Constitution, reveal the evolutionary process of the relationship between the state's educational authority and the right to education, and ultimately propose an interpretive scheme to balance and adjust the two, delineating the normative boundaries of the state's educational authority, ensuring the realization of the right to education, and resolving

---

① The applicability of the "right to education" and "obligation to receive education" as outlined in Article 46 of the current Constitution of our country remains a topic of debate. Some scholars argue that the right to education applies to all stages of education, whereas the obligation to receive education refers only to compulsory education. This viewpoint is supported by references such as Wu Peng's "Interpretation of the Rights and Obligations to Education in the Chinese Constitution," published in the *Journal of Law* in the March 2008 issue, and Wang Jun's "On the Intrinsic Rationality of the Constitutional Right and Obligation to Education," featured in the *Journal of Henan Normal University (Philosophy and Social Sciences Edition)* in the June 2005 issue. Conversely, other scholars believe that both the "right to education" and the "obligation to receive education" apply solely to the compulsory education stage, as discussed by Yuan Wenfeng in "Analysis of the Educational Stages Applicable to Article 46 of the Constitution," in the *Journal of East China University of Political Science and Law* in the 2015 second issue, and Mo Jihong in "The Constitutional Protection of the Right to Education," in the *Jurist* in the third issue of 2003. Some scholars argue that the obligation to receive education lacks direct effectiveness and cannot serve as the basis for regulating the relationship between citizens' rights and obligations to education. This perspective is explored by Chen Junsheng in "Re-examining the Citizen's Obligation to Receive Education Under the Constitution," in the *Journal of Sichuan Police College* in the fifth issue of 2016.

② Indeed, during the drafting of the current Constitution of our country, there were suggestions to simultaneously designate labor and education as both rights and obligations of citizens, which could lead to numerous ambiguities and issues in interpretation and implementation. However, the drafting committee of the Constitution did not adopt this suggestion, ultimately opting for a normative structure that aligns the right and obligation to education. This decision is detailed by Xu Chongde in *History of the Constitution of the People's Republic of China*, published by Fujian People's Publishing House in 2003, page 723.

practical disputes.

1. The Original Meaning of Article 46 of the Constitution

1.1 A labor-centered view of education

In the early years of the founding of the People's Republic of China, a labor-centered view of socialist education was implemented, with the goal of cultivating qualified socialist workers to serve the construction of socialism. This goal is derived from Marxism, which posits that to eliminate exploitation in a socialist society, its members must engage in labor. Therefore, an important purpose of socialist education is to cultivate the concepts of labor in the educated, master labor skills, and develop labor habits, thus becoming qualified workers who serve the socialist construction (Fang, 2002). In late December 1949, the Ministry of Education convened the first national education work conference, which put forward the policy that "education must serve production and construction, serve the workers and peasants, and open schools to workers and peasants." (He, 1998) In 1957, based on the summarization of the laws of socialist educational development, Mao Zedong proposed the guidelines for socialist education in "On the Correct Handling of Internal Contradictions among the People", "Our educational policy should enable those who are educated... to become culturally adept workers with socialist consciousness." (Mao, 1992) In 1958, the "Directives of the Central Committee of the Communist Party of China and the State Council on Education Work" (hereinafter referred to as "Instructions") stated, "The purpose of education is to cultivate culturally adept workers with socialist consciousness, which is uniform across the nation. Violating this uniformity would destroy the fundamental principles of socialist education." Moreover, the "Instructions" announced that in a socialist society, "The Party's educational work policy is to serve proletarian politics and combine education with productive labor." (Directives of the Central Committee of the Communist Party of China and the State Council on Education,1958) In other words, socialist education put forward two requirements: firstly, to cultivate "workers" to serve the construction of socialism and to serve proletarian politics, determined by the socialist nature of our state; secondly, to cultivate "qualified" workers to improve labor productivity. It can be said that in the traditional socialist educational concept, education is closely connected with the state. The purpose of education is to cultivate talents needed for various political tasks of the state, and the most important goal at the beginning of the founding of the New China was to build the socialist cause. Precisely because of this, all historical texts of our country's Constitution reflect the close connection between education and labor. The "Seventy-Fifth

Constitution" stipulated the right to labor and the right to education together in Section 2 of Article 27: "Citizens have the right to work and the right to education."①The "Seventy-Eighth Constitution" Article 13 stipulates: "Education must serve proletarian politics, combine with productive labor, and allow those who are educated to develop in moral, intellectual, and physical education, and become culturally adept workers with socialist consciousness."②

The education view centered on labor carries significant historical inertia, influencing the educational policies at the beginning of the reform and opening up. This is reflected in Article 46 of the current Constitution of our country: firstly, only the labor clause (Article 42 of the Constitution) and the education clause (Article 46 of the Constitution) adopt a "composite norm structure" in the Constitution, treating labor and education simultaneously as both rights and duties of citizens③. Secondly, Clause 4 of Article 42 (the labor clause) specifies the content of "education," namely, "The state shall provide necessary pre-employment training for its citizens."④ Thirdly, Peng Zhen, in explaining the "education clause" of our current Constitution, pointed out: "Receiving education is a right that citizens should enjoy and a duty they should fulfill, including the obligation for school-age children to receive primary education and the obligation for adult workers to receive appropriate forms of political, cultural, scientific, technical, and professional education, as well as the obligation for citizens before employment to receive labor employment training." (Peng, 1982) It can be seen that the scope of "education" in Article 46 of the current Constitution not only includes compulsory education and pre-

---

① The "Seventy-Fifth Constitution" refers to the "Draft Amendment to the Constitution of the People's Republic of China" passed at the First Session of the Fourth National People's Congress on January 17, 1975. Article 27, Clause 2 of this Constitution stipulates: "Citizens have the right to work and the right to education. Workers have the right to rest, and in old age, illness, or loss of working capacity, have the right to receive material assistance." See the Communist Party Members Network: https://news.12371. cn/2015/03/18 /ARTI1426666984513758. Shtml.

② The "Seventy-Eighth Constitution" refers to the "Draft Amendment to the Constitution of the People's Republic of China" passed at the First Session of the Fifth National People's Congress on March 5, 1978. Article 13 of this Constitution states: "The state vigorously develops the cause of education and improves the cultural and scientific level of the whole nation. Education must serve proletarian politics, be combined with productive labor, and ensure that those receiving education develop morally, intellectually, and physically, becoming cultured workers with socialist consciousness." See the Communist Part Network: https://news.12371.cn/2015/03/18/ARTI1426667115741768.shtml.

③ Lin Laifan generalizes the textual structure of "rights and obligations to education" and "rights and obligations to work" as a "composite norm structure." For the convenience of discussion, this article adopts this terminology. See Lin Laifan, "On Constitutional Obligations," in *Law Review of the National People's Congress* (2000 Edition 2), China Renmin University Press, 2000, page 160.

④ When interpreting the education clause of Article 46 of the Constitution, Zhang Youyu includes "vocational training" mentioned in Clause 4 of Article 42 within its scope, which also belongs to the "education" scope of Article 46 of the Constitution. See Zhang Youyu, *Constitutional Discussions (Volume II)*, Mass Publishing House, 1986 edition, page 394.

employment education (secondary and higher education) but also encompasses education for workers (vocational training). It can be said that the original meaning of Article 46 of the current Constitution inherits from the education view centered on labor. Thus, on one hand, it broadens the scope of "education," bringing most educational activities within the ambit of Article 46 of the Constitution, and on the other hand, it emphasizes the obligatory aspect of receiving education, indicating that citizens' pursuit of education is not only a right but also a duty.

1.2 Formation of social responsibility of the educated

The historical examination of educational objectives solidifies the logical connection between "education-labor," while the establishment of the "labor-state" logical chain serves as the logical foundation for forming the social responsibility of the educated. When the "1982 Constitution" was promulgated, the state was still under a highly centralized economic system, with public ownership dominating. State-owned enterprises represented the interests of the state. In this context, the "1982 Constitution" had two reasons for designating labor as a constitutional duty: one is that the interests of the state and laborers are aligned. Zhang Youyu points out, "Laborers are the masters of the state; labor is for socialist production, for the production of all people including laborers, hence it is both a right and a duty." (Zhang, 1986) However, in capitalist countries, capitalists may choose to hire or not hire laborers, and citizens do not have a legal duty to work. The second reason is that socialist states do not allow for unearned income. The "1954 Constitution" did not stipulate "labor duty" because, at the time, the non-working exploiting class was still allowed to exist (Zhang, 1986), but this situation had changed with the completion of the Three Great Remold heralded China. The completion of the Three Great Remold heralded China signified that our country had truly become a socialist state, not allowing for unearned income, and labor became a duty that citizens must fulfill (Xu, 2003).

Therefore, Article 42 of the current Constitution not only designates "labor" as a citizen's duty but also as the "an honorable duty for every citizens who is able to work" (General Office of the Standing Committee of the National People's Congress, 2018). The socialist constitutional view that regards labor as a duty has had a profound impact on Chinese constitutional norms (Yan, 2021). The "labor-state" logical chain becomes the port for citizens' "responsibility" towards the state, society, and other citizens, and on the other side of this port could be many constitutional norms related to labor, with the education clause (Article 46 of the Constitution) being one of them. In other words, through the transmission of the "education-labor-state" logical chain, "responsibility" connects the interests of the educated with those of the state, meaning that education is for cultivating workers, and the interests of socialist state workers are aligned with the interests of the state, laboring to ensure the people are the masters of their own affairs.[①] Liu Shaoqi pointed out, "In our country, the rights and duties of the people are completely consistent. No one is to only fulfill duties without having rights; nor can anyone only enjoy rights without fulfilling duties."(Liu, 1954) In other words, the people become the true masters of the state through labor, and receiving education is an essential step for citizens to become qualified workers, making education naturally also a citizen's duty. Based on this, some scholars argue that citizens' right to education is both a right and a duty, meaning the right to education is an inalienable right (Zhao, 1991). After the establishment of New China, our country began to emulate the Soviet Union in implementing a highly centralized planned education system, with everything from educational objectives to curriculum design and teaching content uniformly set and arranged by the state.

1.3 The State's educational authority and the right to education in the current Constitution

The formation of the "education-labor-state" logical chain signifies the viewpoint of the consistency between the state's interests and the laborers' interests, which extends to the consistency between the state's interests and the interests of the educated. This becomes the logical starting point for the educational obligations stipulated in Article 46 of the Current Constitution, providing a normative basis for the state's educational authority's involvement in educational activities. The state's educational authority represents the state's control over education, meaning the state has the right to shape qualified citizens according to educational objectives (Qin, 1998). Specifically, the state intervenes in the implementation, development, organization, leadership, and management of education by defining education as a civic duty.

Under the guidance of education goals centered on labor, constitution drafters expanded the scope of educational obligations to compulsory education, pre-employment education, and education for workers (Peng, 1982). Peng Zhen's classification of education can be considered as the original meaning of the Constitution. In legislative practice, the education concept centered on labor also has a significant impact. Although the Education Law was not enacted until 1995, its drafting began in 1985 and was thus

---

① The premise of citizens' obligations is the unity of national interests and the people's interests. Liu Shaoqi pointed out, "Since our country is a people's country, where the interests of the state and the people are completely aligned, the people naturally regard their duties to the state as their bounden duty." This is referenced in Liu Shaoqi's "Report on the Draft Constitution of the People's Republic of China," published on the front page of *People's Daily* on September 16, 1954.

influenced by the labor-centered education concept. For example, the Education Law defines its scope of application from the perspective of "broad education." Article 2 of the Education Law (Draft) stipulates, "The present Law shall be applicable to basic education, higher education, vocational education and adult education at all levels within the territory of the People's Republic of China." Article 9 of the Education Law provides that, "Citizens of the People's Republic of China shall have the right and duty to be educated." (Zhu, 1995) Similar to Article 46 of the Constitution, there is no distinction between the right to education and the obligation to education, and the educational obligation is not limited to the compulsory education stage. For instance, Article 41, Clause 1 of the Education Law, stipulates, "Employees shall have the right and duty to receive vocational training and continuous education according to law." (Standing Committee of the National People's Congress, 1996) Furthermore, at the local regulatory level, Article 11 of the "Regulations on Employee Education in Tianjin", adopted by the Standing Committee of the Tianjin Municipal People's Congress in 1990 states, "Employees have the right and obligation to participate in political, cultural, technical and business studies in accordance with the needs of their work." (People's Congress of Tianjin, 1991) This is because "education-labor-state" could be viewed as a dualistic structure of public law of "individual-state" ultimately. When the "1982 Constitution" was promulgated, state-owned enterprises occupied a dominant position, often seen as an extension of the government, and could be considered the "state" end of the "individual-state" structure. It can be said that the broad applicability of "educational obligations" means that the state's educational authority can regulate educational activities from multiple areas.

In summary, the educational clause in our country's current Constitution was deeply influenced by the education concept centered on labor at its drafting. It expanded the scope of educational obligations to compulsory education, pre-employment education, and education for workers, thereby allowing the state's educational authority to influence educational activities. The educational obligations formed by citizens relative to the state become the normative basis for the state's educational authority to determine the content and form of education.

2. Historical Evolution of Article 46 of the Constitution

2.1 Education reform aiming at talent cultivation

The evolution of the goals of education was first hinted at in the "Decision of the Central Committee of the Communist Party of China on the Reform of the Educational

System" (hereinafter referred to as the "Decision") on May 27, 1985. Unlike the labor-centered education view, the "Decision" posited that "the fundamental purpose of the reform of the education system is to improve the quality of the nation, produce more talents, and produce good talents." (People's Daily, 1982) The former emphasizes that education should adapt to the needs of the state's political tasks, cultivating qualified socialist workers in a collectivist education perspective. The latter emphasizes the realization of individual capabilities and values, highlighting the autonomous value of individuals in education.

The change in educational objectives was a practical need of economic system reform. The highly planned education system could not meet the needs of economic system reform. One of the most important reforms in the "Decision" was granting autonomy to universities, especially changing the method of "state assignment of all graduates" (People's Daily, 1982). This reform was facilitated by a written report submitted by Hu Qili to the Central Committee's Document Drafting Leading Group, entitled "Some Suggestions on the Reform of the Educational System" on December 22, 1984. The report states, "Under the guidance of the Party and the state's major policies, gradually change the method where higher education institutions recruit all students according to state plans, and graduates are all allocated by the state, enhancing the dynamism and vitality of universities to actively adapt to social development." (Hu, 2008) This suggestion was made because the biggest drawback of the education system at the time was "the rigid pattern formed under the long-term planned economy system... whether universities were managed by departments, provinces, or the state, they all followed the unified recruitment, distribution, and allocation system. As a result, schools relied on government funding, and students relied on schools, with students feeling secure once they entered university, as if entering a vault." (Hu, 2008) In summary, the labor-centered education view held that the purpose of education was to cultivate qualified workers to serve socialist construction. This concept originated from a highly centralized planned economy system where the state was responsible for people's employment to ensure their livelihood (Zhang, 1986). In turn, people had the obligation to participate in labor to build socialism and become qualified workers through education, meaning the state had to adopt a unified recruitment, distribution, and allocation model. However, the "Decision of the Central Committee of the Communist Party of China on the Reform of the Economic System" on October 20, 1984, proposed reforming the planned economy system and developing a commodity economy. The employment of graduates after education was no longer decided by the state but by the market. The traditional labor-centered education view could not meet the needs of societal development, hence the educational goal shifted to talent cultivation. The difference between the two lies in that the former has a distinct collectivist color; the latter focuses more on improving the individual quality of the educated, emphasizing individual autonomy.

The development of education undertaking in China is affected by the reform of the planned economic system, the development of the commodity economy and the State's encouragement of the private economy. Since 1988, when the "Amendment to the Constitution" which modified the provisions of the economic system, a series of legal norms have been introduced, where significant changes was made to "education", particularly in "pre-employment education" and "education for laborers". The change began with the Company Law of 1993, which, unlike many normative documents previously mentioned that viewed education for workers as both a right and an obligation, Article 15, Clause 2 of the 1993 Company Law only stipulates: "Companies shall adopt various forms to strengthen vocational education and job training for their employees to improve their quality" (Standing Committee of the National People's Congress, 1994), without defining the educational obligation of workers. Article 3 of the Labor Law of 1994 states: "Workers have the right to... receive vocational skills training..." (Standing Committee of the National People's Congress, 1995), viewing education for workers as a right rather than an obligation. The logic behind the change in legal norms is twofold: on one hand, the development of the private economy has led to a change in the main body of labor services. From the traditional public law perspective of the Constitution, state-owned or collective enterprises could still be seen as extensions of the government, but private enterprises, individual businesses, and other non-public-owned enterprises belong to the private economy, making it difficult for the educational obligations and labor obligations in the Constitution to regulate workers in non-public-owned enterprises. Therefore, neither the "Company Law nor the Labor Law" regards pre-employment education and education for workers as a civic duty. On the other hand, the development of the private economy means that "labor" no longer occurs entirely within state-owned or collective enterprises; labor is no longer for the production of all people, including workers, and cannot be seen as a constitutional obligation.

Does the same logic apply to nationally or collectively owned enterprises? The answer is negative. Laborers in such enterprises still have the attribute of serving socialism, but this does not mean that the constitutional obligation of education can be applied continually. There are two reasons for this: one is the need for the principle of equality. If the constitutional obligation of education is only applied to laborers in certain types of enterprises, this would mean that enterprises of different natures are treated differently, namely the imposition of obligations and derogation of rights on laborers in publicly owned enterprises as compared with others. This practice is against the principle of equality in Article 33 of the Constitution (Wang, 2023). The second reason is that the operational autonomy of state-owned enterprises is required to be safeguarded under the background of the market economy reform, therefore it is difficult for public authorities to directly require employees of state-owned enterprises to fulfill their educational duties (Zhou, 2020). State-owned enterprises can no longer be seen as extensions of the government.

2.2 The contraction of the State's scope in regulating educational activities

The extent of the "educational obligation" stipulated in Article 46 of the Constitution is crucial for determining the scope of state intervention in educational activities. Academia has previously offered three different interpretations: "compulsory education stage,"(Yuan, 2015) "compulsory and higher education stages," (Jia & Yu, 2021) and "all types of education." (Zhang, 2016) However, these perspectives have not considered the historical evolution of the state's educational authority. It can be said that the transformation of educational objectives has influenced the interpretation of Article 46 of the Constitution, particularly in terms of understanding its educational obligations, which can no longer adhere to its original meaning.

Firstly, "compulsory education" falls within the scope of educational obligations. Compulsory education is a practical requirement of the national goal of "eliminating illiteracy" stated in Clause 3 of Article 19 of the current Constitution (General Office of the Standing Committee of the National People's Congress, 2018). At the beginning of the reform and opening up, rural areas were gradually implementing the household responsibility system, and many parents were reluctant to spend money on their children's education, leading to a surge in illiteracy. In response, Dong Biwu suggested including in Article 45 of the Constitution: "The People's Republic of China implements compulsory education for its citizens, generally reaching the completion of primary education" (Xu, 2003). This suggestion hit the nail on the head, distinguishing the scope of the right to education and the obligation to education, and clarifying the scope of the latter.[1] The final text of the Constitution did not adopt this suggestion but integrated the

---

[1] Many constitutions around the world, when stipulating both the right and the obligation to receive education, often clarify the normative meaning of "education" to avoid misunderstandings. For example, Article 26 of the "Japanese Constitution of 1947" states: "All people, in accordance with the law, have the equal right to receive an education compatible with their ability; all people, in accordance with the law, have the obligation to have their children receive ordinary education." This provision of the Japanese Constitution differentiates the understanding of "education" between the right and obligation to education: the "education" in the right to education refers to education in a general sense, while the education in the obligation to education is limited to "ordinary education," meaning national education. This is discussed in Nobuyoshi Ashibe's *The Constitution*, revised by Kazuyuki Takahashi, translated by Lin Laifan, Ling Weici, and Long Xuanli, published by Tsinghua University Press in 2018, page 219.

obligation to education into the concept of "broad education" (compulsory education, pre-employment education, and education for workers). Moreover, compulsory education helps improve the quality of the nationals and raise the moral and cultural level of the entire population. Compulsory education is "mandatory" (Xu, 2003), "Implementing compulsory education is both a duty of the state towards the people and a duty of parents towards the state and society" (Li, 1986). Overall, the corresponding relationship between "the educated-state" formed around compulsory education has not substantially changed, and citizens still bear the constitutional obligation to receive compulsory education. However, the change in the purpose of education means that compulsory education begins to focus on fostering the autonomous development of the educated.[①] On one hand, the state can directly adjust the curriculum, school settings, and methods of education based on the realization of national goals; on the other hand, the state has the obligation to provide teaching facilities to ensure the fulfillment of the obligation to education (Xie, 2014).

Secondly, "pre-employment education" is a right of citizens, not an obligation. Pre-employment education, including vocational and higher education, falls within the protection scope of the right to education under Article 46 of the Constitution. However, in the context of economic system reform, this segment of education is left to the autonomous decision of the educated, rather than being a compulsory duty imposed by the state on citizens. This change is recognized by law: Article 9 of the Higher Education Law stipulates, "Citizens have the right to receive higher education according to the law." (Standing Committee of the National People's Congress,1999) Article 5 of the Vocational Education Law states, "Citizens have the right to receive vocational education according to the law." (Standing Committee of the National People's Congress,1997) Both laws do not stipulate an educational obligation. The 2022 revision of the Vocational Education Law, by clarifying the equal status of vocational and general education and perfecting the vocational education guarantee system and measures, further strengthens the state's responsibility from the perspective of realizing the right to education.

Thirdly, "education for workers" is regarded as a right of citizens, not an obligation. The development of the market economy allows enterprises to autonomously decide how to conduct labor skills training for workers, which falls under the business freedom of enterprises. The laws concerning this part are not entirely uniform. On one hand, both the

---

① This change is reflected in the Compulsory Education Law passed on April 12, 1986, Article 3 of which stipulats, "Compulsory education must implement the national education guidelines, carry out quality education, improve the quality of education, and enable children and adolescents of the appropriate age to develop comprehensively in terms of ethics, intelligence, physical fitness, etc." See the PKU law database, http://www.pkulaw. com/PopUp/FulltextTips? status=iperror& logid = e364f73017ac4519a5506a8d2d33cd67& ip = 111.199.87.170.

Vocational Education Law and the Labor Law stipulate that education for workers is a right, not an obligation. For example, Article 3 of the Labor Law stipulates: "Workers have the right to... receive vocational skills training..." (Standing Committee of the National People's Congress, 1995) Additionally, many local regulations have abolished the provision of educational obligations for workers. For example, the "Regulations on Employee Education in Tianjin" of 1990 stipulated the "right and obligation to learn" for workers (People's Congress of Tianjin, 1991), which has been replaced by the "Tianjin Regulations on Vocational Education" implemented in 2007, with the new regulation eliminating the obligation to learn. On the other hand, the basic law in the field of education, the Education Law, considers that employees have both the right and obligation to receive education, i.e., Article 41 of the Education Law stipulates, "Employees have the right and obligation to receive vocational training and continuing education according to the law." (Standing Committee of the National People's Congress, 1996) Future legislative revisions are needed to unify these legal provisions.

2.3 The weakening intensity of State Regulation in educational activities

Guided by the modern educational concept of cultivating talents, the right to education has more autonomous space, and the intensity of the state's educational authority's intervention in educational activities has indeed weakened. On one hand, the educational goal is to cultivate talents and promote the comprehensive development of individuals. The state begins to respect the individual's autonomy in education. The role of the state in educational activities has shifted from a provider to a facilitator, with the state's function being to provide a framework that can achieve educational objectives. Within the educational framework established by the state, the educated have the right to engage in educational activities autonomously, realizing personal value. This value concept is gradually converging with other countries worldwide. Since the inception of the state, the state's educational authority has begun to include content of provision, and correspondingly, the right to education has begun to be seen as the right of citizens to demand from the state the necessary cultural education conditions and equal education plans from an economic perspective, i. e., the right to education is seen as the right to survival, aiming at the full development of individuals. On this basis, the "right to education" begins to rise from a legal right to a constitutional right. Additionally, from an external environment perspective, China's accession to the World Trade Organization (WTO) in 2001 also impacted our country's traditional educational concept. The WTO's principles of fairness, openness, and justice require our higher education to establish concepts of fairness, openness, and justice (Xue, 2001). The diversification of educational providers makes education, as a public service, more selective, highlighting individual autonomy.

The transformation of educational objectives has redefined the role of the state in educational activities. This also poses a challenge to our country's transition from comprehensive control by the state's educational authority to limited regulation. That is, the boundaries of the state's educational authority are not unrestrained; the exercise of the state's educational authority needs to aim at realizing the right to education. The legalization of educational activities is an important way to address this challenge, with the core goal being to balance the state's educational authority with citizens' right to education.

3. Balancing and Adjusting the State's Educational Authority and the Right to Education

Since the establishment of New China, changes in the "right to education-state's educational authority" relationship indicate: Although Article 46 of the Constitution, influenced by the labor-centered view of education, considers education simultaneously as a right and an obligation for citizens, the broad applicability of the educational obligation provided a rationale for the state's comprehensive regulation of educational activities. However, educational system reform demands the standardization of the state's educational authority, i.e., the state's educational authority has regulatory boundaries to protect the autonomous realization of citizens' right to education. This implies a balance between the "right to education-state's educational authority." After the evolution of the "composite norm structure" of Article 46 of the Constitution, it is still possible to construct a normative structure balancing power and rights based on this foundation. However, this balance is no longer merely between the rights and obligations of citizens under a single subject but between the state's power and citizens' rights. Specifically, the intervention of the state's educational authority in the right to education needs to meet the following three requirements.

3.1 Scope and intensity of the intervention of the State's power to education: the distinction between compulsory and non-compulsory education

The exercise of the state's educational authority differs in intensity between compulsory and non-compulsory education stages, with deeper intervention in compulsory education. This is because receiving compulsory education is viewed as a constitutional obligation, while receiving education at other stages is a legal obligation (Lin, 2000). The difference in obligation types means the state's regulatory intensity for compulsory education is higher compared to other educational stages. For example, during compulsory education, the state has the right to decide the curriculum and teaching content of compulsory education to better implement the state's educational guidelines. Schools, students, and teachers have no autonomy in curriculum selection. If school-aged children or their guardians refuse compulsory education, the government can subject them to criticism, education, and order corrective action within a specified period.[1] Although schools have the freedom to conduct teaching activities independently, they cannot unilaterally change the teaching content.[2] In contrast, the high school stage of education grants the educated the freedom to choose. On one hand, students can choose to advance to general high schools or enter vocational high schools for vocational education. On the other hand, there is some flexibility in learning content. For instance, the "Implementation Opinions of the State Council on Deepening the Reform on the Examination and Enrollment System" (Guofa [2014] No. 35) in 2014, by reforming the enrollment examination system, allows students to choose their subjects of study and examination based on their strengths, ensuring educational diversity (State Council, 2014). Therefore, based on the realization of educational objectives, the state can decide on curriculum and teaching content during the compulsory education stage, such as the implementation of the "Double Reduction Policy," the establishment of "sex education" courses, and promoting the teaching of the Chinese common language in schools in minority ethnic regions, all within the scope and intensity of intervention by the state's educational authority.

3.2 Formal elements of the exercise of the State's power to education: legal reservations

The obligation to education constitutes a restriction on fundamental rights. Notably, the educational obligation, unlike other types of obligations in the Constitution such as tax and military service duties, belongs to a new type of obligation in modern constitutions

---

[1] Article 58 of the Compulsory Education Law of the People's Republic of China (amended in 2018) stipulates: "If the parents or other legal guardians of children and adolescents of appropriate age fail to enroll them in school to receive compulsory education without justifiable reasons, in accordance with this law, the local township people's government or the county-level people's government educational administrative department shall provide criticism and education, and order corrections within a specified time limit." See the PKU law database, https://www.pkulaw.com/chl/c8e1992c1d175ed2bdfb.html? keyword=义务教育法& way = listView.

[2] Article 35, Clause 2 of the Compulsory Education Law of the People's Republic of China (amended in 2018) specifies: "Schools and teachers shall carry out educational and teaching activities in accordance with the determined educational content and curriculum settings, ensuring the achievement of the basic quality requirements stipulated by the state." See the PKU law database, https://www.pkulaw.com/chl/c8e1992c1d175ed2bdfb.html? keyword=义务教育法& way = listView.

(Jiang, 2018). Imposing duties on citizens means the state's power limits citizens' freedom. The Constitution's establishment of the educational obligation effectively grants the state the power to regulate educational activities. The state's exercise of this power, for public purposes, effectively restricts the realization of citizens' rights. Therefore, the exercise of state educational authority needs to meet certain legal requirements to ensure the regulated exercise of power. "Legal reservation" is a formal requirement for the state power to limit citizens' rights (Zhang, 2008). First, Article 51 of the Constitution stipulates the "general restriction" clause, meaning all fundamental rights are restrictable, and there are no unrestricted fundamental rights. Basic rights, including the right to education, can be limited by the rights and interests of others, societal interests, and public interests (Li, 2020). For example, the state's educational authority can limit citizens' rights based on the public goal of "socialist spiritual civilization construction" under Article 24 of the Constitution (Chen, 2021). Similarly, the German Federal Constitutional Court has dealt with similar disputes where "state educational supervisory rights" clashed with "religious freedom," acknowledging that the freedom of belief is "diluted" by the state's independent educational supervisory rights, and considering state intervention in freedom of belief as not violating the provisions of the German Basic Law (Zhang, 2018).

Secondly, the restriction of fundamental rights itself should also be limited, at least needing to meet the formal requirements of the law (Zhao, 2011). The reason is that the Legislative Law Articles 11-12 have already established the legal reservation requirements for rights restrictions. Amendments to the Legislation Law in 2015 further established the basic principle that "Local governmental rules may not lay down any regulation impairing the rights of, or increasing the duties of citizens without a basis in law, administrative regulations or local provisions."[1] It can be said that the principle of legal reservation has been preliminarily established in our country's legislative system. Specifically, we can distinguish the activities of the state's educational authority into intervention and provision aspects: the intervention aspect refers to the regulation of educational activities by the state's educational authority should be strictly constrained by the principle of legal

---

[1] The revision of the Legislation Law in 2015 added a provision in Article 80: "The matters specified by departmental regulations should belong to the implementation of laws or administrative regulations, decisions, orders of the State Council. Without the basis of law or administrative regulations, decisions, orders of the State Council, departmental regulations may not set norms that impair the rights of citizens, legal persons, and other organizations or increase their obligations, nor may they increase the powers of the department or reduce its statutory duties." Article 82 was also amended to state: "Without the basis of laws, administrative regulations, or local regulations, local government regulations may not set norms that impair the rights of citizens, legal persons, and other organizations or increase their obligations." These amendments were passed at the third session of the 12th National People's Congress on March 15, 2015. See the NPC Network, http://www.npc.gov.cn /zgrdw/npc/xinwen/2015-03/18/content_1930129. html.

reservation; the provision aspect is different, its main content is the state taking positive measures to realize the right to education. It is not a measure of "impairing rights" as mentioned in the Legislative Law, therefore not constrained by the principle of legal reservation. Currently, the state's educational authority's restrictions on the right to education are often specified in lower-level normative documents such as policy files, like the implementation of the "Double Reduction Policy". These measures await further elevation to the legal level after being tested in practice. The requirement of legal reservation provides a democratic legitimacy basis for the exercise of state educational authority on one hand, and on the other hand, it can stabilize market expectations through the legal certainty of policy solidification.

3.3 Substantive requirements for State educational authority to restrict the right to education: cultivating the comprehensive development of students

The "educational obligation" restricts basic rights, besides meeting the formal requirements of legal reservation, it also needs to satisfy substantive requirements, namely, the constitutional spirit of Article 46, Clause 2 of the Constitution. Article 46, Clause 2 of the Constitution stipulates the normative goal of compulsory education, namely, "The state cultivates youth, teenagers, and children to develop comprehensively in morality, intelligence, physique, etc." (General Office of the Standing Committee of the National People's Congress, 2018) This goal values the individuality and autonomy of the educated, aligning with the needs of educational system reform. And the constitutional spirit itself is a major factor limiting the restriction of fundamental rights. Article 36 of the "Regulations on the Record-Filing and Review of Normative Documents and Judicial Interpretations" requires that normative documents must not violate the constitutional spirit (Regulations Filing and Review Office of the Legislative Affairs Commission of the Standing Committee of the National People's Congress, 2020). With the evolution of the normative goal of the educational clause from cultivating workers to cultivating talents, "cultivating the comprehensive development of students" becomes a substantive requirement for restricting basic rights. This extraction of substantive requirements is more specific compared to public interest, providing clearer guidance for norm implementation, overcoming the conceptual flaw of the too uncertain concept of public interest. For example, in the practical dispute of whether "sex education courses can be introduced to the classroom," the state's setting of educational courses will limit the autonomous choice aspect of the right to education. The Ministry of Education responded positively to the proposal by CPPCC member Ma Xiuzhen on "Proposal on Strengthening Sexual and Reproductive Health Education for China's Secondary School Student

Population," in the future, efforts will be further increased to urge all regions to implement school AIDS prevention education and sexual health education... to improve the quality of health education teaching and students' health literacy" (Ministry of Education of the People's Republic of China, 2021). From the Ministry of Education's response, it can be seen that introducing "sex education" into the classroom aims to improve students' health literacy, meeting the substantive requirements for restricting basic rights. Here, the state's educational authority is not only a state power but also a constitutional responsibility the state undertakes to realize the right to education (Wen, 2008). Additionally, while achieving national goals, the means adopted by the state must be "proportional", meaning the state's adjustment of educational activities must strictly serve the realization of educational objectives, subject to the "principle of proportionality" review (Regulations Filing and Review Office of the Legislative Affairs Commission of the Standing Committee of the National People's Congress, 2020).

In summary, the "composite norm structure" is considered the normative embodiment of the "consistency of rights and duties" socialist constitutional theory. However, this normative structure was born in the era of the planned economy of the 1982 Constitution, emphasizing the balance of citizens' rights and duties. With the development of the private economy and other non-public sectors, the education view centered on labor quietly transformed, making talent cultivation the new educational goal. In this intense transformation process, educational activities began to follow the path of the rule of law. The state's intervention in the right to education is not unrestrained; it needs to meet the above normative requirements, facilitating the balance of the "state's educational authority-right to education" relationship.

4. Conclusion

The "right to education-state's educational authority" is the fundamental relationship hidden behind the "composite norm structure" of Article 46 of the current Constitution of our country. Its historical evolution reveals the history of changes in the legal relationship of education in our country. The original meaning of the "composite norm structure" was limited to balancing the rights and duties of citizens' education. Compulsory education, pre-employment education, and education for workers were all seen as within the scope of the educational obligations under Article 46 of the Constitution. However, in the second year after the promulgation of the current Constitution, amidst the wave of economic system reform, educational concepts were updated, and educational system reform was put on the agenda. Cultivating talents and improving individual quality became the goals of our country's educational endeavors. Citizens' reception of pre-employment education and education for workers were no longer viewed as social responsibilities and constitutional duties. The "right to education-state's educational authority" began to move towards balance gradually. On this basis, we reinterpret the "composite norm structure" of Article 46 of the Constitution, that is, under the "state-citizen" binary structure, the state's educational authority and citizens' right to education are balanced. This balance is primarily reflected in three aspects: the scope and intensity of the state's educational authority's intervention in the right to education, legal reservation, and substantive reasons. This article reveals the historical evolution process of the "right to education-state's educational authority" in our country and attempts to reconstruct this most crucial legal relationship of education based on this. The formulation of educational policies, the compilation of educational codes, and the practice of educational legal governance all cannot be separated from a deep understanding of this relationship. The discussion in this article is merely a simple outline of the relationship between the state's educational authority and the right to education in our country, with various forms and types of educational legal relationships in practice still awaiting further research.

Reference

Mao, Z.(毛泽东). *Comrade Mao Zedong on Educational Work* (毛泽东同志论教育工作). Beijing: People's Education Press(北京：人民教育出版社), 1992.

Liu, S.(刘少奇). Report on the Draft Constitution of the People's Republic of China (关于中华人民共和国宪法草案的报告).*People's Daily*(人民日报), 1954-09-16 (1).

Xi, J.(习近平). Writing a New Chapter in China's Constitutional Practice in the New Era: Commemorating the 40th Anniversary of the Promulgation and Implementation of the Current Constitution (谱写新时代中国宪法实践新篇章——纪念现行宪法公布施行40周年). *The People's Congress of China* (中国人大), 2022(24): 6-8.

Chen, C.(陈楚风). The Formal Requirements of Restriction on Fundamental Rights in Chinese Constitution(中国宪法上基本权利限制的形式要件), *Chinese Journal of Law*(法学研究), 2021, 43(5): 129-143.

Chen, W.(陈伟). Constitutional Relations among the State, Parents and Children in the Sexuality Education for Children: Taking the Controversy over Sexuality Education Materials as an Example(性教育中国家、父母、儿童的宪法关系——以性教育读本争议为例). *Journal of Soochow University (Law Edition)*[苏州大学学报(法学版)]. 2022, 9(1): 123-135.

Decision of the Central Committee of the Communist Party of China on the Reform of the Education System(中共中央关于教育体制改革的决定). *People's Daily*(人

民日报), 1982-05-29(1).

Directives of the Central Committee of the Communist Party of China and the State
Council on Education (中共中央、国务院关于教育工作的指示). *People's Daily*
(人民日报), 1958-09-20(1).

Fang, X.(方晓东). *Outline of the History of Education in the People's Republic of
China* (中华人民共和国教育史纲). Haikou: Hainan Publishing House(海口：海南
出版社), 2002.

General Office of the Standing Committee of the National People's Congress (全国
人大常委会办公厅). *Constitution of the People's Republic of China (2018
Amendments)* [中华人民共和国宪法(2018 年修正)], Beijing: China Democracy
Legal System Publishing House(北京：中国民主法制出版社), 2018.

He, D.(何东昌). *Important Educational Literature of the People's Republic of China
(1949—1975)* [中华人民共和国重要教育文献(1949—1975)].Haikou: Hainan
Publishing House(海口：海南出版社), 1998.

Hu, Q.(胡启立). Before and After the Introduction of the Decision of the Central
Committee of the Communist Party of China on the Reform of the Education
System(《中共中央关于教育体制改革的决定》出台前后), *Yanhuang Chunqiu*(炎
黄春秋), 2008(12): 1-6.

Jia, J.(贾健) & Yu, Y.(余燕娟). On the Criminal Protection of the Right of Chinese
Citizens: with a Review on Article 32 of the Amendment to the Criminal Law(XI)
(论我国公民受教育权的刑法保护——兼评《刑法修正案(十一)》第 32 条),
Human Rights(人权), 2021(1): 103-115.

Jiang, B. (姜秉曦). Normative Analysis of the Basic Obligations of Citizens in
Constitution of the People's Republic of China(我国宪法中公民基本义务的规范
分析). *Law Review*(法学评论), 2018, 36(2): 43-53.

Li, P.(李鹏). Notes on the Compulsory Education Law of the People's Republic of
China (Draft)(关于《中华人民共和国义务教育法(草案)》的说明), *Gazette of the
State Council of the People's Republic of China*(中华人民共和国国务院公报),
1986(12): 403-411.

Li, S. Freedom in Handcuffs: Religious Freedom in the Constitution of China.
Journal of Law and Religion, 2020(1).

Lin, L. (林来梵). On Constitutional Obligations(论宪法义务), *Renmin University
Law Review*(人大法律评论), 2000(2).

Ministry of Education of the People's Republic of China(教育部). Letter of Reply to
Proposal No. 3643 (Education No. 306) of the Fourth Session of the Thirteenth
National Committee of the CPPCC (关于政协第十三届全国委员会第四次会议
第 3643 号(教育类306号) 提案答复的函), Available from: http://www.moe.gov.

cn / jyb_xxgk / xxgk_jyta / jyta_twys / 202111 / t20211104_577678. html [Accessed October 31, 2021].

Peng, Z.(彭真), Report on the Draft Revision of the Constitution of the People's Republic of China(关于中华人民共和国宪法修改草案的报告), *People's Daily* (人民日报), 1982-12-06(1).

People's Congress of Tianjin(天津市人大). Regulations on Employee Education in Tianjin (天津市职工教育条例), *Law Yearbook of China*(中国法律年鉴), 1991(1).

Qin, H.(秦惠民). Analysis of the Basic Patterns of the Right to Education in Modern Society(现代社会的基本教育权型态分析). *Journal of Renmin University of China*(中国人民大大学学报), 1998(5): 85-90.

Regulations Filing and Review Office of the Legislative Affairs Commission of the Standing Committee of the National People's Congress(全国人大常委会法制工作委员会法规备案审查室). *Introduction to the Measures for Reviewing the Filing of Regulations and Judicial Interpretations*(《法规、司法解释备案审查工作办法》导读), Beijing: China Democracy Legal System Publishing House(北京：中国民主法制出版社), 2020.

Regulations Filing and Review Office of the Legislative Affairs Commission of the Standing Committee of the National People's Congress(全国人大常委会法制工作委员会法规备案审查室). *Review of the Filing of Normative Documents: Theory and Practice*(规范性文件备案审查：理论与实务), Beijing: China Democracy Legal System Publishing House(北京：中国民主法制出版社), 2020.

Standing Committee of the National People's Congress(全国人大常委会). Company Law of the People's Republic of China(中华人民共和国公司法), *Law Yearbook of China*(中国法律年鉴), 1994(1).

Standing Committee of the National People's Congress(全国人大常委会). Education Law of the People's Republic of China(中华人民共和国教育法), *Law Yearbook of China*(中国法律年鉴), 1996(1).

Standing Committee of the National People's Congress(全国人大常委会). Higher Education Law of the People's Republic of China(中华人民共和国高等教育法), *Law Yearbook of China*(中国法律年鉴), 1999(1).

Standing Committee of the National People's Congress(全国人大常委会). Labor Law of the People's Republic of China(中华人民共和国公司法), *Law Yearbook of China*(中国法律年鉴), 1995(1).

Standing Committee of the National People's Congress(全国人大常委会). Vocational Education Law of the People's Republic of China(中华人民共和国职业教育法), *Law Yearbook of China*(中国法律年鉴), 1997(1).

State Council(国务院). Implementation Opinions of the State Council on Deepening

the Reform on the Examination and Enrollment System (Guofa [2014] No. 35) [国
务院关于深化考试招生制度改革的实施意见 (国发〔2014〕35 号)]. Available from:
https://www. gov. cn / zhengce / content / 2014-09 / 04 /content_906. html [Accessed
December 24 2021].

The National People's Congress of the People's Republic of China(全国人民代表大
会). Report of the Legal Affairs Working Committee of the Standing Committee of
the National People's Congress on the status of the filing review work in 2021(全
国人民代表大会常务委员会法制工作委员会关于2021年备案审查工作情况的
报告), 2021. Available from: http://www. npc. gov. cn / npc / c2 / c30834 / 202112 /
t20211224_315576.html [Accessed December 24, 2021].

The State Council of the People's Republic of China(中华人民共和国国务院).
Opinions on Further Reducing the Burden of Homework on Students in
Compulsory Education and the Burden of Out-of-School Training(关于进一步减
轻义务教育阶段学生作业负担和校外培训负担的意见), 2021. Available from: https:
//www. gov. cn / zhengce / 2021-07 / 24 / content_5627132. html [Accessed July 24,
2021].

Wang, K. (王锴). Application of the Proportionality Principle in Analysis of
Constitutional Right to Equality(比例原则在宪法平等权分析中的运用). *Law
Science*(法学), 2023(2): 32-46.

Wen, H.(温辉). *The Constitution and Education: Outline of a Study on the National
Right to Education*(宪法与教育——国家教育权研究纲要), Beijing: China
Fangzheng Press(北京:中国方正出版社), 2008.

Xie, L. (谢立斌). Systematic Guarantee of Constitutional Social Rights: from the
Perspective of Sino-German Comparison(宪法社会权的体系性保障——以中德
比较为视角), *Zhejiang Social Sciences*(浙江社会科学), 2014(5)：60-67, 157-158.

Xu, C.(许崇德), *History of the Constitution of the People's Republic of China* (中华
人民共和国宪法史), Fuzhou: Fujian People's Publishing House(福州:福建人民
出版社), 2003.

Xue, T.(薛天祥). WTO Challenges for China's Higher Education(WTO 挑战中国高
等教育), *Higher Education Research*(高等教育研究), 2001(1).

Yan, T. (阎天). The Constitutional Change and Enlightenment of the Obligation of
Citizens to Comply with Workplace Discipling(公民遵守劳动纪律义务的宪法变
迁与启示). *China Legal Science*(中国法学), 2021(4): 165-182.

Yuan, W.(袁文锋), Identification of the Stages of Education to which Article 46 of
the Constitution Applies(《宪法》第四十六条适用的教育阶段辨析), *ECUPL
Journal*(华东政法大学学报), 2015, 18(2): 48-54.

Zhang, H. (张海涛). The Constitutional Interpretation of "Citizens Have the Right and Obligation to Education"(论"公民有受教育的权利和义务"的宪法解释), *Law and Economy*(财经法学), 2016(5):95-104.

Zhang, X. (张 翔). Framework for Reflection on the Question of Limitations on Fundamental Rights(基本权利限制问题的思考框架). *The Jurist*(法学家), 2008 (1):134-139.

Zhang, X.(张翔). *Selected German Constitutional Law Cases: Volume 3*(德国宪法案例选释: 第3辑), Beijing: Law Press China(北京:法律出版社), 2018.

Zhang, Y.(张友渔), *Constitutionalism Series: Book II* (宪政论丛:下册), Beijing: Qunzhong Publishing house(北京:群众出版社), 1986.

Zhao, H.(赵宏). Limiting the Limitation: The Internal Reason of German Fundamental Rights Limitation Mode(限制的限制: 德国基本权利限制模式的内在机理), *The Jurist*(法学家), 2011(2), 152-166, 180.

Zhao, Z.(赵正群). Labor and Education as Non-renounceable Rights of Citizens: A Jurisprudential Reading of the Constitutional Norm of Complexity of Rights and Obligations(劳动与受教育是公民不可放弃的权利——对权利义务复合的宪法规范的法理学读解), *Journal of Liaoning University (Philosophy and Social Sciences Edition)* [辽宁大学学报(哲学社会科学版)], 1991(3): 108-110.

Zhou, L. (周雷), Freedom of Business as a Basic Right: Changes of Norms, Constitutional Basis and Scope of Protection (营业自由作为基本权利: 规范变迁、宪法依据与保护范围), *China Law Review*(中国法律评论), 2020(5): 99-115.

Zhu, K. (朱开轩). Notes on the Education Law of the People's Republic of China (Draft): At the Third Session of the Eighth National People's Congress on March 11, 1995(关于《中华人民共和国教育法(草案)》的说明——1995年3月11日在第八届全国人民代表大会第三次会议上). *Gazette of the Standing Committee of the National People's Congress of the People's Republic of China*(中华人民共和国全国人民代表大会常务委员会公报), 1995(3): 14-20.

Study on the Influencing Factors and Promotion Strategies of Teacher Mobility in Local Universities in Western China: An Analysis Based on Grounded Theory[*]

Chen Qi, Liang Xiaoke[**]

Abstract：In the construction and development of universities, a reasonable and moderate teacher mobility is conducive to promoting the exchange of research results and information among teachers, to improve the quality of higher education in China. However, in the fierce talent competition, local universities in the west are obviously disadvantaged. Therefore, how to introduce and retain excellent talents has become the difficulty and challenge for local universities in western China. This paper takes 14 teachers who flowed out of local universities in the western region as research samples to conduct in-depth interviews. Using the grounded theory research method, this study analyzes the influencing factors that cause the outflow of teachers in western local universities. It is found that the expectations for the development of university and personal career development are the internal factors driving the outflow of teachers; the organizational characteristics of universities are the moderating variables; economic incentives and the development of the cities where the universities are located are the external factors. Based on this, playing the collaborative and coordinated role of the government and market, optimizing the internal management environment of local universities, valuing the "external recruitment and internal training" for teachers, and strengthening the construction of professional ethics of teachers can be helpful for the stable and high-quality development of teachers in western local universities.

Keywords：western local university; teacher mobility; grounded theory; influencing factors

* Date Received: June 20, 2023; Date Revised: March 11, 2024.

** Chen Qi(陈琪), Associate Professor, Ph.D., Faculty of Education, Shaanxi Normal University.Liang Xiaoke(梁笑珂), Postgraduate of Faculty of Education, Shaanxi Normal University.

1. Introduction

As a part of China's higher education, local universities are jointly built (co-managed) by provinces, autonomous regions and municipalities. Local universities are ordinary undergraduate universities that cultivate application-oriented talents for the local economy, with the characteristics of "local management", "local investment", "in local" (He, 2009). According to statistics from the Ministry of Education, as of June 15, 2023, there are 1161 local universities in China, of which 293 local universities in the western region account for 25.92% (Ministry of Education, 2023). Since the 21st century, with the launch of the "211 Project" and "985 Project" in universities, the mobility of universities teachers has entered a relatively active period. In the process of construction and development of universities, reasonable and moderate teacher mobility is beneficial for the exchange of research results and information among teachers and keeping a certain competitiveness in the academic labor market, which will promote academic innovation and prosperity and diversified development of universities teachers, improve the quality of higher education. However, in the fierce talent competition, local universities in the west are obviously disadvantaged. Firstly, the exodus of teachers in local universities has disrupted the discipline echelons, caused profound talent disjunction, and lowered the overall level of teachers. On the other hand, it will seriously affect the normal teaching and talent training, hindering the connotative construction and high-quality development of local universities in the west. Consequently, attracting and retaining outstanding talents has emerged as a significant difficulty and challenge for universities in western China.

The western local universities play an immeasurable role in the local economic construction, social development and spiritual and cultural construction. Reversing the dilemma of teachers' loss has become the top priority for the high-quality development of western local universities. In January 2022, the Ministry of Finance and the Ministry of Education jointly revised the "Measures for the Management of Funds to Support the Reform and Development of Local Universities", which pointed out the support for local universities to focus on connotative development, build high-quality teachers, and enhance their ability to serve economic and social development. It can be said that this pointed out the direction for the construction of western local universities, that is, teachers are the core force and primary resource to promote the high-quality development of local universities. Then, what are the reasons for the outflow of teachers in western local universities? What factors cause them to leave? And how do teachers outflow occur? Based on the research method of grounded theory, this paper conducts semi-structured interviews with 14 teachers who flowed out from local universities in western China, in order to investigate the influencing factors and mechanisms of the outflow of teachers in western local universities, and on this basis put forward countermeasures and suggestions to promote the development of teachers in local universities in western China.

2. Literature Review

Throughout the development history of higher education in China, the rapid development of higher education has driven the growth of teacher flow, which led to the imbalance of higher education development in the eastern and western regions of China and destroyed the fairness of higher education development. In recent years, with the continuous advancement of "Double First-Class" project, the issue of teachers' mobility has once again been concerned by society and scholars. The research of foreign scholars on the universities teachers' mobility mainly focuses on the causes and influencing factors of mobility. For instance, mobility factors include personal behavior (Hinsz,1992), disciplinary differences (Xu,2008), and the influence of national talent policies (Shacher, 2006). At present, domestic scholars have carried out many studies about the issue of universities teachers' mobility from different perspectives. Firstly, scholars mainly discussed the characteristics of universities teachers' mobility. Based on the timing series survey of Chinese universities teachers mobility since the founding of New China 70 years ago, Zhe and Sun (2019) analyzed and summarized the main characteristics of universities teacher mobility in different periods: the purpose and mode of teachers mobility shifts from "government-oriented" to "market-oriented"; intra-occupational mobility is the main type of mobility; the mobility direction is from the academic periphery to the academic center, that is, from local ordinary universities to "211", "985" and "Double First-Class" universities. Based on the analysis of the recruitment announcements of 15 universities at different levels, Chen and Zhi's (2021) research pointed out that universities' teachers' mobility shows the characteristics of poaching teachers with high salaries and high welfare, emphasizing titles over discipline needs, significantly increasing investment in talent introduction by local governments. Secondly, the influencing factors of universities teachers' mobility. Lu and Cao (2019) believed that individual, environmental and organizational factors are the main influencing factors. Dong's (2018) study showed that three factors affected the mobility of teachers in universities. The first is the individual dimension of teachers, such as the inducement of economic interests, and the lack of credit for teachers; the second is the organizational dimension, such as the lack of long-term planning for talent introduction and the poor effect of talent incentive mechanism; the last is the environmental dimension, such as imperfect relevant laws and regulations, and the guidance of external policy environment (Dong, 2018). Based on Victor Froome's "Expectation Theory" and Maslow's Hierarchy of Needs Theory, Chu and other scholars (2022) analyzed the influencing factors of teacher mobility in universities from three dimensions: individual, universities and society. Ding Jing (2022) took teachers in central and western local universities as the interviewees, and then conducted an empirical analysis of the factors affecting the reverse mobility of teachers from the aspects of salary, academic development and the internal environment of universities. Thirdly, the harm of the disorderly mobility of universities teachers. It not only greatly exacerbates the development gap among universities, but also affects the academic output of the academic community (Dang,2018). In addition, in the context of "Double First-Class" construction, teachers' mobility is a normal phenomenon. However, some teachers' disorderly and improper mobility has caused the waste of human resources, the imbalance of discipline structure, regional education inequity, the deterioration of education ecology and other adverse consequences (Dong, 2018). Fourthly, solutions to promote orderly universities teachers mobility. For instance, promote the teacher resource sharing mechanism, establish a diversified co-governance guarantee system (Zhang, 2023), innovate the way of personnel training in order to enhance the scientific research and innovation ability of young teachers in universities, solve the difficulties of system and mechanism to build a sound academic ecological environment for universities in central and western China (Qing,2021).

From the above studies, it can be seen that scholars mainly discussed the teachers' mobility in the central and western universities under the background of "Double First-Class" construction. However, there is little discussion on the mobility and outflow of teachers in local universities. In addition, from the perspective of the research method, the current study pays more attention to theoretical speculation, less qualitative research, and a lack of in-depth inspection of scenes. Under the background of accelerating the construction of a powerful country in education, teachers are the first resource to promote the high-quality development of local universities in western China. Improving the quality of the construction of teachers in western local universities and ensuring the stable development of the teacher team have become critical issues. Based on this, the grounded theory methodology is adopted in this paper in order to study the influencing factors and mechanism models of teacher outflow in local universities in western China, and puts forward policy suggestions to promote the stable development of teachers in western local universities.

3. Research Design

3.1 Research question

Generally, there are three types of teacher mobility of universities. One is that teachers are mobilized from the existing position inside the university to another position;

the second is to leave the current university to work in another university, that is, teachers flow in the different region or different universities; the third is that teachers leave universities and turn to other industries (Lu & Cao, 2019). In this study, teacher mobility refers to teachers who have worked in local universities for various reasons choosing to leave, and flow to other universities in different regions or higher level, it belongs to the intra-career mobility. Therefore, the core question in this paper is: Why do the teachers at local universities in the west choose to flow out to other universities? On this basis, it is decomposed into three sub-problems: (1) What factors affect the outflow of local universities teachers in the west? (2) What is the mechanism of the role of the outflow of teachers in western local universities? (3) How to solve the problem of outflow of local universities teachers in western China?

3.2 Research method

This paper aims to explore the factors affecting the outflow of teachers in western local universities and mainly adopts the grounded theory research method. Grounded theory is a bottom-up theory construction method proposed by Glaser and Strauss in 1967. Its main purpose is to establish a theory based on empirical data. When researchers build the theory, they encode and classify the information, and associate each part to form a logical diagram or model for testing and verification (Glaser et al., 1967). Grounded theory is a qualitative research method, in which researchers collect data and information through actual observation and in-depth situations encode step by step in a top-down way, and summarize and extract concepts and categories from data through abstract and conceptual analysis, that is to find out core concepts reflecting social phenomena based on systematic data collection (Chen, 1999). From the current research status, the influencing factors that affect the outflow of local universities teachers in western China and how these factors interact with each other are not fully understood, which is the reason why this paper uses grounded theory to conduct research.

3.3 Research objects selection

Given that the mobility of teachers in local universities mostly involves personal privacy and has a high degree of concealment. In order to ensure the collected data was valid, representative and authentic, this study followed the principle of purposive sampling and gradually expanded the scope of interviews by utilizing "snowball" approach, and finally 14 teachers were selected as interviewees. They showed differences in the distribution characteristics of age, teaching year, professional title, education background and native place.

The reason for choosing these 14 teachers is because they used to work in local

Table 1　Basic information of interviewees

Teacher coding	Native place	Age	Teaching year	Professional title	Education background	Mobility time	City before mobility	City after mobility	University level before mobility	University level after mobility
T1,20221113	Ankang, Shaanxi Province	36	8	lecture	doctor	2021	An kang	Xi'an	provincial key university	university directly under the Ministry of Education
T2,20221114	Weinan, Shaanxi Province	48	17	professor	doctor	2020	Urumqi	Xi'an	provincial key university	university directly under the Ministry of Education
T3,2022114	Xian yang, Shanxi Province	44	14	professor	doctor	2021	Xi'an	Xi'an	provincial key university	university directly under the Ministry of Education
T4,20221116	Baoji, Shaanxi Province	54	25	professor	doctor	2016	Yinchuan	Xi'an	provincial key university	university directly under the Ministry of Education
T5,20221205	Qingyang, Gansu Province	42	11	Associate Professor	doctor	2018	Lanzhou	Xi'an	provincial key university	university directly under the Ministry of Education
T6,20221206	Yinchuan, Ningxia Province	47	20	Professor	doctor	2017	Xi'an	Xi'an	provincial key university	university directly under the Ministry of Education
T7,20221116	San Menya, Henan Province	38	9	lecturer	doctor	2022	Guizhou	Xi'an	provincial key university	university directly under the Ministry of Education
T8,20221222	Tianshui, Gansu Province	39	13	associate professor	doctor	2014	Tianshui	Xi'an	provincial regular university	provincial key university
T9,20221125	Zhuanglang, Gansu Province	35		associate professor	doctor	2019	Lanzhou	Xi'an	provincial key university	provincial key university

continued

Teacher coding	Native place	Age	Teaching year	Professional title	Education background	Mobility time	City before mobility	City after mobility	University level before mobility	University level after mobility
T10,20221203	Yulin,Shaanxi province	50	22	professor	master	2021	Shangluo	Xi'an	provincial regular university	provincial key university
T11,20221204	Xi'an,Shaanxi province	38	9	associate professor	doctor	2019	Xuchang	Xi'an	provincial regular university	provincial key university
T12,20221205	Baoji,Shaanxi province	55	30	professor	master	2018	Baoji	Xi'an	provincial regular university	provincial key university
T13,20221206	Guyuan,Ningxia province	39	9	associate professor	doctor	2017	Guyuan	Xi'an	provincial regular university	provincial key university
T14,20221204	Zhangye,Gansu province	36	6	lecturer	doctor	2020	Zhangye	Xi'an	provincial regular university	provincial key university

universities in western China and moved to other different levels of universities for various reasons, such as moving from a provincial key university to a university directly under the Ministry of Education, from remote city to city with higher levels of economic development. As a result, an interview with them undoubtedly provides a high degree of credibility for understanding the reasons behind the outflow of teachers and influencing factors (see Table 1).

3.4 Research data collection

In order to clearly understand the real reasons for the flow of interviewees, this paper designed a semi-structured interview outline based on referring to relevant studies (see Table 2). According to the interview outline prepared in advance, we conducted one-to-one in-depth interviews with each research object between November and December 2022. Each interview usually lasted about 40 minutes. In addition, we also conducted a second interview with some research subjects through WeChat, telephone and other means to ensure the integrity and depth of interview information and materials. After the interview, the recording was transcribed, arranged and analyzed to obtain the text.

Table 2   Interview questions

Number	Questions
1	How long have you been working in your present university?
2	In your opinion, what were the reasons that drove you to leave your former university?
3	What is the most important reason for you to leave your former university?
4	What factors have you taken into consideration when choosing the university for which you want to move?
5	How do you feel about your current work situation? Did you achieve your expectations at the time?
6	How do you think work mobility has affected you personally and your family?
7	What work have done in introducing teachers and professional development training for teachers in your current university?
8	What supports do you value more in your work?
9	What do you think needs to be improved in your current university?

3.5 Research ethics

Before the formal interview, we communicated with the interviewees in advance about the research purpose, research content, recording, and other related issues and agreed on the time and place of the interview. In addition, it promises not to involve privacy issues and confidential information. The whole interview process is recorded with the consent of the interviewee. To protect the interviewees' privacy, the order and time of the interviews are used as the code name of each respondent, which is finally presented as T1, 20221113; T2, 20221114, etc.

4. Grounded Theory Coding and Model Construction

Coding is the most critical link for grounded theory, that is, the author compares, analyzes, summarizes the interview materials repeatedly and continuously, from low level to high level, gradually conceptualization, categorization and finally construction of theory (Wei et al., 2017). The grounded theory data analysis includes three steps: open coding, axial coding and selective coding. Through the analysis of interview data, this paper gradually explores the factors that affect the outflow of teachers from local universities in western China and attempts to build a model of the factors that influence the outflow of teachers from local universities.

4.1 Open coding

Open coding, or first-level coding, is an operational process of coding and labelling the original interview data word by word, and then recombining the concepts. Its purpose is to find concept categories from the data, name the categories, determine the attributes and dimensions of the categories, and then name and categorize the phenomena under study (Xu & Wang, 2021). In the process of open coding, the original concepts and statements of teachers' current teaching situation and why they left the local university where they worked were labeled, and the influence of subjective opinion and individual preference was excluded as far as possible. By classifying, comparing, screening and summarizing the original interview data for many times, 24 sentences were summarized from 158 original sentences. Twenty concepts were abstracted from 123 original concepts. At the same time, after refining the original concept of homogenization, 10 variable categories are obtained (see Table 3), which are the factors affecting the outflow of teachers from western local universities.

Table 3　Open coding results

original statement (summarizing, sorting)	initial concept	categories
T2: My major is history, due to discipline adjustment, the department of liberal arts was compressed and no longer set up a separate school of history.	discipline development prospect is not ideal	discipline development expectation
T6: My major was not highly valued in my previous university and had a low sense of existence.	discipline development is not valued	

continued

original statement (summarizing, sorting)	initial concept	categories
T8: The English major of my current university has a strong advantage, which can provide a very sound platform for my professional development.	prospect of discipline development is good	
T8: The university where I used to work had limited resources for teachers and paid little attention to the long-term professional development of teachers.	neglect of teacher growth and development needs	talent training expectation
T12: The university only cares about how to introduce talents and pays little attention to the cultivation and development of talents in the later stages.	neglect of talent training	
T11: The university where I work now is relatively in line with my future career development plan.	in line with personal career planning	for personal development consider
T8: The university where I work now attaches great importance to talents, which will be of great help to my career development and promotion.	career development advantage	
T14: At that time, my husband was working in a university in Shaanxi Province. Later, I resigned to study for a doctor's degree and find a job here, so I settled here.	for the spouse's sake	for family happiness
T10: Provincial capitals have more excellent educational resources, which can provide more educational opportunities and choices for children.	for the next generation's sake	
T4: Personnel management system in my previous university was more rigid, and did not put the fundamental interests of teachers first. T3: The university's evaluation of professional titles was chaotic, sometimes not following the implementation of policy documents, and the management mode was also very chaotic. T11: The management style of leadership is more rigid and lacks humanity.	management system	university management
T5: I was unhappy in my former university where the cultural environment was very poor.	poor humanistic environment	humanistic environment
T12: The working atmosphere in my previous university was not satisfactory. The academic atmosphere was not very strong.	work atmosphere depression	
T14: Transportation, medical care, education and other high-quality resources are concentrated in the provincial capital city, it is very attractive to me.	the trend of urban development is good	city and geographical advantage
T2: The university where I used work also located in the provincial capital, but further northwest. T13: The university where I used to work was also a comprehensive university with good overall strength, but it is located in a remote place and not in the provincial capital.	superior geographical location	

continued

original statement (summarizing, sorting)	initial concept	categories
T1: Now the university has the opportunity of a house purchase policy, which is one of the important reasons that attracts me. After all, it can relieve the economic pressure to some extent.	home-buying and housing allowance	provide welfare protection
T7: Housing subsidies are a very big attraction for young teachers. T5: I didn't get an apartment when I first came here, but the university provided me housing subsidies for three consecutive years.		
T10: There are primary and secondary schools attached to this university, so that my children can receive a favorable basic education.	welfare	
T1: The salary at my previous university was a little low, which is why I left.	low pay	salary incentive
T6: In the past, the university didn't pay much attention to talent, so the salary of teachers with doctoral degrees was no more than 7000 yuan a month.		
T11: The salary was much higher than the previous university. I needed money at that time, so I went to the university that offered the best salary.	high pay	
T4: Now this university is very close to my hometown. After retirement, I can live in my hometown. After all, there is little possibility for me to move in the future.	getting home	regression hometown
T2: For me, staying in my hometown is generally more comfortable than staying in a place where I am not familiar with.	sense of belonging	

4.2 Axical coding

The main task of axial coding is to discover and establish various connections between concepts and categories to represent the organic correlation between various parts of the data. As shown in Table 4, "humanistic environment of university" and "internal management of university" are combined into the second-level code "organizational characteristics of university." According to this method, the 10 categories obtained by open coding are analyzed and classified again at this stage. They can be summarized into 5 main categories, which are the expectations for the development of the university, organizational characteristics of the university, individual career development, economic inducement and regional economic level.

Table 4   Category relations formed by axial coding

Main categories	Corresponding category	Connotation of relationship
expectations for the development of the university	discipline development potential	The university cannot provide an ideal subject platform for teachers, but teachers expect to have a platform with more development potential.
	comprehensive development strength of the university	The conditions and resources provided by the university are conducive to teachers' personal career development, and the prospect of professional development is clear.
	talent training expectation	Teachers expect universities to pay attention to the cultivation of talents as well as the introduction of talents to avoid the waste of talent resources.
organizational characteristics of the university	humanistic environment of the university	Through mobility, teachers avoid the interpersonal environment they don't like and pursue a comfortable humanistic environment that conforms to their personality.
		Teachers hope to engage in teaching and scientific research in a relatively free and relaxed environment.
	internal management of the university	Some functional departments are rigid in managing matters in the interests of teachers, system design not humanized, official standards are not met, and there is administrative atmosphere.
		The establishment of reward and incentive mechanism, flexible assessment, and evaluation affect teachers' sense of identity in the university.
individual profession development	professional development expectation	Teachers hope to obtain the supports in terms of professional title promotion, scientific research and teaching level improvment.
	career advancement opportunity	Teachers expect universities to provide more resources and opportunities for promotion.
	return to hometown	Choosing a university close to home is the reason for some teachers.
economic incentives	salary incentive	High salaries and superior treatment are major incentives for the mobility of teachers.
	welfare guarantee	Whether the university provides various benefits, such as medical care, housing, and children's enrollment, is also a factor for teachers to consider.
regional economic level	geographical location advantage	Shaanxi is in a relatively advantageous geographical position.
	urban development prospect	The external environment of the city where universities are located is superior, and the quality and quantity of hardware facilities coexist, which is conducive to the survival and development of individuals.

4.3 Selective coding

Selective coding is based on the main axis coding, in the way of storylines to link the main category and category, extract and summarize the logical relationship between categories, and through data and existing theories to improve the various categories and their mutual relations, clarify the storyline and then build a new theoretical framework. According to the content of the relationship between the main category and the corresponding category, this paper first investigated the connection between the main category and the corresponding category and the outflow of teachers from local universities in the western region, and found that five core categories, including the expectations for the development of the university, organizational characteristics of the university, individual career development, economic inducement and regional economic level, had a significant impact on the outflow of teachers from local universities. Among them, the academic potential and personal career development are the internal factors. The organizational characteristics of universities, such as the humanistic environment and internal management system universities, are the moderating variables, which promote the transformation of local teachers' mobility intention into behavior. External factors include economic incentives and the development of the cities where the universities are located.

Based on three-level coding, according to the storyline and the connection relationship between class and main class, this paper has built a model of the factors influencing teacher outflow in western local universities, namely the "willingness-condition-mobility" action mechanism model (see Figure 1). According to the model, the factors affecting the outflow of teachers in local universities mainly involve universities, individuals and society, among which the university includes the development expectation of universities and the organizational characteristics of universities; the individual includes the professional development of teachers, promotion opportunities and factors such as returning to their hometown; the social aspects mainly involve economic incentives and regional economic level.

4.4 Theoretical saturation test

In this study, the interview records of 4 teachers were randomly selected for theoretical saturation test. The results show that the concepts of record mining are covered by 10 existing categories. No new concepts and categories in the five core categories that affect the outflow of teachers from western local universities. It indicates that the coding has basically reached saturation, and the "influencing factor model of teachers outflow in western local universities" obtained by following the story line of "willingness-condition-mobility" has theoretical saturation.

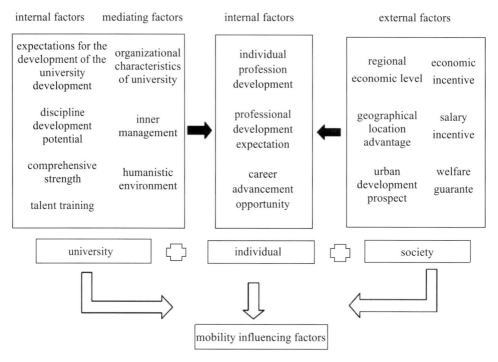

internal factors | mediating factors | internal factors | external factors

Figure 1   Influencing factors and mechanism models of teacher mobility in western local university

5. Analysis on Influencing Factors of Teachers' Mobility in Western Local Universities

In 1977, Bronfenbrenner proposed Social Ecological Theory, emphasising "the complexity and dynamics of the environments in which people live and work. It consists of four nested word systems, from the inside out the microsystem, the middle system, the outer system and the macro system. Among them, the innermost microsystem refers to the direct environment of individual activities, the intermediate system is the environment under the interaction between microsystems, the outer system is the environment that individuals are not directly involved in but have a direct impact on them, and the macro system is the social ideology and cultural environment" (Zhang & Xia,2022). For teachers in western local universities, the occurrence of their willingness to flow not only lies in personal career development decisions but also reflects the interaction of various influencing factors such as teachers' macroscopic external environment, middle-view organizational situation and microscopic psychological state.

5.1 Internal factors: the discipline strength and individual professional development

The construction of teachers is related to the sustainable and high-quality development of the university. Teachers' normal and reasonable mobility provides a steady stream of fresh blood for the university's development. According to the Push-Pull Theory, the generation of mobility behavior is jointly affected by the organization's internal structure and the pull of the external environment. Teachers' mobility behavior is the result of rational choice, and the result of the "push" factor of the teachers' original university and the "pull" factor of the target university. Non-external forces usually drive the orderly mobility of teachers in local universities. Teachers pursue status, higher honor, academic development opportunities and space in the academic field through career flow, so as to realize self-value. T8 interviewee mentioned:

> *When the development strength of a subject is insufficient, teachers'*
> *dependence on the university will be reduced. At that time, due to the consideration*
> *of personal value and economic return, I felt that my ability have not been maximized*
> *and reflected in the previous university, so I took the initiative to seek a new platform*
> *to realize my value.(T8, 20221121)*

Generally speaking, a university is a collection of "people", "literature" and "things", in which "people" and "things" together constitute the entity part of the university, is the hard power of the university, "literature" is a university of enduring precious resources. That is, "literature" not only refers to the running culture and humanistic environment of the university, but also includes the good prospect of discipline development and the construction of scientific research platform, which is the main factor for the local undergraduate teachers to choose the mobility for their own development. The status quo of discipline development in universities and the level of scientific research platforms have an impact on the development prospects of local university teachers, which can not only generate strong siphon power in talent introduction, but also become a "stepping stone" for the development of teachers, especially in the application and approval of national or key scientific research projects, academic papers published and access to academic resources (Gu & Xia, 2021). Burton Clark, an American scholar, once said that the discipline rather than the institution dominates the power of a scholar's work and life. In general, there is a close correlation between a university's discipline construction and teachers' development. A good discipline development platform can bring a higher starting point and more development opportunities for teachers, and first-class teachers are the fundamental guarantee for the construction of first-class disciplines in the university. Only by employing high-quality and high - level teachers can the university creates a higher level of scientific research results, high-quality personnel and training efficient social services. For many western local university teachers, their knowledge reserve and ability have matured after years of professional learning and scientific research accumulation, which makes them pay more attention to whether the university will provide a better platform for further development and promotion opportunities. If the university cannot meet these aspirations, most of them may have the idea of leaving. As many teachers mentioned in the interview, they are in the rising and golden stage of career development. When their academic capital has accumulated to a certain extent, they will have higher expectations for future development, and then they maybe consider choosing a university with stronger comprehensive strength than the previous one. Two interviewees indicated:

> *My major is history and I used to work at a comprehensive university with an emphasis on science and engineering. In the first few years, the university still attached great importance to the development of humanities and social disciplines, but the overall development level and momentum of the School of History and Culture were not particularly good, and the discipline advantages were not obvious and prominent. As a result, schools do not give sufficient funds and resources to historical subjects. Therefore, under the pressure of "Double First-Class" construction, the university adjusted relatively weak disciplines or departments. As a result, the School of History and Culture was abolished and the history major was merged into the School of Arts. (T2,20221114)*

> *Three years ago, it was a critical period of my professional development and promotion, and I hoped to make further progress. However, the university where I used to work is a provincial university in a prefecture-level city, with poor comprehensive strength and lagging behind in the national comprehensive professional level ranking. Besides, it had no qualifications for postgraduate admission, so on second thought I left. Now it seems that this decision is correct. Now I have obtained the qualification of master tutor, which makes me full of expectations for my future career development. (T11, 20221204)*

5.2 Key factors: organizational characteristics of university

Organizational Behavior believes that the environment or atmosphere created by an organization greatly impacts its members' behavior. As a special form of organization, university organization has a significant effect on the mobility of teachers. In the research on teacher mobility, the organization theory is mainly used to analyze the influence of university organization characteristics on teacher mobility. For example, Torres et al. found that a school's requirements on teacher performance, working hours, teaching facilities, management system and administrative support all affect teachers' views on work (Torees, 2016). The organizational characteristics of the university mainly refer to the internal management system, the cultural construction and the ideology of running a school at the spiritual level, various rules and regulations, values, the behavior of teachers and students, etc, which are the hidden invisible environment of the university. In general, teachers in a positive organizational environment are more likely to love their work and students, be proactive, and constantly pursue excellence. One of the teachers in the interview said:

At present, under the market economy's value orientation, university teachers' work pressure is increasing. Many teachers feel powerless, while some teachers even lack working motivation, low interest, decreased job satisfaction, and fatigue in teaching. These problems are influenced by various factors, one of which is the university's organizational structure and management system. Suppose university administrative departments can establish a "people-oriented" sense of service, break away from the ideological bondage of "official standard," and establish a warm and caring administrative working model for safeguarding the fundamental interests of teachers as a starting point. In that case, it will improve teachers' trust and satisfaction in the university. (T4, 20221116)

Western local universities' organization characteristics are imperfect, which mainly manifests in three aspects. Firstly, universities are becoming increasingly bureaucratic, with redundant institutional settings and entrenched section hierarchies. This phenomenon is prevalent and a common problem in Chinese universities. Under the Chinese system, the bureaucracy highlights the tendency of administration, which is incompatible with the university governance structure that emphasizes professional authority and professorial rule and an organizational culture focusing on academic freedom (Zhang, 2015). Therefore, under the management mode of bureaucracy, the "administrative power" of university far exceeds the "academic power," which weakens academic power and jeopardizes the academic freedom of universities and the academic-based university organization structure. Secondly, the internal management system of western local universities is not sound enough, and the democratic management atmosphere is increasingly fading. Some administrators' strong-power leadership, unfair management methods, imperfect performance appraisal mechanism, and interference in teaching and scientific research with administrative power, to some extent, caused a poor atmosphere of academic freedom, which makes it difficult to arouse the enthusiasm and initiative of teachers, and even makes teachers distrustful of the university. Thirdly, negative culture affects teachers' enthusiasm in their work. Under the joint action of social and cultural tradition and various institutional factors, there is a widespread bureaucratic culture in Chinese universities. In addition, pursuing the realistic and immediate benefits, especially the excessive emphasis on economic indicators at the expense of academic and moral standards (Zhang,2015). The transition and excessive prevalence of these two cultures in western local universities have contributed to the alienation of university development organizations, which is not beneficial to the long-term healthy development of university. As the interviewee mentioned:

> *A favorable environment can make the work efficient and get twice the result with half the effort. The main reason for my resignation was that the former university had a strong ideology of official standards, and many evaluation and assessment mechanisms were based on the size of administrative power. Moreover, the university's administrative management overlapped, and departments passed the blame to each other, resulting in low efficiency. In addition, the style of management was inflexible, in the long run, it will decrease the enthusiasm of teachers for work. (T11, 20221204)*

> *I used to work in a university with a poor cultural environment, and some department leaders failed to perform their duties and do practical things for teachers. Besides, the relationship between colleagues was not harmonious, and I felt uncomfortable when we worked together sometimes, which was one of the reasons why I chose to leave. (T12, 20221205)*

5.3 Direct factors: the high salary and welfare guarantee

In 1966, Herzberg pointed out in his research that hygiene and motivators factors affected teachers' satisfaction with their work, including salary, academic promotion, higher honors, and other incentive mechanisms (Chen, 2013). The Rational Choice Theory in economics holds that the behavior of individuals is to maximize their "utility". Teachers measure the gains and losses of exchange behavior in terms of their strengths and values and exchange the benefits and resources they expect to receive by their abilities. Therefore, high salary and welfare guarantee have a strong explanatory power to the occurrence of teachers' mobility behavior.

At present, some universities in China attract high level teachers through high salary and high welfare, which has become the main reason for inducing teachers' chaotic mobility. It can be found that both universities directly under the Ministry of Education and local universities, whether they are in the eastern region with a high level of economic development or in the western region with a relatively backward level of economic development, all provide attractive annual salaries, research start-up fees and settlement fees to poach teachers. At the same time, it also provides generous welfare protection such as apartment housing for experts, medical protection and services, and schooling for children (Chen & Zhi, 2021). Therefore, when western local universities cannot provide generous salary and welfare protection for teachers, it may lead to the mobility of teachers. But higher salary, improvement of working conditions and stable welfare protection are conducive to reducing the possibility of teachers' mobility in western local universities. In interviews, several faculty members talked about salary and benefit security as one of the reasons they considered mobile to another university.

I chose this university at that time because the salary and various benefits were relatively good. Besides, the university also provided me with research start-up and settling expenses. At the same time, I could have the priority to buy a house in the university at a significantly reduced cost compared to the market value. (T1, 20221113)

One of the reasons why I came to this university was that I valued the welfare conditions they provided. The primary and middle schools attached to the university have high educational level and teaching quality, ranking among the primary and middle schools in Xi'an. So if I work here, it means that the problem of my children's schooling was solved, which was very attractive to me. (T13, 20221206)

5.4 External factors: the level of regional economic and social development

The "Center-Periphery" Theory believes that there is an obvious center and periphery in the academic labor market, and the teachers in the peripheral academic system tend to flow towards the central academic system (Liu,2016). Generally speaking, economically developed regions or provincial capitals are in the center of teacher mobility, which can attract more high-level talents. For instance, according to a news report, Xinjiang Medical University has lost 197 teachers in a decade (Chai & Jin, 2017). Regional factors include the level of regional economy development, urban environment conditions, and talent attraction policy. Regional economic and social development level can generate a higher degree of economic efficiency, that is, to have better infrastructure construction, convenient transportation, better quality medical resources and educational opportunities, which has become an important external condition affecting the recruitment and retention of talents in university.

Theoretically, the more capable teachers are, the more likely they are to obtain job opportunities and rewards. When western local universities fail to meet teachers' expectations, the intention of teacher outflow will be stronger. A study showed that the mobility intention of teachers in western and central universities was about 9 percent higher than that of teachers in the east (You, 2014). Therefore, due to the influence of economic conditions, living environment and other regional factors, teachers in western local universities have been flowing from second-and third-tier cities to the provincial cities, and from northwest cities to more developed midwest or eastern cities. In the interview, several teachers with a doctoral degree or in the rising carer development period mentioned that:

> *As my professional title level continued to rise, I sprouted the idea of going to another university. The university where I used to work was not located in a provincial capital city. It is a prefecture-level city with relatively backward economic development level. The development potential of the university was not great, and many high-quality academic resources could not be leaned towards these universities. (T13, 20221206)*

> *Before I came to this university, a university in Guizhou also offered me an olive branch, but I didn't choose it in the end, mainly because of its remote location and relatively low development level of transportation, medical care and education, which can hardly meet my needs.(T8, 20221121)*

6. Countermeasures and Suggestions

In order to promote the rational mobility of teachers in western local universities, reduce the brain drain, and achieve the mutual benefit and win-win development between universities and talents, this paper puts forward the following countermeasures and suggestions from the three perspectives of market and government, universities and teachers.

6.1 Government and market should collaborate and coordinate to promote the reasonable mobility of teachers in western local universities

The mobility of teachers in universities is an important path for allocating human resources in the labor market. In order to prevent aggravating the issue of the disorder in university teachers' mobility brought on by the failure of market regulation, it is imperative that the government play the guiding role in the macro-control of teachers' mobility in addition to fully allowing the market to play its fundamental role in the allocation of human resources in a timely and appropriate manner. We should grasp both hands, regulation with one hand and freedom with the other. "Regulation" has obvious administrative interference, highlighting the function of the government, with more emphasis on the government's restrictions on the mobility of teachers in universities, while "freedom" manifests in the opposite direction as the government's laissez faire behavior towards teachers' mobility, with the market playing a more regulatory role. Therefore, it is necessary to grasp the contradiction and unity between regulation and freedom accurately.

On the one hand, we should establish and improve the system construction for the outflow of teachers from local universities in the western region. The government should strengthen macro-control and not completely let market mechanisms play a role. By improving the mobility mechanism and evaluation incentive mechanism, the stable development of teachers can be promoted. At the same time, the government should pay attention to controlling the outflow of local universities in the western region, establish a flexible mechanism for the outflow of teachers, prevent excessive intervention and complete release, and return teachers to a certain degree of autonomy. On the other hand, we should follow the general law that the market determines the allocation of human resources, promote the rational flow of teachers in local universities with effective market and promising government, creating a healthy ecology of university teachers' mobility.

6.2 Management environment of western local universities should be improved to enhance teachers' sense of identity

A good internal ecological environment is the criterion that promotes the stable development of teachers in local universities. The loss of teachers in western local universities is mostly due to voluntary or forced departure, which is closely related to the rigid management system of the university and the educational environment. For this reason, first of all, western local universities should emancipate their minds, transform the management concept of "official standard," and create a clean and positive campus cultural atmosphere. Local universities in the western region follow the basic logic of universities and the law of academic talents development, providing teachers with an independent, open, and innovative academic stage so that they can devote themselves to academic research without distractions, focus on teaching and scientific research with peace of mind. Only in this way can teachers' career development be filled with a sense of happiness and struggle.

Secondly, western local universities should establish a people-oriented management environment and break down teacher management barriers. Local universities should adhere to the service concept of "people-oriented," fully attach importance to and ensure teachers' subjectivity, and constantly meet the needs of teachers' self-development and self-achievement. At the same time, western local universities should form a "flexible" management model featuring flexibility, respect and inclusiveness, establish an effective competitive incentive mechanism, and eliminate inappropriate management methods such as "egalitarianism" and "seniority-based" system, so as to build a good ecology of "employing-managing- retaining people", which will make teachers actively, consciously and automatically contribute to the development of universities. In addition, the secondary departments of western local universities should make great efforts to stimulate teachers' endogenous motivation and establish a sound teacher training support system. Universities and teachers should follow the concept of joint construction, sharing, mutual benefit, and win-win as a community of interests. The secondary departments should pay attention to the needs and trends of teachers' career development, strengthen pre-job training and development guidance for new staff, and solve all the problems they encounter. Thirdly, western local universities should establish the organizational culture of humanization, institutionalization and multi-participation, actively advocate teamwork, create a cooperative environment of mutual assistance, tolerance and harmony, stimulate teachers to creatively carry out teaching activities, and guide teachers to closely combine their personal career development with the development of the school, so as to realize the organic unity of personal development and school development.

6.3 It is necessary to concerned "external recruitment and internal training" to solve the problem of unbalanced allocation of teachers

The mobility of university teachers is a kind of market behavior. As the main body of cultivating, attracting, and using talents, universities bear the governance responsibility of employers (Dan,2017). The Report of the 20th National Congress of Communist Party of China pointed out: "Deepening the reform of the system and mechanism for talent development, sincerely love talents, cultivate talents, attract talents, and use talents meticulously. We will be eager to seek talents, not stick to one style, and gather outstanding talents from all aspects into the cause of the Party and the people." The construction of teaching staff is the foundation of all work in universities. The shortage of teachers from outside and the loss of existing teachers, to some extent, will affect the normal teaching activities of the university and reduce the level of education and teaching, which is detrimental to the healthy and long-term development of university. Therefore, local universities in western China should actively expand the channels for introducing teachers and strengthen the training of existing teachers to maintain the stability of the structure of teachers.

On the one hand, western local universities should do a good job in talents introduction. Local universities should reasonably formulate plans and requirements for introducing teachers according to the actual development and the demand for personnel in disciplines, especially to increase the introduction of teachers in scarce disciplines and continue to promote the strategy of strengthening schools with talents. In addition, in the process of introducing teachers, local universities should take the principle of "demand-driven" and adopt an open, transparent, and honest approach to avoid conflicts with teachers again in management, such as salary, professional title promotion, scientific research conditions, evaluation and assessment, etc.

On the other hand, local universities in western China should strengthen the cultivation of existing teachers and formulate long-term talent development plans. They should give necessary humanistic care to teachers and comprehensively understand the development needs of teachers in various ways, such as housing, children's enrollment and other issues related to the stability of teachers' life, so as to ensure the retention of teachers in terms of life security. In addition, local universities should retain staff in terms of salary and take multiple measures to raise the overall salary of teachers as one of the important measures to stabilize the teaching team. Specifically, it includes raising teachers' basic salary, expanding the autonomy of higher income distribution, establishing and improving the post income distribution system within university, etc.

6.4 It is important to boost teachers' development of professional ethics to optimize the academic ecological environment

Rational Selectivism believes that people have economic attributes and will automatically pursue the maximization of interests (Zhang & Tian, 2020). At present, "some teachers in universities have alienated their value orientation because of being induced by outside interests when they examine their own values; Some provide false resumes for personal interests and obtain greater economic benefits by constantly changing jobs; Even though the university has committed a significant amount of material resources, financial resources and careful cultivation, there are certain teachers who abruptly quit at a crucial juncture in its development." (Dong, 2018) These individual behaviours and disorderly mobility are to some extent due to the problems of teachers' professional ethics.

Therefore, it is of great significance for university teachers to establish the correct concept of professional development and strengthen the construction of teachers' professional ethics, in order to solve the problem of reasonable mobility of teachers in western local university and scientifically avoid the brain drain. First of all, local university teachers in the western region should improve their own professional ethics, academic ethics and will quality. Teachers in local universities should strengthen their academic faith, abide by their professional ethics, strengthen their sense of responsibility and reduce the occurrence of profit-seeking mobility behaviour. Secondly, teachers in western local universities should take the initiative to make personal career development plans, rationally analyze the relationship between mobility cost and mobility premium, and focus on improving personal teaching levels and publishing scientific research results. Thirdly, teachers in western local universities should actively participate in various professional training and learning activities in various ways, constantly improve their own knowledge structure, take the initiative to improve their teaching level, scientific research ability and comprehensive quality, resolutely undertake the responsibility of "preaching and accepting learning", and fulfill the responsibility of teaching and educating people.

References

Chai, R.(柴如瑾) & Jin, H.(晋浩天). The Hidden Worry of "Poaching" Talents to Create First-class: Perspective on the Phenomenon of "Peacock Flying Southeast" of University Talents("挖"人才创一流的隐忧:高校人才"孔雀东南飞"现象透视). *Guangming Daily*(光明日报), 2017-03-20(1).

Chen, W.(陈文博) & Zhi, T.(郅庭瑾). Rational Analysis and Institutional Norms of Disorderly Flow of University Teachers: Based on the Perspective of Rational Choice Institutionalism under the Background of Multi-Dimensional Evaluation(高校教师失序流动的理性分析及制度规范——基于多维评价背景下理性选择制度主义的视角).*Fudan Education Forum*(复旦教育论坛), 2021(6): 72-79.

Chen, X.(陈向明). Ideas and Methods of Grounded Theory(扎根理论的思路与方法).*Educational Research and Experiment*(教育研究与实验), 1999(4): 288-303.

Chen, Y.(陈玉芬). A Review of Theories on Faculty Turnover(高校教师流动行为理论综述).*Fudan Education Forum*(复旦教育论坛), 2013(2): 42-45.

Chu, F. (储凡静) Guo, H.(郭号林) & Sun, X.(孙晓玲). Analysis of the Loss of High-Level Talents in Colleges and Universities in the New Period(新时期高校高层次人才的流失分析).*China Education of Light Industry*(中国轻工教育), 2022(3): 9-18.

Dan, L.(丹聆). Construction of Credit System for Talents in Colleges and Universities and Reasonable Flow of High-Level Talents(高校人才诚信体系建设与高层次人才合理流动).*China Higher Education*(中国高等教育), 2017(5): 4-6.

Dang, Y.(党彦虹). College Teachers' Job-hopping, Problems and Countermeasures Under Background of "Double- First-Class" Construction("双一流"建设背景下高校教师流动现状、问题与对策).*Heilongjiang Researches on Higher Education*(黑龙江高教研究), 2018(9): 1-4.

Ding, J.(丁晶). From the East to the Midwest: Retroactive Causes and Suggestions for the Reverse Flow of Talents in Colleges and Universities(从东部到中西部：高校人才逆向流动溯因与献策).*Higher Education Exploration*(高教探索), 2022(5): 37-42, 62.

Dong, S.(董树军). Faculty Mobility and Its Governance in Universities under the Background of "Double First-Class" Construction("双一流"建设背景下高校教师流动及其治理).*Journal of Higher Education*(高等教育研究), 2018(10): 63-67,74.

Glaser, B. G., & Strauss, A. L., & Strutzel, E. The Discovery of Grounded Theory: Strategy for Qualitative Research.*Nursing Research*,1967(4): 378.

Gu, H.(顾和军) & Xia, Y.(夏艳娇). Analysis of Benign Flow Factors of Talents in Colleges and Universities under the Background of "Double First-Class" : Take 18 Case Interviews of Colleges and Universities in Jiangsu as Examples("双一流"背景下高校人才良性流动因素分析——以江苏高校的 18 个案例访谈为例). *Chinese University Science & Technology*(中国高校科技), 2021(6): 1-5.

He, J. (贺金玉）. *The Orientation of New Local Universities in China*（中国地方新建本科院校的办学定位）. Beijing: Higher Education Publishing(北京：高等教育出版社), 2009.

Hinsz, V. B., & Nelson, L. C. Testing Models of Turnover Intentions with University Faculty.*Journal of Applied Social Psychology*, 1992(1): 68-84.

Liu, F. (刘凤祥). *Reform of Regional Economic Development Mode from the Perspective of Growth Efficiency(*增长效率视角下区域经济发展方式变革）. Beijing:Enterprise management Press(北京：企业管理出版社), 2016.

Lu, H.(陆慧玲) & Cao, H.(曹辉). Flow of University Teachers and Its Rationality in the Context of "Double First-Class" Construction("双一流"建设背景下高校教师流动及其合理性判别).*Journal of Hebei Normal University(Educational Science)* [河北师范大学学报(教育科学版)], 2019(6): 57-63.

Ministry of Education of the People's Republic of China. List of National Universities,2023. Available from:http://www.moe.gov.cn/jyb_xxgk/s5743/s5744/A03/202306/t20230619_1064976.html[Accessed July 20, 2023].

Qing, S.(卿素兰). Current Situation Investigation and Countermeasures of Teacher Mobility in Universities and Colleges in Central and Western China: Based on the Analysis of "One Province, One School" Key Universities in Central and Western China(中西部高校教师流动的现状考察与对策建议——基于中西部"一省一校"重点建设大学的分析). *Journal of Southwest University (Social Science Edition)*[西南大学学报 (社会科学版)], 2021(6): 93-100.

Shacher, A. The Race for Talent：Highly Skilled Migrant and Competitive Immigration Regimes.*New York University Law Review*, 2006(1): 148-206.

Torres, A. C. Is This Work Sustainable? Teacher Turnover and Perceptions of Workload in Charter Management Organiazaions.*Urban Education*, 2016(8): 891-914.

Wei, S.(韦斯林),Wang, Q(王巧丽), Jia, Y.(贾远娥) et al. A Model of Subject Teaching Competencies: Based on the Grounded Theory and In-depth Interviews with 10 Superfine Teachers of Secondary School(教师学科教学能力模型的建构——基于扎根理论的10位特级教师的深度访谈).*Teacher Education Research*(教师教育研究), 2017(4): 84-91.

Xu, J.(徐娟) & Wang, J.(王建平). Influencing Factors of High-Level Young Talent Mobility in Chinese Universities: A Political Study Based on Talent Resume Tracking of Five Types of Projects(中国大学高层次青年人才流动的影响因素——基于5类项目人才履历追踪的实证研究).*Modern University Education*(现代大学教育), 2021(3): 78-87.

Xu, Y. J. Faculty Turnover: Discipline-specific Attention is Warranted. *Research in Higher Education*, 2008(1): 40-61.

You, Y.（由由）. Opportunity Costs and Faculty Turnover Intention：An Empirical Investigation(机会成本与高校教师流动意向的实证研究).*China Higher Education Research*(中国高教研究), 2014(3): 60-67.

Zhang, J.(张佳) & Xia, M.(夏美茹).Leaving or Straying: a Review of International Literature on Factors Affecting Teacher Mobility(离开还是留任:国际教师流动影响因素研究述评).*Journal of Comparative Education*(比较教育学报), 2021(3): 135-151.

Zhang, J.(张继明). On the Features of the University Organization and the System Reform of Chinese Universities(大学的组织特征、组织异化与制度变革).*Journal of Jinan University(Social Science Edition)*[济南大学学报(社会科学版)], 2015(2): 70-74, 92.

Zhang, X.(张曦琳) & Tian, X.(田贤鹏). Teacher Mobility Management in the Construction of "Double First-Class": Challenges, Difficulties and Measures("双一流"建设中的教师流动治理:挑战、困境与举措).*Higher Education Exploration* (高教探索), 2020(3): 108-114.

Zhang, Z.(张卓).Dilemma and Outlet: Research on the Orderly Flow of University Teachers from Perspectives of Stakeholders(困局与出路:基于利益相关者视角的高校教师有序流动研究).*Heilongjiang Researches on Higher Education*(黑龙江高教研究), 2023(1): 84-90.

Zhe, H.(者卉) & Sun, B.(孙百才). The Course and Characteristic of University Teacher Mobility of our Country: Based on the Historical Analysis of 70 Years since the Founding of New China(我国大学教师流动的历程与特征——基于新中国成立 70 年的历史分析).*Education and Economy*(教育与经济), 2019(6): 57-62,78.

Enhancing Economic Cooperation between Western China and Central Asian Countries within the Belt and Road Initiative Framework[*]

Wang Xiaohong[**]

Abstract: In response to the complex and evolving international landscape, exacerbated by various crises in the post-pandemic era, enhancing economic collaboration between Western China and Central Asian countries has become imperative within the framework of the Belt and Road Initiative (BRI). Despite encountering challenges, positioning Western China as a pivotal player and fostering economic ties with Central Asian nations is deemed indispensable for forging a community of shared future for humanity. This paper underscores the significance of prioritizing infrastructure development, bolstering trade and investment, fostering agricultural cooperation, and leveraging energy partnerships to maintain diplomatic equilibrium among major powers. Additionally, the paper advocates for intensified collaboration in diverse engineering projects to strengthen regional connectivity and prosperity.

Keywords: Belt and Road Initiative, western China, Central Asia, economic cooperation, route

The Belt and Road Initiative has energized into the deepening relations between China and Central Asian countries. Scholars are closely examining the economic cooperation between China and Central Asian countries through the lens of the Belt and Road Initiative, resulting in a continuous stream of research findings. However, most scholars tend to focus on the economic cooperation between China and the entire region. More targeted studies include Wu Hongwei's Economic and Trade Cooperation between China and Central Asian Countries from the Perspective of "The Belt and Road"(2018),

* Date Received: March 10, 2023; Date Revised: Feburary 21, 2024.

** Wang Xiaohong(王晓红),Ph. D. Candidate, The Institute of Collaborative Innovation of Belt & Road and Central Asia, Shaanxi Normal University.

Li Jianmin's "30 Years of Economic Cooperation between China and Central Asia: Policy Evolution, Progress in Key Areas and Future Development Path" (2022), and Wang Haiyan's "Comparative Study on Geo-Economic Cooperation between China and Central Asian Countries from the Perspective of the Belt and Road Initiative." (2020)

Few articles specifically address the unique geographical advantages of cooperation between western China and Central Asian countries and the particular significance of this cooperation for the Belt and Road Initiative. Currently, there are no monographs on this aspect in China. Relevant academic articles include Li Qi's "Current Situation and Development Trend of Local Cooperation between Shaanxi Province of China and Central Asian Countries"(2020) and Zhang Ru's "Prospective Research on Economic and Trade Cooperation between western China's Provinces and Central Asia under the New Development Pattern - Taking Xinjiang, Gansu, and Shaanxi as Examples."(2022) The former examines Shaanxi as a case study of a western province of China to explore the achievements in various fields of local cooperation with Central Asian countries and introduces key projects in the realm of economic and trade cooperation. The latter primarily investigates the accomplishments of cooperation between China's western provinces and Central Asian countries across various domains under the dual-cycle development pattern. It briefly summarizes the notable achievements in economic cooperation, analyzes the unfavorable factors hindering the development of bilateral economic and trade relations, and proposes recommendations for optimizing trade structures and establishing extensive logistics channels.

Given the shifting dynamics in Central Asia due to the conflict between Russia and Ukraine, it has become imperative to leverage the geographical advantages of western China and thoroughly explore the path of economic cooperation between western China and Central Asian countries to promote the development of economic and trade cooperation between China and Central Asian countries.

Geopolitical uncertainty and turbulence have prompted the exploration and development of new forms and projects aimed at enhancing economic cooperation between western China and Central Asian countries. Heightened competition within the region, coupled with the convergence of various global actors vying for dominance in economic, political, and humanitarian realms, underscores the necessity of considering innovative approaches and structures to forge robust connections for the community with a shared future.

The inception of the Belt and Road Initiative (BRI) in 2013 has significantly boosted trade and economic cooperation between western China and Central Asia. Nonetheless, several obstacles must be systematically addressed and overcome to enhance the quality of interaction.

Issues such as "debt trap diplomacy" in Kyrgyzstan and Tajikistan, ensuring the safety of Chinese enterprises, the profitability of specific projects (particularly in Kazakhstan), and the predictability of the political regimes in the region, among others, remain unresolved.

Central Asian countries are of economic interest to the People's Republic of China (PRC) for several crucial reasons. Firstly, they offer supplementary reservoirs of raw materials for the Chinese economy, particularly oil, gas, and metals, which collectively account for more than half of China's imports.

Secondly, with the initiation of the Belt and Road Initiative (BRI), the Central Asian region is emerging as a pivotal transport and transit nexus facilitating the passage of goods from China to western markets. Thirdly, fostering mutual trade and the engagement of Chinese entrepreneurs in Central Asia positively contribute to the economic advancement of western China's regions.

Moreover, enhancing economic cooperation entails the advancement of infrastructure projects, financial initiatives, investment ventures, and various other forms of collaboration. In this regard, it is prudent to examine these areas collectively.

1. Implementation of a Diversified Approach to Constructing Transportation Infrastructure and Establishing New Logistics Routes

As aptly highlighted in the report by the Eurasian Development Bank (EDB) titled "The Economy of Central Asia: A Fresh Perspective," the Central Asian region is poised for economic growth through the expansion of existing routes such as the International Transport Route "North-South," "Europe-Western China," Trans-Caspian International Transport Route, CAREC corridors, among others, and the establishment of new railway corridors including China - Kyrgyzstan - Uzbekistan, Kazakhstan - Uzbekistan - Afghanistan - Pakistan, and Tajikistan - Afghanistan - Turkmenistan (2022).

1.1 Kazakhstan has assumed a pivotal role in facilitating connectivity between western China and the Central Asian countries

Kazakhstan plays a paramount role in bolstering connectivity between Western China and the Central Asian countries. According to data from Kazakhstan Railways, from January to October 2022, China continues to be a key destination for both exports and imports. During this period, the volume of cargo transportation across the border between China and Kazakhstan increased by 12%. A total of 19.4 million tons of cargo were transported through the Dostyk-Alashankou and Altynkol-Khorgos railway crossings. Transit from China saw a 16% increase, while the export of Kazakhstani goods rose by 12%.

However, since the onset of the war between Russia and Ukraine, the infrastructure of Central Asia has struggled to keep up with the escalating flow of goods. Despite the favorable trends in Kazakh-Chinese logistics cooperation, it is crucial to acknowledge that both western China and Central Asian countries must explore new avenues for development. The current routes have become congested and fail to meet modern standards, resulting in delays in the delivery of goods. Consequently, Kazakhstan has initiated the construction of an additional railway line along its border with China.

The second track on the Dostyk-Moiynty line, adjacent to the Alashankou border crossing with China, aims to increase the capacity of this vital route by fivefold, from 12 pairs of trains to 60 pairs per day. Concurrently, construction of a new railway line has commenced as part of the National Project "Strong Regions - Driver of the Country's Development," beginning on November 17, 2022. Kazakh authorities estimate that the project's implementation will generate an additional 8.6 billion euros in budget revenues over 20 years. Moreover, this project is expected to address the transportation challenges faced by Kazakhstani exporters in this direction.

Furthermore, Kazakhstan is contemplating the opening of a third railway crossing between Kazakhstan (Bakhty) and China, along with the subsequent construction of the Ayagoz-Bakhty railway line featuring a border crossing terminal. This initiative is anticipated to result in a potential increase in shipments to China, potentially reaching 20 million tons.

During the summit of the leaders of the Organization of Turkic States (OTS) in Samarkand, the President of the Republic of Kazakhstan, Kassym-Jomart Tokayev, announced plans to attract $20 billion in investments by 2025 for the development of the Trans-Caspian International Transport Route (TCITR). The TCITR facilitates the transportation of goods from China to Europe via the territories of Kazakhstan, Azerbaijan, Georgia, and Turkey (2022).

1.2 The implementation of multiple railway projects will concurrently diversify trade and logistics connections between western China and Central Asia

The events in January 2022 in Kazakhstan highlighted certain deficiencies in the logistics routes linking western China and the Central Asian countries, particularly the excessive dependence on Kazakhstan. Therefore, special attention and emphasis should be placed on routes such as China-Kyrgyzstan-Uzbekistan, for which a memorandum on construction was signed during the SCO summit in Samarkand earlier this year. Presently, a feasibility study is ongoing, with a preliminary cost estimate for the route. According to recent reports, the commencement of railway construction is scheduled for autumn 2023.

The implementation of the China-Kyrgyzstan-Uzbekistan transport corridor project will eventually facilitate the connection of Uzbekistan and the People's Republic of China (PRC) through a single railway, spanning from the western borders of the PRC to the eastern borders of Uzbekistan via Kyrgyzstan. This initiative aims to establish the shortest and most efficient transport route for the PRC to access Central Asia, enabling the connectivity of Xinjiang - Uighur Autonomous Region of China with countries in the Persian Gulf and Transcaucasia, ultimately providing access to the Mediterranean Sea.

For Uzbekistan and Kyrgyzstan, this project holds significant importance as it offers an opportunity to integrate the countries into the global network of logistics routes that pass through China's seaports. The construction of this route will contribute to diversifying trade and logistics connections between Western China and the region, fostering stronger ties and expanding both the scope and quality of trade and services.

Another promising infrastructure endeavor is linked to the inauguration of the multimodal corridor "Tajikistan - Uzbekistan - Turkmenistan - Iran - Turkey," enabling the transportation of goods via water, air, and land routes. The advantage of this corridor lies in its ability to connect Tajikistan with the People's Republic of China through roadways, thereby revitalizing the Great Silk Road and promoting regional economic integration.

2. Enhancing Trade and Investment

In 2022, there has been a consistent rise in mutual trade among all Central Asian countries. From the standpoint of trade volume influenced by objective factors, Kazakhstan stands out as China's most significant trading partner in Central Asia.

According to the latest data, trade turnover between Kazakhstan and the PRC "in the nine months of 2022 grew by an annualized rate of 22.5%, reaching $23.2 billion." The PRC Ambassador to Kazakhstan anticipates that with these dynamics, a new record will be set in 2022, reaching $30 billion, which could potentially mark "the highest figure in the past 30 years." (Zhang, 2022)

By the end of 2022, the volume of trade between Kyrgyzstan and China is projected to reach $9 billion, reflecting an increase compared to the previous figure of $7.5 billion. However, a persistent issue in the economic interaction between the two countries is the unchanged commodity structure of exports and imports over many years. Kyrgyzstan primarily supplies China with raw materials such as wool, ores, and concentrates of precious metals, as well as scrap and waste of ferrous and non-ferrous metals. Conversely, imports from China typically include fabrics, clothing, footwear, engineering products, plastics, organic and inorganic chemicals, foodstuffs, vehicles, and more.

As statistics demonstrate, there remains a disparity in trade cooperation between countries, notably in favor of China. Consequently, there is a burgeoning negative balance for the Kyrgyz Republic, characterized by an abundance of raw materials in its exports compared to finished products in China's exports. It is imperative to underscore the most crucial areas of cooperation, including transport communication infrastructure, the fuel and energy sector, mining, agriculture, construction, border trade with the Xinjiang Uighur Autonomous Region (XUAR), as well as tourism. Bishkek expresses a keen interest in broadening this scope of cooperation.

According to the Ministry of Investment and Foreign Trade of Uzbekistan, the trade turnover between China and Uzbekistan reached $6.8 billion in the first nine months of this year, compared to $7.4 billion for the whole of 2021. Uzbekistan is also a significant supplier of natural gas to China, earning $768 million for gas supplies in the first nine months of 2022, a 60% increase from the same period last year. Notably, China ranked first in the import of cars to Uzbekistan during the same period. Between January and September 2022, Uzbekistan imported 8,682 cars from China, surpassing imports from South Korea (7,117 cars) and Kazakhstan (4,431 cars). The ministry further clarified that approximately 1,629 electric cars have been imported to Uzbekistan since the beginning of the year, with 1,422 of them originating from China.

In addition to car imports, China also leads in the export of phones to Uzbekistan. Out of a total volume of 2.4 million devices worth $162.1 million, China supplied 1.8 million mobile phones to Uzbekistan.

According to the Center for Strategic Studies of Tajikistan, "the volume of foreign trade turnover between the Republic of Tajikistan and the People's Republic of China for the first 7 months of 2022 amounted to $766.1 million, marking an increase of $313.9 million or 69.4% compared to the same period in 2021. China's share in Tajikistan's foreign trade turnover reached 18.5%, ranking third." Notably, nearly a third of foreign investment inflows into Tajikistan between 2007 and 2021 originated from China, accounting for 29.5% (2022). By 2017, China had surpassed and outpaced Russia, which had been a consistent leader and investor in Tajikistan's recent history.

From January to September 2022, the bilateral trade turnover between Turkmenistan and China reached $7.993 billion. Over this period, the mutual trade turnover between the two countries surged by 51.7%. China's exports to Turkmenistan increased by 65.3%, while imports from Turkmenistan rose by 50.6%.

Turkmenistan maintains its position as the largest supplier of natural gas to China, providing over 20% of China's total imports of natural gas in August, amounting to 2.9

billion cubic meters out of 13.2 billion cubic meters. From January to October 2022, Turkmenistan earned $8.23 billion from gas supplies to China, marking a 53% increase compared to the same period in 2021.

As reported by *People's Daily*, total Chinese investment in Central Asia reached approximately $40 billion by the end of 2020, with Kazakhstan receiving $21.4 billion of this investment. Furthermore, by the end of 2021, 7,700 Chinese firms were operating in Central Asia.

It is noteworthy that the primary areas for investment allocation in Central Asian republics include the development of the energy sector and the provision of oil and gas supplies to China, as well as infrastructure development in the context of the Belt and Road Initiative (BRI) project. Additionally, Beijing provides funds for the creation and renovation of infrastructure facilities such as railways, highways, logistics centers, and border checkpoints, which enhance connectivity between Central Asia and the western regions of China.

3. Agriculture is of Mutual Interest

All Central Asian countries are keen on expanding and diversifying their export deliveries to China. Notably, the agro-industrial sector is experiencing active development between Kazakhstan and China. For instance, over 1,100 enterprises in Kazakhstan have been granted the authorization to export their products to China.

In 2022, Kazakhstan seized the opportunity to export oilseed meals and oilcakes derived from oilseeds, camel milk, and other organic products to China. Notably, Kazakhstan has witnessed a significant uptick in the production and export of vegetable oils over the past year. Processing volumes for sunflower seeds have surged by 40% from October 2021 to September 2022. Correspondingly, exports have also seen a notable increase, with sunflower oil exports doubling and rapeseed exports rising by 38%.

China emerges as the primary consumer of Kazakhstani rapeseed oil, having received 24,000 tons of this product over the specified period. Additionally, China ranks second, after Uzbekistan, in the import of Kazakhstani sunflower oil, with an import volume of 59,000 tons. Moreover, Kazakh producers are eager to expand fish exports to China.

Kazakh millers have been endeavoring to enter the markets of western China for several years, but various challenges persist in this regard, particularly concerning Chinese tariffs on flour imports.

Kyrgyz producers are Keen to export food products such as fruits, nuts, honey, water, meat, and fish to China. Notably, on November 14, China lifted the ban on the supply of Kyrgyz honey, which was introduced in 2020 due to the coronavirus pandemic. However, deliveries will be conducted exclusively by companies listed in the register of the veterinary service under the Ministry of Agriculture of Kyrgyzstan and China, and possessing a 5G veterinary and sanitary passport.

4. Energy Cooperation to Balance Russia

China has emerged as a significant player in the energy industry, which is crucial for the modernization efforts of both Kyrgyzstan and Tajikistan. China has notably contributed to the construction and modernization of combined heat and power plants in both countries.

In 2013, China revitalized its oil and gas cooperation with the Kyrgyz Republic by announcing plans to construct the fourth line of the gas pipeline (line D), known as "Turkmenistan - China" pipeline, which would pass through the territories of Uzbekistan, Tajikistan, and Kyrgyzstan. This line is an integral component of the gas pipeline "Central Asia-China" and aims to increase its total capacity to 85 billion cubic meters.

The agreement between the governments of China and Kyrgyzstan regarding the construction of the main gas pipeline was signed on September 11, 2013, in Bishkek during the summit of the Shanghai Cooperation Organization. Although construction in Kyrgyzstan was scheduled to commence as early as 2016, delays in the construction of the pipeline in Tajikistan have caused the Kyrgyz part of the gas pipeline lagging the announced work schedules.

The construction of Line D represents one of the most challenging engineering projects in the history of pipeline construction worldwide. This project aims to integrate the China-Central Asia gas pipeline network, closely connecting the five countries of Central Asia with China. This integration will deepen energy cooperation between western China and the Central Asian countries, thereby stimulating trade and economic exchanges and strengthening traditional friendships based on mutual benefit.

Oil and gas cooperation with China, including pipeline construction, enables Kyrgyzstan and Tajikistan to pursue energy development and contributes to the establishment of paths for economic growth. Additionally, energy cooperation with China has the potential to balance Russia's strong position in the region and its participation in the Eurasian Economic Union (EAEU), showcasing alternative opportunities for cooperation with geopolitical power centers.

Given mutual interests, oil and gas cooperation can yield a synergistic effect, benefiting both the diversification of the oil sector in the region and China's energy security. In conclusion, upon the completion of Line D construction, a new, more fruitful, and active stage of strategic cooperation between Central Asia and China is expected to commence.

5. Project Cooperation in Other Fields

Kazakhstan is demonstrating interest in leveraging China's expertise in oil storage. Currently, Kazakh oil is promptly exported due to technological requirements, and halting production is not feasible. In contrast, China has established extensive oil storage facilities, enabling the country to meet internal needs for 3-4 months without additional supplies. Consequently, Kazakh authorities have directed KazMunayGas to explore a project for constructing a large oil storage facility in the Atyrau region, while the Ministry of Energy is tasked with negotiating with major mining companies for the construction of additional storage facilities.

Given China's proficiency in constructing complex facilities, sulfur production also presents promising opportunities. For instance, the Chinese company CAMC Engineering secured a $289 million contract from Uzbek authorities for constructing the Olympic Village near Tashkent, scheduled for the IV Summer Asian and V Para-Asian Youth Games in 2025. This follows CAMC Engineering's previous significant contracts in Uzbekistan, including the launch of a chemical plant in Navoi in 2019, for which it received $440 million, and winning a contract in September of this year for constructing a cable car near the Charvak reservoir.

China's economic model, often referred to as the "Chinese economic miracle," has long been a source of fascination for Central Asian countries. As such, China is well-positioned to share its experience in poverty alleviation, particularly with countries like Kyrgyzstan and Tajikistan. For instance, discussions between the Ministry of Labor of the Kyrgyz Republic and the Permanent Representative of China to the FAO in Rome explored the potential of developing the "social contracts" program. Under this initiative, low-income families would sign social contracts with the state, receiving 100,000 Kyrgyz soms (approximately $1,200 USD) to establish small businesses. This initiative is inspired by Deng Xiaoping's reforms, which introduced loan repayment programs for impoverished families. Additionally, collaboration with the Chinese Academy of Agriculture and Science, renowned for its research capacity in poverty alleviation and productivity improvement, is under consideration.

In summary, the PRC is committed to cooperation based on the "win-win" principle, aiming to strengthen bilateral relations in economic and trade spheres.

6. Recommendations

In light of pressing overwhelming environmental challenges, such as global warming and summer droughts, collaboration on in "green projects" and the advancement of a "green economy," including projects for renewable energy sources, hold significant promise for all countries in the region. The diversification of trade between western China and the Central Asian countries, including the expansion of eco-products for export to western China, can yield synergistic effects. However, this requires further efforts to establish a modern ecosystem for trade.

To enhance economic relations, it is crutial to support the organization of events for stakeholders, including bilateral business forums, SCO summits, C5 + 1 platforms, and BRI forums.

Regarding the challenges in economic cooperation, discrepancies in trade data between Central Asian countries and China persist, partly due to different methods of calculating imports and exports and the existence of smuggling. Accelerating digitalization, particularly at border checkpoints, can streamline trade flows and enhance transparency in tax revenues for the budgets of Central Asian countries. China's expertise in expanding non-cash trade operations is particularly valuable, offering the potential for increasing income and reducing shadow economy in Central Asian countries.

Cooperation in high technologies and digitalization, such as creating e-commerce platforms and digitalizing trade operations, deserves special attention. These efforts can enhance transparency and tax compliance. Amidst global players' confrontation in the region, establishing a new financial system based on the Yuan or trade in national currencies emerges as a promising direction for the future.

The effectiveness of trade and logistics centers, exemplified by "Khorgos" in Kazakhstan, underscores their role in strengthening trade and economic cooperation. This experience holds significant potential for Kyrgyzstan and Tajikistan, offering opportunities for cross-border trade, local employment, and increased freight flows between China and the region. Renewed negotiations on constructing a logistics center in the Naryn region of Kyrgyzstan could pave the way for the successful realization of this project.

In the realm of high-tech cooperation, addressing information security vulnerabilities in Central Asia suggests a promising project: the construction of fiber optic lines from western China. This initiative aims to reduce regional internet dependence on a single country, enhance internet speed, and bolster information security.

Considering China's growing presence in the Central Asian electric car market, collaboration in establishing infrastructure for eco-friendly transport holds promise. This indudes joint ventures for manufacturing electric batteries and chargers utilizing Chinese technologies. The capitals of Kazakhstan, Kyrgyzstan, and Uzbekistan grapple with air pollution issues, positioning China's assistance in bolstering electric transport infrastructure to address environmental concerns and enhance its regional image.

China's leadership in global innovation and artificial intelligence presents opportunities for fostering long-term economic ties between regions. Given the shortage of skilled personnel in Central Asia and challenges in human capital development, establishing Lu Ban workshops across the region can facilitate the training of technical specialists, particularly in STEM fields, to meet the demands of the technical sectors of the economy.

Creating a conducive environment for economic cooperation entails addressing challenges such as the debt trap and social unrest. Efforts to mitigate the debt trap and minimize its impact are essential, along with fostering people-to-people connections and leveraging soft power to promote the positive outcomes of Chinese economic projects and cooperation initiatives. These measures can contribute to fostering a favorable atmosphere for sustainable economic cooperation.

7. Conclusion

An analysis of the trade and economic cooperation between Central Asian countries and China over the past three decades reveals several key conclusions.

Firstly, China has emerged as into the primary trade and economic partner of Central Asian countries. The trade turnover between China and the Central Asian states has demonstrated consistent growth.

Secondly, Central Asian countries have secured their status as suppliers of hydrocarbon and natural resources to China. In Beijing's energy policy, the Central Asian region has gained independent strategic importance, with the share of oil and gas supplied from Central Asia to China increasing significantly. Consequently, all Central Asian countries are keen on leveraging the Belt and Road Initiative (BRI) to boost national industrial production and reduce dependence on raw materials. However, achieving this goal necessitates developing relevant industries, investing in science and personnel, and gaining wide access to markets, particularly in China.

Thirdly, China has established a network of transportation routes in Central Asia aimed at accessing markets in the Middle East and Europe. The extensive routes being constructed by Beijing, through Central Asian countries, have the potential to significantly reduce time, financial, and logistical costs in the future.

Amid ongoing global economic turbulence, China has emerged as a crucial source of investment and technology for almost all Central Asian states. Beijing's emphasis on mutual development lays the groundwork for enhancing the economic potential and infrastructure base of the region, creating a diversified network of transport and communication routes facilitating access to global markets.

While the extent of Central Asian participation in the Belt and Road Initiative varies, the overall trend toward deepening ties between Central Asia and China across all spheres remains consistent. Thus, strengthening economic cooperation between western China and Central Asian countries emerges as a prevailing trend.

References

China Promises More Investment at Central Asia Summit(中国在中亚峰会上承诺进行更多投资),2022. Available from: https://eurasianet. org/china-promises-more-investment-at-central-asia-summit [Accessed March 20, 2023].

Eurasian Development Bank(欧亚开发银行).The Economy of Central Asia:A Fresh Perspective(中亚经济:一个全新的视角),2022. Available from: https://eabr.org/upload/iblock/1fe/EDB_2022_Report-3_The-Economy-of-CA_eng.pdf[Accessed March 20, 2023].

Kazakhstan lays second track on railway line to China(哈萨克斯坦在通往中国铁路线上铺设第二条轨道), 2022. Available from: https://www. railfreight. com / beltandroad/2022/11/22/37838[Accessed March 20, 2023].

Kazakhstan Temir Zholy(哈萨克斯坦铁路公司).Demonstrates a Positive Trend in Freight Trafflc(货物运输上展现了积极态势).Available from: https://railways. kz/articles/company/news/_ktj_demonstriruet_polojitelnuu_dinamiku_gruzovyh_perevozok[Accessed March 20, 2023].

Li, J.(李建民).30 Years of Economic Cooperation between China and Central Asia: Policy Evolution, Progress in Key Areas and Future Development Path (中国与中亚经济合作30年——政策演进、重点领域进展与未来发展路径) . *Russian Studies*(俄罗斯研究) , 2022(5): 74-94.

Li,Q.(李琪).*Current Situation and Development Trend of Local Cooperation between Shaanxi Province of China and Central Asian Countries*(中国陕西与中亚国家地方合作现状与发展趋势).Beijing: Social Sciences Academic Press(北京:社会科学文献出版社), 2020.

Wang, H.(王海燕), Comparative Research on Geo-economic Cooperation between China and Central Asian Countries under the Perspective of OBOR ("一带一路"视域下中国与中亚国家地缘经济合作比较研究). *World Regional Studies*(世界地理研究), 2020, 29(1): 18-29.

Wu,H.(吴宏伟) . Economic and Trade Cooperation between China and Central Asian Countries from the Perspective of "The Belt and Road"("一带一路"视域下中国与中亚国家的经贸合作).*Journal of Xinjiang Normal University*(新疆师范大学学报), 2018(39): 92-101.

Zhang, R. (张 如), Prospective Research on Economic and Trade Cooperation between Western China's Provinces and Central Asia under the New Development

Pattern：Taking Xinjiang, Gansu, and Shaanxi as Examples(新发展格局下中国西部省份与中亚经贸合作前瞻研究——以新疆、甘肃、陕西为例). *Foreign Trade Practice*(对外经贸实务), 2022(8): 74-79.

Встреча с чрезвычайным и полномочным послом китайской народной республика в республике Таджикистан(同中国驻塔吉克斯坦特命全权大使会谈). Available from:https://mts.tj/ru/4187/news/[Accessed March 20, 2023].

Главное таможенное управление КНР сообщило, что среди поставляющих Китаю топливо по газопроводу государств первое место продолжает занимать Туркмения(中国海关总署通报,土库曼斯坦在对华输气的国家中依然占据首位). Available from:https://salamnews.tm/ru/section/ykdysadyyet/sowda/ turkmenistanyn - we -hytayyn - sowdadolanysygy -9 - ayda - 8 - milliard - dollara - golaylady-cf0640[Accessed March 20, 2023].

Давлат статистика қўмитаси маълумотларига кўра, 2022 йилнинг январь-сентя- брь ойларида Ўзбекистон 25 та хорижий давлатлардан енгил автомобиллар импорт қилган(根据国家统计局数据,乌兹别克斯坦2022年从25个国家进口轻型汽车). Available from:https://t.me/statistika_rasmiy/2785[Accessed March 20, 2023].

Давлат статистика қўмитаси маълумотларига кўра, Ўзбекистонга 2022 йилнинг январь-октябрь ойларида хориждан қиймати 162,1 млн. АҚШ долларига тенг бўлган қарийб 2,4 млн. дона мобил телефон импорт қилинган(根据国家统计局数据,2022年1月—10月,乌兹别克斯坦从国外进口240万辆小汽车,共计162 100 000 美元). Available from:https://t.me/statistika_rasmiy/2887[Accessed March 20, 2023].

Казахстан планирует открыть третий ж/д переход на границе с Китаем (哈萨克斯坦计划在中国边境开通第三条铁路通道). Available from:https://ru.sputnik.kz/ 20221128/kazakhstan-planiruet-otkryt-tretiy-zhd-perekhod-na-granitse-s-kitaem- 29809716.html[Accessed March 20, 2023].

Казахстан продолжит наращивать объемы производства и экспорта раститель-ных масел в 2022/23 МГ(哈萨克斯坦在2022—2023年继续增加植物油的生产和出口). Available from:https://www.oilworld.ru/news/335408[Accessed March 20, 2023].

Как Китай догнал и перегнал Россию в Таджикистане?(中国将在塔吉克斯坦赶上并超过俄罗斯？). Available from: https://asiaplustj. info / news / tajikistan / economic/20220630/investitsii-kak-kitai-dognal-i-peregnalrossiyu-v-tadzhikistane [Accessed March 20, 2023].

Министр труда обсудил поддержку Китая новой программе преодоления бедности(劳动部长讨论中国支持新扶贫计划).Available from:https://mlsp.gov.

kg / 2022 / 11 / 15 / ministr - truda - obsudil - podderzhku - kitaya - novoj -
programmepreodoleniya-bednosti/[Accessed March 20, 2023].

Первый объект газопровода «Центральная Азия - Китай» в Таджикистане
практически готов(塔吉克斯坦首个中亚—中国天然气管道项目基本建成).
Available from: https://www. ritmeurasia. org / news -- 2019 -07 - 16 - pervyj -obekt -
gazoprovoda - centralnajaazija - kitaj - v - tadzhikistane -prakticheski - gotov - 43829
[Accessed March 20, 2023].

Поставки СПГ в Китай из России в январе-сентябре выросли на 29%(1 月—9 月
俄罗斯对华液化天然气的供应量增加 29%). Available from: https://tass.ru /
ekonomika/16136707[Accessed March 20, 2023].

Президент Касым - Жомарт Токаев принял участие в саммите Организации
тюркских государств(哈萨克斯坦总统托卡耶夫准备出席突厥语国家组织峰
会). Available from: https://www.akorda.kz / ru / prezident - kasym - zhomart - tokaev -
prinyal - uchastie - v - sammite - organizaciityurkskih - gosudarstv - 11104851[Accessed
March 20, 2023].

Сайфиддин Караев(塞弗金·卡拉耶夫). В Душанбе представители маршрут«Китай-
Турция»через Территорию Таджикистана(在杜尚别建成中国—土耳其航线的
代表).Available from:https://asiaplustj.info/ru/news/tajikistan/economic/20221020/
v - dushanbe - predstavili - marshrut - kitaiturtsiya - cherez - territoriyu -tadzhikistana
[Accessed March 20, 2023].

Товарооборот Казахстана и Китая может достигнуть в этом году $30 млрд(本年
度中哈贸易额达到 300 亿美元).Available from:https://kz.kursiv.media/2022-11-
09 / tovarooborot - kazahstana - i - kitayamozhet - dostignut - v - etom - godu-30 - mlrd/
[Accessed March 20, 2023].

Товарооборот Кыргызстана с Китаем до конца года может достигнуть $9 млрд
(中吉贸易额年底可能达到 90 亿美元). Available from: https://kabar. kg / news /
tovarooborot - kyrgyzstana - s - kitaem - do - kontca - goda - mozhet - dostignut-9 - mlrd/
[Accessed March 20, 2023].

Товарооборот между Казахстаном и Китаем за девять месяцев вырос на 22,5%
(中哈贸易额 9 个月内增长 22.5%).Available from:https://www.inform.kz/amp/
tovarooborot - mezhdu - kazahstanom - i - kitaem - za - devyat - mesyacev - vyros -na-22-
5_a3995538.

Товарооборот Туркменистана и Китая за 9 месяцев вырос до 8 млрд. Долларов
США(土库曼斯坦和中国的贸易额在9个月内增长到80亿美元).Available from:
https://salamnews.tm/ru/section/ykdysadyyet/sowda/turkmenistanyn-we-hytayyn-
sowdadolanysygy-9-ayda-8-milliard-dollara-golaylady-cf0640[Accessed March 20,
2023].

Укрепление Нового шёлкового пути. Строительство очередной линии из Казахстана в Китай(巩固新丝绸之路。建设从哈萨克斯坦至中国的新干线). Available from: https://trans. info / ru / ukreplenie - novogo - shelkovogo - puti - stroitelstvo - ocherednoy - linii - iz - kazahstana - vkitay - 314524[Accessed March 20, 2023].

Theoretical Logic and Practical Path of Income Distribution for Original Data Providers: The Investigation from the Perspective of Common Prosperity[*]

Wang Yanchuan, Lyu Junzhi[**]

Abstract: The report of the 20th CPC National Congress presents clear requirements for improving the policy system of distribution based on elements. As a vital component of the fundamental system of data elements, the income distribution of data elements holds significant importance in advancing distribution system reforms in the new era and fostering the collective prosperity of all citizens. The original data providers, exemplified by platform consumers and employees, wield decisive influence in shaping data elements, supplying raw materials for data elements, and serving as "laborers" in data element production. Their involvement should be a focal point of data element income distribution. Additionally, there exists inherent alignment between the participation of original data providers in factor income distribution and the logical basis, development objectives, and value standards of common prosperity. Nevertheless, in the current era, due to data ownership ambiguities, the involvement of original data providers in distribution is imperfect, and they face technical challenges. Thus, it is imperative to bolster the establishment of laws and regulations to safeguard the income of original data providers' data elements; enhance organizational mechanisms to forge a new framework for data element distribution; and accelerate digital technology innovation to surmount barriers to data element distribution. Pioneering the practical avenue for original data

---

* This article was originally published in *Journal of Shaanxi Normal University (Philosophy and Social Sciences Edition)*, Vol. 52, No.3. Original Title:原始数据提供者参与数据要素收益分配的理论逻辑与实践路径——以共同富裕为视角的考察.

Translators: Wang Qi(王琦), Doctoral Student of International Business School, Shaanxi Normal University. Her research focuses on the Digital Economy and Economic Resilience. Wang Qinmei(王琴梅), Professor of International Business School, Shaanxi Normal University. Her research focuses on Economic Development of Western China.

** Wang Yanchuan(王延川), Ph. D. of Law, Professor of School of Marxism, Northwestern Polytechnical University, Doctoral Supervisor, Researcher of Shaanxi Provincial Key Public Opinion Information Research Center of Northwestern Polytechnical University. Lyu Junzhi(吕君枝), Ph.D. Candidate, School of Marxism, Northwestern Polytechnical University.

providers to engage in data element distribution is the sole path for our nation to achieve substantial strides in common prosperity in the digital age.

Keywords: original data providers; data elements; benefit distribution; common prosperity; "Data Twenty"

At different stages of socialist revolution, construction, reform, and development, the Communist Party of China has consistently regarded achieving common prosperity as the fundamental value guiding the continuous struggle of the entire people.[①] The 20th National Congress report of the Party explicitly states, "Common prosperity is the fundamental requirement of socialism with Chinese characteristics." (Xi et al., 2022) Through theoretical exploration and practical accumulation, China has continuously taken solid steps on the path of promoting common prosperity, laying a solid foundation for achieving common prosperity for all the people in the new era (Guo, 2021). As China's socialist practice with Chinese characteristics deepens, it is necessary not only to implement the concept and practice of common prosperity in various aspects of social production, distribution, exchange, and consumption but also to explore new forms and methods to achieve common prosperity. The 20th National Congress report proposes to "improve the policy system of factor distribution, explore various channels to increase the factor income of middle and low-income groups, and increase the property income of urban and rural residents through multiple channels." (Xi et al., 2022) It emphasizes "efforts to promote common prosperity for all the people and resolutely prevent polarization." (Xi et al., 2022) In other words, perfecting the policy of factor distribution has become an important means to increase the income of Chinese workers and promote common prosperity.

The utilization of data as a critical factor of production has introduced new variables to China's economic growth and serves as a crucial source for creating material wealth.

---

① The concept of "common prosperity" was first proposed by Mao Zedong in the 1953 Resolution of the Central Committee of the Communist Party of China on the Development of Agricultural Production Cooperatives. The resolution states: In order to further improve agricultural productivity, the most fundamental task of the Party's work in rural areas is to be good at using clear and understandable principles and methods that are acceptable to farmers to educate and promote the gradual joint organization of farmers, gradually implement socialist transformation of agriculture, and transform agriculture from a backward small-scale individual economy to an advanced large-scale cooperative economy, in order to gradually overcome industry and agriculture "The contradiction between the development of these two economic sectors and the gradual and complete elimination of poverty for farmers to achieve common prosperity and universal prosperity." Please refer to *Reference Materials on the History of the Communist Party of China (8) Socialist Transformation of the Ownership of Production Materials and the First Five Year Plan Period of the National Economy*, People's Publishing House, 1980 edition, page 11.

The market value of data elements is becoming more prominent. As of 2021, the scale of China's data trading market has exceeded 50 billion yuan, and it is predicted by the China Academy of Information and Communications Technology that the scale will reach 220 billion yuan by 2025 (Yang, 2023). In addition to generating important economic value on its own, data elements are also crucial for strengthening the digital economy, accelerating the deep integration of the digital economy and the real economy, empowering industrial digitization and digital industrialization, and leading high-quality economic and social development through digital innovation (Chen & Yin, 2019). In the process of forming enterprise data elements, original data providers, represented by consumers and employees, play a decisive role. On the one hand, the information provided by original data providers constitutes the foundation of data elements. On the other hand, the labor of original data providers stimulates the generation of the original data sets that make up data elements. Based on this, it is reasonable for original data providers to participate in the distribution of benefits related to data elements. However, the reality is that original data providers not only fail to receive data benefits commensurate with their contributions, but consumers also encounter phenomena such as data-driven price discrimination (Hu & Feng, 2022), and delivery personnel are trapped in platform algorithm systems (Wang & Wu, 2022). The protection of the data interests of original data providers is urgently needed.

On December 19, 2022, the Central Committee of the Communist Party of China and the State Council issued the "Opinions of the Central Committee of the Communist Party of China and The State Council on Building a data basic System to Better Play the role of data elements" (hereinafter referred to as the "Twenty Articles on Data"). It explicitly states the need to "establish a data element benefit distribution system that reflects efficiency and promotes fairness" and "emphasis should be placed on protecting the input-output benefits of all parties involved in data elements, safeguarding the rights and interests of data resource assets in accordance with laws and regulations, exploring ways for individuals, enterprises, and the public to share value and benefits from data, establishing and improving a more reasonable market evaluation mechanism, and promoting the matching of labor contributions and remuneration for workers." (State Council, 2022) This indicates that in the era of the digital economy, ensuring the interests of all parties involved in data elements has become a top-level design at the national level. The contribution and return of laborers should be safeguarded. However, the "Data Twenty" only provides principled regulations on whether original data providers should participate in the distribution of benefits related to data elements, lacking clear design in terms of the mechanisms and pathways for original data providers to participate in and secure the distribution of benefits. Further exploration and research should be conducted in this regard. Currently, there is limited literature focused on the participation of original data providers in the distribution of benefits related to data elements, which is not conducive to the advancement and realization of common prosperity in the digital age. Discussing the legitimacy of the participation of original data providers in the distribution of benefits related to data elements, the relationship between the distribution of benefits related to data elements and common prosperity, and how to ensure that original data providers receive corresponding benefits through mechanism design all have important theoretical and practical significance.

1. Analysis of the Legitimacy of Original Data Providers Participating in the Distribution of Benefits Related to Data Elements

The data element promotes the enormous growth of social material wealth, and the distribution of this wealth directly affects whether ordinary people can truly share the dividends of the digital economy. The original data provider is a participant in the production of data elements, who has contributed to the value generation of data elements and should receive a corresponding distribution of data element benefits, but this phenomenon has not appeared. There are many reasons involved, one of which is the significant controversy over whether the original data provider should participate in the distribution of data element benefits. Opponents argue that the original data provider cannot participate in the distribution of data benefits, and the main reason for their opposition is that individuals are actually unable to participate in the distribution of data benefits because the value of individual data is essentially zero (Chen, 2020). Although the rights to individual data information belong to individuals, as the aggregation and analysis of individual data information are completed by the platform, the relevant data rights should belong exclusively to the platform (Wang, 2020). After being desensitized, data information can no longer be associated with individuals and no longer belongs to personal information. The platform uses personal information reasonably in commercial scenarios, and the profits generated from this do not need to be distributed to the original data owner (Luo, 2023). Recognizing that individual users have property rights over data lacks theoretical support in traditional legal theory, and the interests of user data are not feasible. Supporters believe that original data providers, such as platform consumers and workers, are eligible to participate in the distribution of data benefits (Wang et al, 2021).

The main reasons for their support are: the ownership of original data elements should be distinguished from the ownership of secondary development and utilization data. As the source of data elements is selfish data, the former belongs to an individual who enjoys the corresponding right to benefit from data elements, Individuals can enjoy profit commissions from the use of data production factors through the ownership of source data; The profits generated by internet platforms based on data products and services should be allocated to various entities involved in the data production process, and 20% or 30% of the data element income should be returned to the data producers (Research Group of the Macroeconomic Research Institute of the National Development and Reform Commission, 2021; Yan et al., 2021; Huang, 2023). In addition to the clearly opposing views mentioned above, there is another view that the production of data elements involves two types of entities: data processing enterprises and original data information providers, and requires a return to the original data information provider. However, this return is not a distribution of benefits, but a reasonable compensation (Wang et al., 2020). Due to controversy, it is necessary to analyze the production process of data elements, clarify the legitimacy of the participation of original data providers in the distribution of data element benefits, and clarify the logical premise for the participation of original data providers in the distribution of data element benefits.

1.1 Raw data is the foundation for the formation of data elements

Although a single source of raw data cannot generate value, only the data elements can generate value. However, raw data provides the raw materials for the formation of data elements and is the foundation for their formation. The raw data is processed to form a data product, which meets the requirements of production materials and becomes a data element. Specifically, the production of data elements is mainly carried out on the platform. Through the log collection system of sensors and online apps, the raw data is obtained and used as raw materials to enter the data production platform. After being processed by an electronic data collector (EDL), it is stored in the platform's data warehouse. After cleaning, filtering, and aggregating in the data warehouse, this data will enter the data application layer of the platform and produce data products that meet different business needs in the data application layer. The platform gains data benefits by using and selling these data products. At this point, data products belong to data elements, which obtain sustained data value through participation in production and sales. Raw data is the foundation for the value of data elements. The value of data elements depends on the quantity, scale, and diversity of the original data.

Related studies have shown that when data elements are applied to prediction models and machine learning models, the amount of raw data directly affects the accuracy of the prediction model (Zhou et al., 2016). Similarly, the performance of machine learning models is highly dependent on the amount of data. The larger the amount of data, the stronger the neural network it feeds, and the higher the accuracy of the machine learning model (Halevy et al., 2009). The scale of raw data has a scalability effect on the value of data elements. The larger the scale of raw data, the more potential value of data elements can be stimulated, thereby maximizing the development of the digital industry (The Economist, 2017). As the saying goes, "a clever woman cannot cook without rice." Without raw data to provide a continuous source of raw materials for the production of data elements, the production of data elements only has theoretical possibilities and does not have practical feasibility. It can be seen that raw data plays a decisive role in the formation and value of data elements, and is the basis for the formation of data elements.

1.2 The original data provider acts as a laborer in the production process of data elements

In the production process of data elements, knowledge workers such as programmers and data analysts contribute to the production of data elements through their knowledge and technical capabilities. This labor contribution is recognized and safeguarded through relevant contracts signed with platform enterprises, entitling them to a portion of the revenue distribution of data elements. However, original data providers do not typically sign specific contracts related to data revenue distribution. Where does the legitimacy of their data revenue distribution lie? According to Marx, the labor process involves laborers using labor materials to process and produce the use-value of labor objects, encompassing three elements: laborers, labor objects, and labor materials. Laborers are individuals participating in labor production activities, and labor objects refer to all material resources necessary for labor production. The process of generating original data essentially constitutes a labor process, manifesting not only in tangible material production processes but also in data production processes occurring in the digital realm, such as registering, logging in, searching, clicking, and browsing. For instance, when using a platform, original data providers often need to fill in personal information for registration before accessing the platform's services. The actions of filling out forms and clicking are forms of "labor" in themselves. Consumers purchasing goods or using services on a platform also generate consumption data for the platform. Similarly, ride-sharing drivers and food delivery riders produce comprehensive original data, including consumer data, pricing data, and location data, while performing their work. Comparing this to Marx's concept of the labor process, original data falls under the category of labor objects, and original data providers participating in data labor production are considered laborers in the context of data elements.

Therefore, in the initial distribution, based on the principle of distributing according to production factors, laborers can use their labor input as a basis for participation in distribution and earning income. Naturally, original data providers can participate in the revenue distribution of data elements based on their labor contributions. However, in the current stage, the distribution received by original data providers is often limited to "free" use of platform services for consumers and wages for laborers based on physical labor. In practice, these distributions do not adequately compensate original data providers for their contributions to the value generation of data elements. In summary, whether providing personal information or contributing a substantial amount of original data to the platform through labor, both constitute contributions to data elements. Therefore, in the initial distribution, original data providers are entitled to a share of the revenue from data elements.

1.3 This constitutes an inevitable requirement for establishing a fair and efficient data element revenue distribution system

Including original data providers in the scope of data element revenue distribution can further promote fairness and efficiency in data element allocation, aligning with the spirit of the "Data Twenty" Measures. The "Data Twenty" Measures explicitly state the need to "establish a data element revenue distribution system that reflects efficiency and promotes fairness" and to "promote a reasonable tilt of data element revenue towards creators of data value and utility value." (State Council, 2022) From the "Data Twenty," it is evident that the data element revenue distribution system emphasizes fairness and efficiency in distribution. This fairness and efficiency are manifested in the fact that all entities can enjoy data element revenue distribution based on their contributions. Not only should enterprises that invest in data element production receive corresponding data revenue distribution, but also individual contributors, including ordinary workers, should receive rewards commensurate with their data contributions, achieving a "match between labor contributions and labor rewards (State Council, 2022)." Furthermore, the data element revenue distribution should achieve a balance of interests among various entities through profit-sharing, balancing the distribution benefits among different entities involved in data collection, processing, circulation, and application. As emphasized in the "Data Twenty" Measures, it calls for "strengthening incentive orientation based on data value creation and realization. Through various forms of profit-sharing, such as dividends and commissions, balance the interests of different entities involved in different stages of data content collection, processing, circulation, and application (State Council, 2022)." China's data element revenue distribution system should have the function of harmonizing the interests of different entities. Through a reasonable data element revenue distribution system, it can effectively balance the data interests among different entities, continuously narrow the income gap between various entities, and achieve a "win-win" situation for all participants while promoting economic growth. Properly utilizing the role of platform consumers and ordinary workers in balancing the interests of various entities is of great significance for promoting fairness and efficiency in data element revenue distribution.

In conclusion, the legitimacy of the participation of original data providers in data element revenue distribution is beyond doubt. Including original data providers in the subjects of data element revenue distribution can increase their income, achieve fairness and efficiency in data revenue distribution, and establish a solid foundation for promoting common prosperity.

2. The Inherent Logic of Original Data Providers' Involvement in Data Element Revenue Distribution and Common Prosperity

Marx emphasized that "the structure of distribution is entirely determined by the structure of production" (Marx & Engels, 2009a). With the development of the digital economy, data elements play an increasingly crucial role in advancing the accumulation of total material wealth in society. However, the unjust distribution of data element benefits prevents original data providers from sharing in data dividends, exacerbating the "digital divide" and income wealth polarization, which goes against the development principle of common prosperity. The involvement of original data providers in the income distribution of data elements is a new avenue to promote the common prosperity of all people while upholding Marxist labor values. It is an inherent requirement for implementing the "Data Twenty" in the new era and realizing an efficient and fair data element income distribution system, which holds significant importance for advancing the practical application of data elements.

2.1 Common logical foundation

The common logical basis is embodied in: firstly, the common historical logic. The realization of common prosperity is the essential requirement of socialism, but achieving common prosperity is a historical process, evolving alongside the continuous development of productive forces and sustainable progress. Marx and Engels pointed out that "the sum of the productive forces achieved by men determines the social condition" (Marx & Engels, 2009b). The productive forces are the decisive factor in the development of social history, and the advancement of material productive forces also ultimately determines the achievement of social common prosperity. In the early stage of China's socialist construction, through the "three major transformations," China has essentially built a relatively complete industrial system, yet the level of social productive forces remains relatively underdeveloped, and the material wealth of society is comparatively scarce, lacking the material foundation for common prosperity. Following the reform and opening up, China's social productivity has significantly improved, and social wealth has rapidly increased, laying a certain material foundation for the realization of common prosperity. Deng Xiaoping explicitly stated that the essence of socialism is to "liberate productive forces, develop productive forces, eliminate exploitation, eliminate polarization, and ultimately achieve common prosperity"(Deng, 1993). Moving into the new era, China's economic development has made significant historical strides, with productivity steadily increasing and the "cake" of common prosperity expanding, thus paving the way for substantial progress in achieving common prosperity. Data, as a new factor of production following land, capital, labor, and technology, represents the highest level of productivity development and has a profound impact on transforming production relations and advancing common prosperity. The participation of the original data provider in the distribution of data elements is an inevitable outcome of productivity development and a necessary step toward achieving common prosperity. In this sense, the two follow the common logic of historical development.

Secondly, common theoretical logic. Guided by the theory of "distribution is subordinate to production," our country has established the foundation of distribution system construction—public ownership of means of production. Based on adhering to Marx's labor theory of value, China has gradually established the basic distribution system of "distribution according to work as the main body, and a variety of distribution methods coexist" and "production factors determine remuneration according to their contribution"(Lan & Long, 2022). Balancing efficiency and fairness, it is also proposed to establish a fundamental institutional arrangement that coordinates and supports primary distribution, secondary distribution, and tertiary distribution to promote common prosperity (Xi, 2021). Simultaneously, the "Data Twenty" clearly regards establishing a data factor income distribution system as a crucial part of constructing a data basic system and proposes to "strive to eliminate the digital divide between different regions and groups of people, enhance social fairness, ensure people's livelihood, and promote common prosperity" (State Council, 2022). The participation of original data providers in the distribution of data elements is not only a significant attempt at distribution system reform in the digital economy field but also an inevitable requirement for constructing a fair and efficient income distribution system of data elements. It is evident that the participation of original data providers in the distribution of data elements and common prosperity both entail the theoretical need for building a more perfect distribution system, demonstrating consistency in theoretical logic.

Thirdly, common practical logic. The goal of achieving common prosperity is clear, yet there is no fixed template for the specific path to attain it. Only by continuously exploring in the process of material production practice can common prosperity gradually manifest its form. Similarly, the participation of original data providers in the distribution of data elements is also a new attempt to construct the income distribution system of data elements, which will undoubtedly challenge people's traditional understanding of income distribution systems. Building a new mechanism for original data providers to participate in the distribution of data elements requires breaking through the shackles of traditional thinking through bold experimentation (Jiang, 2023). In this sense, both the realization of common prosperity for all people and the construction of a new data factor income distribution system, wherein original data providers participate in the distribution of data factors, need to follow practical logic to promote realization. Therefore, it is of great significance to correctly grasp that the original data providers' participation in the income distribution of data elements is consistent with common prosperity in terms of historical logic, theoretical logic and practical logic.

2.2 Common development goals

With the continuous deepening of the development of the digital economy, the proportion of original data providers in society will continue to increase. Including original data providers as the main body of data element income distribution can greatly enhance the income level of the people and narrow the income gap. This aligns with the development goal of common prosperity. At the Fifth Plenary Session of the 19th Central Committee of the Communist Party of China, the Party Central Committee proposed the long-term goal of achieving "more significant substantive progress in achieving common prosperity for all people" by 2035 (The 19th Central Committee of the CPC, 2020), clarifying that the development goal of achieving "common prosperity" in China in the new era is to attain common prosperity for all people. At the 10th meeting of the "817" Central Committee of Finance and Economics, the issue of solidly promoting common prosperity was further discussed. It was proposed to focus on expanding the scale of middle-income groups and promoting more low-income groups to enter the middle-income category (Xi, 2023a). This indicates that to achieve the development goal of common prosperity for all people, it is necessary to prioritize "reducing income and increasing income." "The Opinion of the Central Committee of the Communist Party of China and the State Council on Supporting the High-Quality Development and Construction of Zhejiang Province as a Demonstration Zone for Common Prosperity" clearly states that the development goal of common prosperity is to "continuously narrow the gap between urban and rural regional development, the income and living standards gap between urban and rural residents, and significantly improve the income increasing ability and social welfare level of low-income groups (State Council, 2021)." The "Data Twenty" once again emphasizes that the development goal of common prosperity is to increase the income of low-income groups and enhance social welfare levels (State Council, 2022).

From a series of decisions made by the Party Central Committee, it can be seen that to achieve the development goal of common prosperity for all people, it is necessary to begin by increasing the income of low-income groups, expanding the scale of middle-income groups, and narrowing the income gap. The goal and value pursuit of socialism with Chinese characteristics are to achieve common prosperity for all people, and the scope of "all people" includes all members of society (Xiang & Wang, 2022). The common prosperity of all people cannot be achieved without the improvement of income levels. In the process of promoting common prosperity for all people, special attention should be paid to enhancing the proportion and quality of middle-income groups. Establishing a new system for data element allocation with the participation of original data providers can provide new channels for achieving the development goal of common prosperity because including this group in the scope of data element income distribution is conducive to achieving the goal of increasing the income of low-income groups. The realization of a prosperous life for the people depends on the continuous improvement of income levels, and various measures need to be taken to encourage low-income groups to move towards middle-income status (Guo, 2022). According to "The 50th Statistical Report on the Development of China's Internet," as of June 2022, the number of internet users in China has reached 1.051 billion, accounting for over 75% of the total population (CNNIC, 2022). From the data, it can be observed that the scale of internet users is continuously expanding, and with the development of the digital economy, these internet users will become original data providers, indicating that the scale of original data providers as low-income groups is continually expanding. If the income of original data providers cannot be effectively improved, as the market returns of data elements continue to expand, most of the data benefits will be occupied by platforms, data developers, and other entities. The income gap between original data providers and these groups will continue to increase, leading to a larger wealth gap. Therefore, increasing the income of raw data providers can reduce the size of low-income groups within a certain range, increase the income of low-income groups to a greater extent, and achieve the goal of expanding the size of middle-income groups and narrowing income gaps, which inherently aligns with the development goal of common prosperity.

2.3 Common values

By adjusting the distribution relationship of data benefits, we can enhance the fairness of social and economic development, so that contributors and participants of data elements can equally enjoy the economic benefits brought by data elements. This aligns with the principle of fairness and justice pursued by common prosperity in terms of value. This consistency in value can form a strong centripetal force between the two, enabling the original data provider to participate in the distribution of data element benefits and achieve resonance and mutual promotion between common prosperity. Xi Jinping pointed out that, "China aims to achieve common prosperity, but not through egalitarianism. Instead, it needs to first make the 'cake' bigger, and then divide it well through reasonable institutional arrangements, so that the fruits of development can benefit all people more fairly and fairly" (Xi, 2023b). The pursuit of the value of common prosperity is social fairness and justice, which strengthens the cultural identity of all citizens and promotes overall social progress through the pursuit of fairness and justice. The first essence of fairness and justice is to "enhance the well-being of the people" and enable the people to share the fruits of economic development. Common prosperity always emphasizes the implementation of the value principles of fairness and justice throughout the entire process and various fields of socialist construction, and strives to eliminate unfair phenomena in various fields such as social economy and politics. The production of data elements has created one wealth myth after another for human society, and has also created one business tycoon after another, but at the same time, it has also created a new vulnerable group of raw data providers in this production relationship. This is the duality of data elements, and the key to this duality lies in the unfair distribution of data benefits. As Marx said, "The production mode of material life constrains the entire process of social, political, and spiritual life" (Marx & Engels, 1998). The production of data elements has triggered a profound transformation in the economic field, and will also have important impacts on various fields of society. Only by adhering to the principles of fair and just development, can the digital economy led by data elements continue to develop healthily. Fair distribution of benefits from data elements will also promote the realization of justice in the distribution of overall social benefits. The establishment of a data element profit distribution system involving original data providers is to practice the value principle of fairness and justice, allowing original data providers to enjoy data fairly based on their contributions, improving the production efficiency of data elements while also considering the fairness of market transactions, and promoting the healthy development of data elements. At the same time, this method of distributing the benefits of data elements will also allow more people to fully enjoy the economic dividends brought about by data element distribution, enhance the sense of gain for all people, and eliminate the economic development risks caused by unreasonable distribution. Based on this, when constructing a data element benefit distribution system, highlighting the position of the original data provider is to further implement the principle of fairness and justice for common prosperity on the basis of following a fair data element benefit distribution system, and the two have a common value criterion.

In summary, there are many common characteristics between the participation of original data providers in data element allocation and common prosperity. It is necessary to grasp the inherent relationship between the two and promote the continuous benefits of the digital economy for people's livelihoods.

3. The Practical Dilemma of Original Data Providers participating in the Distribution of Data Element Benefits

While enhancing the data benefits of original data providers can boost the income of numerous groups and serve as a vital factor in advancing common prosperity for all and attaining fairness and justice in social development, the establishment of mechanisms for original data providers to engage in the distribution of data element benefits encounters numerous difficulties and challenges. These include unclear data ownership, insufficient organizational mechanisms for data benefit distribution, and deviations in platform technology design.

3.1 Unclear data ownership prevents the original data provider from asserting their data rights

The original data provider participating in the distribution of data element benefits first needs to prove their data contribution. However, due to legal lag and other reasons, the original data provider is currently unable to claim their rights. Specifically, this is reflected in two aspects: firstly, the lack of data ownership results in the original data provider not having a basis for enjoying the distribution of data element benefits. The process of data formation is very complex, and there are both original data providers, data developers, and platform enterprises who provide technical and capital support to contribute to the value of data elements. Therefore, the difficulty of data ownership is very high. At the same time, data is non-exclusive, non-competitive, and can only generate value maximization effects in circulation and sharing. Blindly confirming ownership will, to some extent, hinder the release of data value. So, data authentication is a "world problem", and currently, no country has legislated for data authentication, and the academic community also does not approve of it as data authentication (Determann, 2022). The lack of data ownership makes it difficult for the original data provider to obtain legal proof of their own rights, making their participation in the distribution of data element benefits a challenging issue. Secondly, unequal agreements deprive the individual rights of the original data provider. The platform requires users to sign a so-called "user agreement" when using the APP. In this agreement, the platform will make agreements on the ownership of user identity data, network behavior data, and account information. Some companies even explicitly emphasize in the agreement that the behavior data and account information generated by users using the enterprise platform belong to the enterprise, while users only have the right to use. Under such unequal treaties, it is even more difficult for original data providers to prove their data rights. The final result is that the platform "actually" occupies all the value generated by the data elements for free, while the original data provider cannot obtain any value from the data elements.

3.2 The organizational mechanism for the participation of original data providers in the distribution of data element benefits is not yet robust

An effective organizational mechanism is a crucial means to safeguard the interests of the original data provider. The distribution of benefits for data elements involves multiple entities such as original data providers, data developers, and platform enterprises. Data developers and platform enterprises have already garnered significant benefits for themselves through technology and capital. However, original data providers lack corresponding support, especially effective organizational mechanisms, making it challenging for them to secure a favorable position in data element distribution. There are four reasons for this: Firstly, the consensus mechanism is not robust. The group of original data providers is large and widely dispersed, with different individuals having varying demands for data benefits. For original data providers to participate in the allocation, they must first reach an internal consensus to form a strong collaborative force to pursue greater benefits. Establishing such consensus is nearly impossible without a certain organizational mechanism to facilitate it.

Secondly, the negotiation mechanism is inadequate. The value of the data provided by the original data provider fluctuates with changes in technology, application scenarios, and market demand, making it challenging to maintain a constant allocation share for the original data provider. In such cases, the data revenue of the original data provider needs to be negotiated with other relevant parties, necessitating corresponding negotiation organizations to safeguard the interests of the original data provider. Currently, the negotiation mechanism is not fully developed.

Thirdly, the leadership mechanism is lacking. Platform enterprises and data developers often hold advantageous positions in data element allocation, making it difficult for them to actively engage in interest negotiations with the original data providers. This calls for specialized government organizations to take a leading role, coordinating the interests and needs of various parties to reach a consensus on allocation. However, there is currently no mechanism in place for this purpose.

Fourthly, the organizational policy basis is inadequate. The principles, regulations, and negotiation mechanisms for the participation of original data providers in distribution have not yet been established, rendering the entire distribution negotiation process rule-less to some extent, which affects the interests of original data providers. It is evident that the absence and insufficiency of internal consensus mechanisms, external negotiation mechanisms, corresponding organizational structures, and policy bases hinder the original data providers from obtaining the necessary data benefits.

3.3 The involvement of original data providers in the distribution of benefits from data elements encounters technical challenges

The original data providers, data developers, and platform enterprises all contribute to the generation of data value. However, measuring the contributions of different entities and ensuring fair distribution of data benefits depends on certain technical means. However, the current platform technology design is not conducive to fair measurement of contributions from all parties. Specifically, there are technical challenges in proving the contribution of the original data provider. From a practical perspective, the value generation of data elements inevitably involves the data contribution of the original data provider, but there is still some difficulty in proving the contribution of the original data provider from a technical perspective. This is because the original data undergoes a data desensitization process after entering the platform. During this process, the personalized characteristics of the original data provider will be covered. Even if the original data creates value for the platform, strong technical support is necessary to track the source of value contribution from a technical perspective.

Secondly, platform enterprises can conceal the data contributions of the original data providers. The value generation process of data elements is completed on the platform. Platform enterprises collect data from the original data provider through interfaces like sensors and online apps, and then perform technical processing on the data such as using data desensitization technology to anonymize the personal data of the original data provider. With strong technical support, the platform can silently conceal the traces of the original data provider, making it impossible for the original data provider to provide proof of their contribution to the data, and thus unable to participate in the distribution of data element benefits.

Thirdly, the immaturity of data pricing technology leads to unclear data value. Mature data pricing techniques can dynamically adjust data prices based on application scenarios and market demands, enabling data elements to obtain true market value. This is of great significance for evaluating the value of raw data and promoting the distribution of data benefits to raw data providers. However, existing data pricing techniques are not yet mature. The current data pricing methods mainly rely on traditional methods such as pre-pricing and agreement pricing. For example, more than half of the more than 20 existing data trading platforms in the United States still use pre-pricing, which is based on time rather than market value itself, making it difficult to accurately evaluate the market value of data. Due to technological limitations, existing data pricing models are also relatively single, making it difficult to accurately evaluate the value of increasingly complex data scenarios, which to some extent affects the data interests of the original data providers. The technical difficulties faced by data element allocation hinder the realization of the interests of the original data providers. In summary, if the difficulties faced by data element allocation are not effectively resolved, the data interests of the original data providers will never be guaranteed, and promoting the common prosperity of all people through data element allocation will become a "fantasy". After all, data elements will become one of the main sources of value in the future society, and raw data providers occupy the vast majority of data element allocation entities in terms of quantity. If the data element allocation dilemma faced by raw data providers cannot be solved well, it will to some extent affect the realization of common prosperity in the digital age.

In summary, if the challenges encountered in data element allocation are not effectively addressed, the data interests of the original data providers will never be assured, and the endeavor to foster common prosperity for all through data element allocation will remain a mere "fantasy". After all, data elements are poised to become one of the primary sources of value in future society, and raw data providers constitute the overwhelming majority of data element allocation entities in terms of quantity. If the predicament surrounding data element allocation faced by raw data providers is not adequately resolved, it will, to some extent, impede the realization of common prosperity in the digital age.

4. The Practical Approach for Original Data Providers to Engage in the Distribution of Data Element Benefits

To effectively safeguard the data benefits of original data providers, foster the robust growth of the digital economy, and make tangible strides in common prosperity, it is imperative to investigate the practical approach of original data providers engaging in the distribution of data element benefits. This exploration can proceed from the following three facets.

4.1 Enhance the development of laws and regulations to guarantee the data element benefits of original data providers

Given the numerous controversies surrounding data rights confirmation, it is possible to establish a legal system that safeguards the interests of the original data provider without data rights confirmation. Currently, one of the reasons why original data providers find it difficult to prove their data contribution is the lack of clear legal provisions to protect them. This absence makes their participation in distribution unable to receive legal support, leading to the continuous expansion of the boundaries of personal data infringement. Laws and regulations are the fundamental guarantee for safeguarding individual rights and interests. To construct a system for distributing benefits from data elements, it is necessary to start by strengthening the construction of laws and regulations and ensuring that the original data providers enjoy benefits through improved laws and regulations. Firstly, enhance constitutional provisions. The Constitution is the fundamental law of a country, with the highest legal effect and the basis for formulating other laws. Establishing the legal principle of fair distribution of data benefits at the constitutional level can guide other legislation towards benefiting the original data providers. To fundamentally protect the data rights and interests of original data providers, relevant content safeguarding the interests of data contributors can be added to the constitution. Additionally, the Constitution can clearly state that any distribution method contributing to achieving common prosperity is protected by law, and the specific distribution form should align with improving the income level of the entire populace. No person or organization should infringe upon the distribution benefits deserved by others in any way.

Secondly, when formulating special legislation on data elements, provisions should be added for the distribution of benefits from data elements. In this legislation, it should be evident that all entities participating in the production of data elements should enjoy the benefits, with the original data provider being one such entity. The data benefits of the original data provider should be continually adjusted with changes in the value of data elements. It should also be clarified that the original data provider can participate in the net profit distribution of the platform through methods such as "data shareholding." Efficiency and fairness should be the guiding principles of data element allocation, stipulating that the original data provider can enjoy more data benefits through secondary and tertiary allocation based on initial allocation.

Thirdly, improve existing laws and regulations. In relevant labor regulations, it should be explicitly stated that platform employees, including ride-hailing drivers and delivery riders, have the right to receive distribution of data benefits. These benefits should be independent of the employees' normal income, such as wages and bonuses. Additionally, in relevant consumer rights protection regulations, it should be clear that platform consumers have the right to distribute data element income. Platform enterprises should not use "user agreements" to privately occupy consumer data interests. Agreements involving actual user interests should be highlighted to ensure their right to know. Users should be given corresponding choices and cannot be forced to agree; otherwise, the agreement should be deemed invalid. Those who encroach on profit distribution should compensate consumers to ensure their data interests are not harmed. Revise relevant regulations such as the "Data Security Law" and the "Personal Information Protection Law" to clarify that no individual or organization shall illegally steal or resell the personal data of the original data provider through technological means. Otherwise, severe penalties will be imposed, and the data interests of the original data provider will be compensated. Lastly, enhance coherence and unity among various laws, improve law applicability, facilitate legislative, law enforcement, and judicial channels, and provide convenience for original data providers to protect their rights and interests.

4.2 Enhance organizational mechanism construction and establish a new framework for distributing data element benefits

A robust and effective organizational mechanism is crucial for establishing a standardized and orderly allocation of data elements. Firstly, establish a robust consensus mechanism. Original data providers, being numerous and dispersed, make it challenging to incorporate all viewpoints into distribution plans. To ensure smooth formulation and implementation of these plans, it's vital to establish corresponding consensus mechanisms. This can be achieved by organizing original data providers to engage in discussions through the establishment of the "Original Data Provider Benefit Alliance" and appointing representatives to collect opinions and suggestions. Additionally, worker and consumer rights protection institutions can act as agents to negotiate with original data providers, facilitating dialogue and negotiation among stakeholders to seek common ground while respecting differences and jointly pursuing data interests. Secondly, establish a robust negotiation mechanism. Official government agencies should be established to coordinate data benefit distribution, enabling stakeholders like original data providers, data developers, and platform enterprises to negotiate for their interests. Agents representing original data providers should participate in these negotiations, ensuring each entity agrees on specific allocation shares based on mutual recognition of contributions, thus safeguarding the interests of original data providers. Furthermore, enhance the leadership mechanism. Leveraging the Party's core leadership role in overseeing the overall situation and coordinating all parties, regulatory agencies should dynamically review data revenue distribution plans and implementation by platform enterprises. This guidance ensures platforms fulfill social responsibilities and actively engage in interest negotiations with original data providers. Implementing a "black and white list" system for platform enterprises incentivizes compliance—those excelling in data element allocation join the "white list", while those performing poorly face appropriate penalties, fostering self-correction and protecting the interests of original data providers. Lastly, enhance the organizational policy foundation. Swiftly improve principles, rules, and negotiation mechanisms for original data providers' participation in distribution, promoting active involvement in constructing data element income distribution mechanisms through policy incentives. Adhering to the principle of "consultation, co-construction, and sharing", enhance interactivity among organizational mechanisms to maximize original data providers' interest protection.

4.3 Speed up digital technology innovation and overcome obstacles to the distribution of profits from data elements

The creation, circulation, consumption, and distribution of data elements are intricately tied to digital technology advancement. Addressing the challenges confronted by original data providers in participating in data element allocation requires a focus on technical solutions. Thus, it's crucial to expedite digital technology innovation, continually surmount technical hurdles restricting data element allocation, and furnish robust technical backing to safeguard the data interests of original data providers. Firstly, blockchain technology can be harnessed in the data element production process to achieve traceability, tamper resistance, and segregation of the original data provider's contributions. By integrating blockchain timestamp technology into the data element production process, every stage of data element production can be meticulously documented. This timestamp technique generates a unique "hash value" for the stored records, ensuring temporal inheritance with the preceding hash value, thereby furnishing evidence for ascertaining the data source. The signature technology of blockchain can sign the produced hash value, linking the sender's identity and information data, and thwarting attempts by others to impersonate the sender. Implementing signature technology in data element production can authenticate the original data provider's identity and prevent its tampering. The utilization of blockchain timestamp and signature techniques can differentiate various entities contributing to data elements, thereby elucidating the original data provider's contributions and providing a foundation for their involvement in data element allocation.

Secondly, leveraging information technology and algorithm technology in refining data pricing models to enhance the precision of data pricing technology and ensure accurate evaluation of data element value. By establishing the efficacy function and decision-making model of stakeholders, the contribution of different entities to the value of data is ascertained. Subsequently, quantitative evaluation is conducted based on the economic value of different entities, providing a basis for consensus formation on pricing, addressing the issue of data element profit distribution, and realizing the measurable effect of the original data provider's contribution. Moreover, owing to the impact of various uncertain factors on data element value, a single data pricing model cannot precisely reflect the market value of data elements, let alone meet the equitable distribution of data elements. Machine learning algorithms can dynamically adjust data prices by leveraging their advantages in factor selection and dimensionality reduction techniques, enabling the actual benefits of the original data provider to continually increase with the market value of data elements.

Thirdly, utilizing smart contracts to safeguard provider interests. A smart contract is an automatically executed transaction protocol via a code program, involving transaction stakeholders who meet the contract terms and can autonomously execute transactions sans third-party oversight. Converting the pre-negotiated data element allocation plan into a smart contract allows the smart contract to automatically execute the allocation plan in accordance with the agreement, directly allotting the benefits belonging to the original data provider to the designated account, simplifying the process for the original data provider to collect benefits. Additionally, the execution status of smart contracts is automatically recorded and monitored throughout the entire process, providing favorable evidence for the original data provider to raise queries and appeals, altering the subordinate position of the original data provider in data element allocation.

It is evident that the innovation and application of digital technology can offer more intelligent solutions for the feasibility of data element allocation, thereby further safeguarding the interests of original data providers. In the future, as data application scenarios continue to expand, the specific methods by which original data providers participate in the distribution of data element benefits should also evolve to keep pace with the times, ensuring better protection of the data interests of original data providers.

5. Conclusion

In the new era, the role of data elements in driving the development of the digital economy, empowering the real economy, and promoting high-quality economic development is becoming increasingly prominent, with strong and compounding effects on social and economic growth. Data, as a factor of production, is playing an increasingly crucial role in fostering national economic growth and increasing national income. Addressing the issue of income distribution related to data elements is not only a necessary step to foster the orderly development of the digital economy but also a new approach and method to enhance income sources for the people.

The "Twenty Data Points" clearly emphasizes the need to establish an efficient and equitable distribution system for data element benefits. On one hand, a data element benefit distribution system that embodies efficiency and fairness is a crucial component in constructing a robust data element foundation system, which holds significant importance in fostering the healthy and sustainable growth of the digital economy. On the other hand, an income distribution system for data factors that reflects efficiency and fairness plays a pivotal role in implementing mechanisms that allow for the distribution of production factors based on their contributions, enhancing redistribution adjustment mechanisms, fostering third-party distribution, and ultimately driving substantial progress towards the common prosperity of all individuals.

Exploring the practical approach for original data providers to engage in the distribution of data element benefits can further protect the rightful data interests of original data providers. This is a necessary step to enhance market evaluation mechanisms and advance the efficiency and equity of data benefit distribution systems. To achieve this goal, it is imperative to establish viable pathways for the involvement of original data providers in the distribution of data element benefits through the development of laws and regulations, organizational mechanism enhancement, and innovation in digital technology. This will ensure that data element benefits serve to benefit all individuals more effectively, thereby promoting common prosperity for all.

Funding Statement

This study is financially sponsored by the Major Project of the National Social Science Foundation of China (20&ZD177).

References

Marx, K.(马克思) & Engels, F.(恩格斯). *Complete Works of Marx and Engels: Volume 13*(马克思恩格斯全集:第13卷), Beijing: People's Publishing House(北京:人民出版社),1998.

Marx, K.(马克思) & Engels, F.(恩格斯). *Complete Works of Marx and Engels: Volume 46(Part 1)*[马克思恩格斯全集:第46卷(上)], Beijing: People's Publishing House(北京:人民出版社),2009a.

Marx, K.(马克思) & Engels, F.(恩格斯). *Complete Works of Marx and Engels: Volume 3*(马克思恩格斯全集:第3卷), Beijing: People's Publishing House(北京:人民出版社),2009b.

Deng, X.(邓小平). *Selected Works of Deng Xiaoping: Volume 3*(邓小平文选:第3卷), Beijing: People's Publishing House(北京:人民出版社), 1993.

Xi, J.(习近平). Solidly Promoting Common Prosperity(扎实推动共同富裕). *Qiushi*(求是), 2021, (20): 4-8.

Xi Jinping presided over the 10th meeting of the Central Committee of Finance and Economics, emphasizing the promotion of common prosperity in high-quality development and overall planning to do a good job in preventing and resolving major financial risks. Li Keqiang, Wang Yang, Wang Huning, and Han Zheng attended the meeting(习近平主持召开中央财经委员会第十次会议强调 在高质量发展中促进共同富裕 统筹做好重大金融风险防范化解工作 李克强汪洋王沪宁韩正出席), 2021. Available from: https://baijiahao. baidu. com / s? ID= 17083505317629080&wfr=spider&for=pc [Accessed August 17, 2021].

Xi Jinping's Speech at the 2022 World Economic Forum Video Conference(习近平在2022年世界经济论坛视频会议的演讲), 2023. Available from: http://www. xinhuanet.com/2022-01/17/c1128271799.html [Accessed January 7, 2023].

Chen, J.(陈劲) & Yin, X.(尹西明). The Rise, Characteristics, and Mission of the Fourth Generation of Management Studies from the Perspective of Paradigm Leap (范式跃迁视角下第四代管理学的兴起、特征与使命). *Journal of Management*(管理学报), 2019, 16(1): 1-8.

Chen, T.(陈涛). Exploration of the Ownership of Data Property Rights(数据产权的归属问题探究). *Market Weekly*(市场周刊), 2020, (4): 163-165.

CNNIC(中国互联网络信息中心). The 50th Statistical Report on the Development of the Internet in China was Released(第50次《中国互联网络发展状况统计报告》发布), 2023. Available from: http://www.cnnic.net.cn/n4/2022/0914/c88-10226. html [Accessed January 7, 2023].

Determann, L. No One Owns Data, 2022. Available from: http://ssrn.com/abstract =

or http://dx.doi.org//. ssrn [Accessed December 15, 2022].

Guo, R.(郭瑞萍). On the Centennial Evolution of the CPC's Thought of Common
Prosperity(论中国共产党共同富裕思想的百年演变). *Journal of Shaanxi Normal
University (Philosophy and Social Sciences Edition)* [陕西师范大学学报(哲学社
会科学版)], 2021, 50(6): 26-34.

Guo, R. (郭瑞萍). The Inner Logic and Realistic Path of Promoting Common
Prosperity through High Quality Development(以高质量发展促进共同富裕的内
在逻辑与现实路径). *Introduction to Ideological and Theoretical Education*(思想
理论教育导刊), 2022, (9): 64-70.

Halevy, A., Norvig, P. & Pereira F. The Unreasonable Effectiveness of Data. *IEEE
Intelligent Systems*, 2009, 24(2): 8.

Hu, Y.(胡元聪) & Feng, Y.(冯一帆). Research on the Protection of Consumer Fair
Trade Rights in Big Data Killing(大数据杀熟中消费者公平交易权保护研究).
Journal of Shaanxi Normal University (Philosophy and Social Sciences Edition)
[陕西师范大学学报(哲学社会科学版)], 2022, 51(1): 161-176.

Huang, Q.(黄奇帆). The platform should return 20% -30% of the data transaction
revenue to the original data producer(平台应把数据交易收益的20%—30%返还
给原始数据生产者), 2021. Available from: https://finance.sina.com.cn/money/
bank / bank_hydt / 2021-10-24 / doc-iktzqtyu3244021. shtml [Accessed March 25,
2023].

Jiang, Y. (姜英华). Political Economic Analysis of the Thought on Common
Prosperity(共同富裕思想的政治经济学分析). *Contemporary Economic
Management*(当代经济管理), 2023, 45(2): 9-16.

Lan, N. (兰楠) & Long, Z. (龙治铭). The Historical Process and Theoretical
Achievements of the Construction of the Distribution System of Socialism with
Chinese Characteristics : Promoting the Centenary Struggle for Common
Prosperity(中国特色社会主义分配制度建设的历史进程和理论成就——推动共
同富裕的百年奋斗). *Research on Marxist Theory in Universities*(高校马克思主
义理论研究),2022,8(3):34-48.

Luo, P.(罗培新). Basic Categories of Data Legislation(数据立法的基本范畴),2023.
Available from: http://www. Chinaweekly. cn / html / sxzhuanjia / 32633. html
[Accessed March 25, 2023].

Research Group of the Macroeconomic Research Institute of the National
Development and Reform Commission(国家发展改革委员会宏观经济研究院课
题组). Research on the Mechanism of Improving Factors through Market
Evaluation Contribution and Determining Rewards Based on Contribution(健全要
素由市场评价贡献、按贡献决定报酬机制研究). *Macroeconomic Research*(宏观经济研究),2021,(9):5-23,85.

State Council(国务院). Opinions of the Central Committee of the Communist Party of China and the State Council on Building a Data Infrastructure System to Better Play the Role of Data Elements(中共中央 国务院关于构建数据基础制度更好发挥数据要素作用的意见),2022. Available from: http://www.gov.cn/zhengce/2022-12/19/content_5732695.html [Accessed December 19, 2022].

State Council(国务院). Opinions of the Central Committee of the Communist Party of China and the State Council on Supporting the High Quality Development and Construction of Zhejiang Province as a Demonstration Zone for Common Prosperity(中共中央 国务院关于支持浙江高质量发展建设共同富裕示范区的意见), 2023. Available from: http://www.xinhuanet.com/politics/zywj/2021-06/10/c_1127551386.html [Accessed January 7, 2023].

The 19th Central Committee of the CPC(中国共产党第十九届中央委员会). Proposal of the Central Committee of the Communist Party of China on Formulating the 14th Five Year Plan for National Economic and Social Development and the Long Range Objectives for 2035(中共中央关于制定国民经济和社会发展第十四个五年规划和二〇三五年远景目标的建议). *People's Daily*(人民日报), 2020-11-04(1).

The Economist. The World's Most Valuable Resource is no Longer Oil, but Data, 2017. Available from: https://www.economist.com/news/eaders/21721656-data-economy-demandsnew-approach-anti-trust-rules-worlds-mostvaluable-resource [Accessed May 6, 2017].

Tutorial Reading for the Report of the 20th National Congress of the Communist Party of China(党的二十大报告辅导读本). Beijing: People's Publishing House (北京：人民出版社), 2022.

Wang, L.(王黎黎). The Ethical Basis and Rights Design of Collective Negotiation with Chinese Characteristics(中国特色集体协商的和合伦理基础及权利设计). *Ethical Research*(伦理学研究), 2021, (2): 24-29.

Wang, R. (王燃). On the Distribution Rules of Data Benefits on Open Network Platforms(论网络开放平台数据利益分配规则). *Electronic Intellectual Property* (电子知识产权), 2020, (8): 45-55.

Wang, S.(王颂吉), Li, Y.(李怡璇) & Gao, Y.(高伊凡). Definition of Property Rights and Income Distribution Mechanism of Data Elements(数据要素的产权界定与收入分配机制). *Fujian Forum (Humanities and Social Sciences Edition)*[福建论坛(人文社会科学版)], 2020, (12): 138-145.

Wang, W.(王伟玲), Wu, Z. (吴志刚) & Xu, J.(徐靖). Key Points and Paths to Accelerate the Cultivation of Data Factor Markets(加快数据要素市场培育的关键

点与路径). *Economic Review*(经济纵横), 2021, (3): 39-47.

Wang, Y.(王延川) & Wu, H.(吴海燕). Construction of a Protection System for the Rights and Interests of Employers on Digital Labor Service Platforms(数字劳务平台就业者权益保障体系构建). *Journal of Shaanxi Normal University (Philosophy and Social Sciences Edition)*[陕西师范大学学报(哲学社会科学版)], 2022, 51(4): 155-166.

Wang, Y.(王延川), Chen, Z.(陈姿含) & Yi, R.(伊然). *Blockchain Governance: Principles and Scenarios*(区块链治理：原理与场景), Shanghai: Shanghai People's Publishing House(上海：上海人民出版社), 2019.

Wang, Y.(王延川). Analysis of Blockchain Empowered Emergency Material Support System for Emergencies(区块链赋能突发事件应急物资保障系统探析). *Journal of Beijing Institute of Technology(Social Science Edition)*[北京理工大学学报(社会科学版)], 2020, 22(5): 126-133.

Xiang, J.(项久雨) & Wang Y.(王永杰). The Scientific Connotation, Development History, and Era Approach of Common Prosperity for All People(全体人民共同富裕的科学内涵、发展历程和时代进路). *Fujian Forum(Humanities and Social Sciences Edition)*[福建论坛(人文社会科学版)], 2022, (10): 5-16.

Yan, J.(闫境华) & Shi, X.(石先梅). Political and Economic Analysis of Data Production Factorization and Data Rights Confirmation(数据生产要素化与数据确权的政治经济学分析). *Inner Mongolia Social Sciences*(内蒙古社会科学), 2021, 42(5): 113-120.

Yang, J.(杨洁). The size of the data circulation market is expected to exceed 220 billion yuan by 2025, and the core technology of metadata elements urgently needs to be broken through(2025年数据流通市场规模将超2200亿元 数据要素核心技术亟待突破), 2023. Available from: https://www.cs.com.cn/cj2020/202304/t20230418_6337829.html [Accessed April 18, 2023].

Yao, Q.(姚期智). Core Technologies in the Field of Digital Economy(数字经济领域的核心技术), 2023. Available from: http://new.qq.com/rain/a/20211217A08M6300 [Accessed January 7, 2023].

Zhao, Z.(赵正), Guo, M.(郭明军), Ma, X.(马骁), et al. Research on the Governance System and Supporting Systems of Data Elements in the Context of Data Circulation(数据流通情景下数据要素治理体系及配套制度研究). *E-government* (电子政务), 2022, (2): 40-49.

Zhou, W.(周文杰), Yang, L.(杨璐) & Yan, J.(严建峰). A Complaint Prediction Model Driven by Big Data(大数据驱动的投诉预测模型). *Computer Science*(计算机科学), 2016, 43(7): 217-223.

The Development of National Emergency Language Capacities: A Perspective from Language Planning[*]

Shen Qi, Kang Minghao[**]

Abstract: Language plays an important role in responding to major public emergencies and national emergency language capacities have increasingly attracted much attention. However, due to the absence of the perspectives of language planning, current studies fail to effectively improve national emergency language capacities. Informed by the theory of language planning, there are three types of orientations in language planning in the development of national emergency language capacities: language-as-tool, language-as-right and language-as-resource. This paper classifies the fundamental content of language planning for the development of national emergency language capacities into eight groups: language corpus planning, language status planning, language acquisition planning, language prestige planning, discourse planning, language usage planning, translation planning and language technology planning.

Keywords: public emergencies; language planning; national emergency language capacities; national language capacity; emergency language

1. Introduction

The world is now undergoing momentous changes unseen in a century. In such an era, the development of national emergency language capacities plays an important role in pursuing a holistic approach to national security. The report of the 20th National Congress of the Communist Party of China emphasizes the need to improve the national security system and enhance public security governance. Meanwhile, it regards the national emergency management system as a vital component of the national security system and proposes for the first time to establish an overall safety and emergency response framework. All of these fully demonstrates the high importance that the Central

* This article was originally published in *Journal of Shaanxi Normal University (Philosophy and Social Sciences Edition)*, Vol. 51, No.6. Original Title:语言规划视域下的国家应急语言能力建设.

** Shen Qi(沈骑), Ph.D., Professor, School of Foreign Languages, Tongji University. Kang Minghao(康铭浩), Lecturer, School of Foreign Studies, East China University of Political Science and Law.

Committee of the Party attaches to emergency management work. "A National Master Plan for Responding to Public Emergencies" categorizes public emergencies into four parts : natural disasters, calamitous accidents, public health accidents, and public security incidents, each of which is inextricably linked to language. Whether dealing with earthquakes, mining disasters, mass food poisoning or terrorist attacks, the work related to emergency rescue, information release, rumor prevention and control, psychological comfort, etc., all require strong language capacities. In addition, major public emergencies are difficult to predict and when they occur, the time is always tight and the impact is always wide. Therefore, there is an increasing demand for national emergency language services. The development of emergency language capacities is supposed to be a fundamental project in the national emergency management system in the face of major public emergencies. In April 2022, National Emergency Language Service Corps of China was jointly established by 29 universities, enterprises and associations.[1] It is an important force in the modernization of the national emergency management system and capacities. This indicates that the development of national emergency language capacities has aroused high attention from our country, and relevant theoretical and application research needs to be accelerated urgently.

From a worldwide perspective, emergency language research started early and focused on practical operations, which has become an integral part of emergency management and crisis response system. Relevant foreign research can be divided into four categories. The first is the normativity and practicality of language, such as the naming rules of viruses and diseases in public health (Gesser-Edelsburg et al., 2016) and the plain language emergency alerts (Winger, 2017) , etc. The second is the emergency translation of language, focusing on the positive role translation played in the information release of major public emergencies, emergency rescue, disaster prevention and management (Cadwell, 2015; Tesseur, 2019; O'Brien & Federici, 2020), etc. The third is the technical aspects of language services, which involves the application of voice translation technology (Nallasamy et al., 2008), voice response technology (Forrester et al., 2010), and emotion analysis and processing technology (Choi et al., 2017) in major public emergencies. The fourth is research on crisis communication and discourse dissemination, mainly concentrating on the effect and management of social media and news media discourse such as Twitter (Odlum & Yoon, 2015; Rudra et al., 2018; Sousa et al., 2018; Squiers et al., 2019). It is worthwhile to learn from foreign research for its diverse perspectives and its focus on practicality.

---

[1] National Emergency Language Service Corps of China was established in Beijing(国家应急语言服务团在京成立): http://www. moe. gov. cn /jyb_xwfb/gzdt_gzdt/moe_1485 /202204/t20220428_623075. html.

Relatively speaking, the development of China's emergency language capacities has just started. At present, research on national emergency language is mainly divided into three categories. The first is theoretical construction research. This type of research is primarily concerned with the definition of emergency language capacities (Li, 2011; Wen, 2016; Wang, 2020a; Wang & Sun, 2020), the division of emergency language service research domains (Zhao, 2020), the construction of dimensions, target systems and capacity analysis models for emergency language capacities (Li & Rao, 2020), and retrospect and prospect on domestic emergency language research (Xiao & Zhang, 2022). The second is international comparative research. Some scholars introduce the experience and practices of emergency language services and capacity construction in countries such as the United States and Japan (Zhang, 2016; Teng, 2018; Bao, 2020; Wang & Qu, 2020), and systematically sort out the main approaches and methods of emergency language research abroad (Zhang, 2020). The third is the research and exploration of strategy. The academic community attaches importance to exploring effective ways to improve the quality and capacity of national emergency language services (Teng, 2020; Shen & Kang, 2020; Wang, 2020b; Li et al., 2020; Wang et al., 2020; Liu, 2022; Wei & Qian, 2022; Yang & Du, 2021). The above research has laid a solid foundation for the construction of national emergency language capacities. However, there is a discrepancy between theory and practice in existing research. In other words, the existing research lacks a suitable disciplinary perspective that connects theory with practice. The construction of national emergency language capacities is essentially an act of language planning with strategic characteristics, which reflects the national will and has a distinct value orientation, basic content and planning goals. We hold the opinion that in the process of strengthening national emergency language capacity construction, it is urgent to clarify language planning orientation of national emergency language capacity building and define its basic content and strategic objectives from the perspective of language planning, so as to provide theoretical foundation and practical reference for promoting the development of national emergency language capacities.

2. Orientations in Language Planning in the Development of National Emergency Language Capacities

To strengthen national emergency language capacities, clarifying the orientation in language planning is the first step. The orientation in language planning is a value orientation of special nature. The value orientation of language planning refers to the fundamental understanding of the essence of language value in the process of language planning. Value orientation is the core and driving factor of language planning, which determines the success or failure of language planning. In the past 40 years, scholars at home and abroad have paid close attention to this issue and have successively put forward three different value orientations : "language-as-tool," "language-as-right" and "language-as-resource,"[①] which to some extent decides the obvious differences in the view of language in the development of national emergency language capacities.

2.1 Language-as-tool

Language-as-tool in language planning regards language as a tool to obtain social resources to realize the actual use function of language and solve language communication problems through language planning. Based on language-as-tool, the construction of national emergency language capacities primarily addresses practical issues in emergency management such as language communication barriers, emergency information dissemination and crisis communication, which highlights the value orientation of language-as-tool in emergency language services. However, there are two practical problems in language-as-tool. The first problem is that it tends to tackle emergencies while neglecting the quality and capacity of language services. When an emergency occurs, relevant departments prioritize the urgency of emergency language services over the source and language level of emergency language supply. One of the important reasons is that there is no objective criterion for the quality and capacity of emergency language services. As a result, under the guidance of language-as-tool, emergency language services emphasize urgency while neglecting the construction of cultivation mechanism and evaluation standard of emergency language capacities. The second problem is that it tends to meet the needs of the mainstream population while neglecting the needs of the minority groups. Under the guidance of language-as-tool, when selecting language, emergency language services are likely to utilize national or international lingua franca to satisfy the basic language needs of the mainstream populations. The multilingual needs of minority populations cannot be fully considered, which means customized language services are not provided. Overall, language-as-tool cannot meet the demands of national emergency language services in terms of language categories and quality.

---

① e.g., Li, Y. (李宇明), 2019. Theories and Practices of China's Language Resources(中国语言资源的理念与实践). *Chinese Journal of Language Policy and Planning*(语言战略研究)(3). Li, Y.(李宇明), Wang, C.(王春辉), 2019. On Functional Classification of Languages (论语言的功能分类). *Contemporary Linguistics* (当代语言学)(1). Ruiz R, 1984. Orientations in Language Planning. *NABE* Journal (2). Ruiz R, 2010. Reorienting Language-as-resource. In J. Petrovic(ed). *International Perspectives on Bilingual Education, Information Age*.

2.2 Language-as-right

Language-as-right in language planning is a significant component of national social planning in the context of globalization. Since the end of the 20th century, economic globalization has accelerated interpersonal communication of different ethnic groups. Driven by the trend of multiculturalism, language planning focuses on the language rights of multilingual groups, which account for only a small proportion of total population. In the meantime, language planning focuses on the human being: the core of language life in multilingual society, which shows that language planning regards language as a basic right for everyone. In national emergency language services, on the basis of organized and systematic planning activities, language-as-right conceptualizes real-world linguistic diversity as an issue of emergency information dissemination, so as to respect and protect the rights of the mother tongue and avoid language discrimination. Besides, language-as-right ensures the people's rights to be informed and to be heard in their mother tongues through language services. In China's emergency language services, governments at all levels always adhere to the concept of "people first, life first" and attach importance to the protection of multilingual rights. Since 2020, Chinese linguists have formed the Epidemic Language Service Corps to develop a series of emergency language products, such as *Hubei Dialect Glossary for Fighting Epidemic and Foreign Language Glossary for Fighting Epidemic* (Li et al., 2020), which to some extent reflects the country's concern for language rights of different groups of people. Moreover, coping with problems of special crowds, such as language expression and information transmission of elderly people in major public emergencies (Huang, 2020), communication needs of hearing-impaired people in major public emergencies (Zheng, 2020) and information acquisition of foreigners coming to China, is also an important part of language-as-right. Language-as-right highlights the protection of language interests of minority groups, which is related to the basic rights of citizens. It is not limited only to the construction of national emergency language capacities. It shows more a kind of people-oriented thought: social fairness and justice. However, we should also be soberly aware that language-as-right poses unprecedented challenges to the efficiency and input of language services because no country or government can objectively provide emergency language services for all languages or dialects. Existing research in China emphasizes the urgency of increasing national input while neglecting the limits and benefits of government financial investment. Confronted with the complicated and volatile international situation, our country is inclined to prioritize limited resources in more important areas, such as improving medical conditions and strengthening public health education. Emergency language service planning requires accurate urban language population surveys and language economics data. Blindly increasing government and market resource investment will bring unbearable pressure to the country and society. Therefore, instead of emphasizing the increase in national investment in emergency language services, the linguistic community is supposed to take into account the efficiency and effectiveness of national investment and conduct detailed and in-depth investigations to identify the specific language needs of different regions and formulate corresponding scientific plans for emergency language services.

2.3 Language-as-resource

Language-as-resource in language planning not only highlights the instrumental orientation of language, but also advocates the multiple values of language as human intelligence, culture, politics, society and rights. It fully respects the multiple values of different languages and proposes to deal with various language problems from the angles of humanism and ecologism (Ruiz, 2010; Li, 2019). Language-as-resource views different languages as social public goods and ecological resources from a multilingual perspective, and proposes to construct a space for the harmonious coexistence of multilingual resources.

Based on language-as-resource, the development of national emergency language capacities regards language as an important resource and respects various languages and their users. Furthermore, it is committed to preserving language diversity, including but not limited to the instrumental value of language. It reflects more the resource value of language. The resource value of language is first reflected in its public product attributes. In the construction of national emergency capacities, language is not entirely a tool, but should be positioned as a public product with infrastructure attributes. It is like the street lights arranged on both sides of the road in the construction of municipal facilities, seemingly inconspicuous but indispensable. In consequence, language-as-resource requires ensuring the safety of language as a public product and guaranteeing the infrastructure construction of language resources. This is the manifestation of the bottom-line thinking of modern countries at the level of public society and policy.

Language-as-resource needs to take into consideration the external resource value of language in the economic, cultural, political and other fields. For example, the number of languages for emergency language services should be increased in conjunction with the actual emergency needs of different fields or regions, such as the increasing of Less Commonly Taught Languages in the Belt and Road Initiative; Emergency language services for ethnic minorities in ethnic areas are provided; Multilingual planning services are developed to meet the emergency language needs in special fields such as public service field, medical field, judicial field or security field. These all reflect the planning and service features of language-as-resource.

Language-as-resource also involves the intrinsic value of language in identity construction, self-esteem building, national security, media and public relations (Hult & Hornberger, 2016). In the construction of emergency language capacities, the intrinsic value of language can be realized through the implementation of psychological intervention of language, the development of language technology, the creation of language products and the building of international emergency discourse system. Exploring how to implement psychological intervention of language, giving full play to the soothing role of language in public emergencies (Liu, 2022; Zhao & Deng, 2020; Liu, 2020) and safeguarding national security through translanguaging practices on social media (Zhu, 2020) are all good examples to realize the intrinsic value of language.

However, it should not be overlooked that the value of language resources has not yet been fully exploited. The investigation, collation, development and utilization of language resources need to be carried out urgently (Fang, 2020). Specifically, there is a lack of systematic statistics on the number, distribution and ability of domestic emergency language service talents. The national working mechanism for emergency language service has not been established. The development and utilization of existing language resources are mostly carried out spontaneously by some scholars and volunteers. It is believed that the instruction of the National Language Service Corps of China will contribute to the construction of the system and mechanism of national emergency language capacities. Additionally, it is extremely urgent to establish a global discourse system to deal with major public emergencies. To construct the discourse for China's participation in global governance and to carry out global discourse communication in foreign affairs and diplomacy, we need to actively take advantage of the resource value of language and improve the discourse planning ability. From the perspective of language-as-resource, the language planning for the development of national emergency language capacities demands prompt solution.

3. Fundamental Content of Language Planning for the Development of National Emergency Language Capacities

Based on language-as-resource and classical theories of language planning, we classify the fundamental content of language planning for the development of national emergency language capacities into eight groups: language corpus planning, language status planning, language acquisition planning, language prestige planning, discourse planning, language usage planning, translation planning and language technology planning.

3.1 Language corpus planning

Language corpus planning mainly contains three aspects. The first aspect is to ensure smooth language communication. On the one hand, it is necessary to establish standards for the use of emergency language and develop national emergency terminology capacities according to the principles of scientificity, sociality, unity and timeliness (Tao & Zhao, 2020), which is beneficial to guarantee the core terms in major public emergencies are scientific, standardized and unified. For instance, the naming of diseases and viruses is not only a matter of medical expertise, but also a test of wisdom and level of social governance. Improper naming will hinder economic and social development and even cause social conflicts. The most typical examples are "Spanish flu," "Middle East respiratory syndrome" and "swine flu," which have brought huge negative effects and prompted the World Health Organization (WHO) to update the nomenclature of viruses and diseases in 2015. On the other hand, the naming efficiency and rationality at home and abroad need to be further improved to meet the actual needs of dealing with major public emergencies. Before the official name is issued, many different versions of the name will appear in the society. Once it is circulated, it will be more difficult to make further changes (Wang, 2020c). The second aspect is to safeguard the language communication rights of minority groups. For example, language products such as *Hubei Dialect Glossary for Fighting Epidemic* and *Foreign Language Glossary for Fighting Epidemic* take into account the actual needs of relevant groups and effectively safeguard their language rights; *Concise Chinese for Fighting Epidemic* has played a positive role in promoting the language communication of citizens with weak ability in Mandarin reading and understanding as well as foreigners in China, but the problems such as the selection of words, the formulation of standards and norms, and the rapid transmission of emergency information still need to be further studied (Li & Rao, 2020). The third aspect is to make good use of language comforting (Liu, 2022) and give full play to the resource value of language. Major public emergencies will not only cause physical and mental trauma to injured patients, but also affect other groups such as police, medical staff and their families. Therefore, applying language, words and related methods to comfort and guide these people is of paramount importance. However, the principles of language comforting and how to combine them with mental health measures need to be discussed in depth (Li & Rao, 2020).

3.2 Language status planning

The language status planning mainly includes four parts. The first part is to carry out a survey on the demand for emergency language services and provide customized language services. For China, the National Language Commission, the Ministry of Emergency Management and other relevant departments should jointly survey the demand for emergency language services in different regions and effectively understand the basic information on the number, distribution, language ability and needs of multilingual people (Mandarin, dialect, ethnic language and foreign language) in different regions to draw local "language maps." These maps can provide customized language services to various groups of people in different regions and practical reference for national emergency language services, which is conducive to avoid emergency language service planning that lacks field consideration, reduce resource waste and ensure the maximization of national input-output benefits.

The second part is to overcome the communication challenges brought by language diversity for emergency language services. The government should take the lead in establishing a multilingual information release channel covering common languages, dialects, ethnic languages, foreign languages, sign language and braille, and develop an optimal language selection scheme to respond to public emergencies (Li & Rao, 2020). Language is a bridge that connects people and things. In general conversations, the utilization of the listener's native language is more advantageous. When it comes to prevention and preparation, monitoring and early warning, emergency response and rescue, and post-event recovery and reconstruction, the choice of "emergency languages" from Mandarin, dialects, ethnic languages and foreign languages needs to be systematically studied. The government is supposed to improve the ability to choose and use these "emergency languages" to release information in time, so as to eliminate communication barriers.

The third part is to create an environment for the harmonious development of multiple languages and uphold the right of "emergency languages" to provide emergency language services. On the one hand, it is necessary to explore the allocation and positioning of language function in the relationship between Mandarin and dialects in the development of national emergency language capacities. Japan has accumulated rich experience in making good use of the advantages of dialects in promoting cultural identity and employing dialects to provide emergency language services for disaster victims (Wei & Qian, 2022). In contrast, the ability of Chinese governments at all levels to provide such language services is still very limited, which is also worth our reflection to a certain extent. From the perspective of national language governance, we must scientifically and reasonably position the relationship between Mandarin and dialects in the development of national emergency language capacities. On the other hand, we should pay attention to the improvement of the capacity of emergency foreign language services. As China plays an increasingly important role in global governance, the number of international cooperation and exchanges China organizes and participates is also gradually increasing. In order to deal with global crises, strong emergency foreign language service capacity is desired. However, the current emergency foreign language service capacity in China doesn't match our international status and image. Therefore, the improvement is in urgent need. In addition, it is crucial to advocate giving priority to publishing scientific research results in Chinese and pay attention to the improvement of the status of Chinese in dealing with major public emergencies. Li Yuming and Wang Chunhui put forward the proposal of "Publishing in Chinese as a Priority," calling for reforming the existing scientific research evaluation system and transforming scientific research achievements into China's real productivity in the first place, especially in response to major public emergencies and other emergency issues (Li & Wang, 2020). With China's active participation in global governance, Chinese status planning in international public health and public security will be a new project.

The fourth part is to give full play to the functions and roles of languages in different fields or industries in emergency language services. The emergency language capacity varies from one field or industry to another, including emergency medical language, aviation language, maritime language and internet language (Wang, 2020a). The emergency language capacity of each field or industry has its own characteristics and is somewhat specialized. The government should take notice of the cultivation of these categories of emergency language capacities and combine them with the emergency language capacities of different languages to promote the development of national emergency language capacities.

3.3 Language acquisition planning

Language acquisition planning refers to the language education planning provided to develop the emergency language capacities required to deal with major public emergencies. It includes language education planning in formal areas such as schools, as well as language education planning in informal areas, mainly involving four aspects. The first aspect is to promote language emergency training and enhance language emergency awareness. Nowadays, language emergency training has not been given much attention and carried out effectively. Apart from language researchers and learners, few people know or understand the emergency language capacity in the field of public services, including public security, municipal administration or health. The training work in these fields is even less. The language emergency training cannot be conducted in emergencies. Instead, relevant departments, professional institutions and schools ought to take precautions and accumulate experience at ordinary times.

The second aspect is to plan emergency language education for public (community) to improve their emergency language capacities (Teng, 2020), guide and help them exercise their language rights. This type of language education belongs to pre-disaster prevention education and special attention should be paid to ensuring the right of the elderly, hearing-impaired people, foreigners in China and other special groups to receive emergency language education. For example, by communicating with these special groups, language service volunteers can obtain their information. These groups can also make feedback on the quality of emergency language services. This not only conveys disaster prevention information, but also improves the public's sense of self-esteem and agency (Teng, 2020), thus achieving the goal of safeguarding the public's language rights and improving their emergency language capacities.

The third aspect is to strengthen the training of emergency language service talents and reserve human resources to deal with major public emergencies. Emergency language service talents play an important role in responding to public emergencies, but at present, there is still a large shortage of emergency language service talents in China. Emergency language service talents (specifically refer to emergency language service professionals) include talents with language related emergency language service specialized knowledge, skills and experience, such as translation talents, language technology talents, language training talents and other professional language talents, as well as professional talents in other domains, such as psychiatrists, journalists, news editors and community grid members (Zheng & Xu, 2020).

Based on the teaching system of relevant professional talents in colleges and universities, it is imperative to build a talent training system among the government, universities and industries, where talents have a clear division of labor and cooperate with each other, and explore effective paths for training different types of emergency language service talents. The fourth aspect is to promote the standardization construction of emergency language service personnel training. On the one hand, establishing a database of emergency language service talents and making a list of talents to systematically count the number, distribution, language, occupation and other basic information of domestic emergency language service talents, so as to scientifically and reasonably allocate talents to carry out emergency language services in response to major public emergencies. On the other hand, to classify and manage these talents, we should clarify the talent access and exit mechanism, strengthen the selection and assessment of emergency language service talents and focus on establishing the evaluation criterion of emergency language service capacity. At the same time, incentive measures, such as benefits in employment, education and medical treatment, should be taken to encourage and call on more talents to devote themselves to emergency language services. Only in these ways can we create a new training mode of emergency language service talents in which "professional talents" and "language service volunteers" complement each other.

3.4 Language prestige planning

Language prestige planning is carried out around the language image, which primarily covers three aspects. The first aspect is to eliminate language violence, maintain the language image and purify the language environment. In particular, in the Internet era, when some "opinion leaders" make irresponsible remarks without knowing the truth about public emergencies, it is easy to stir up tempo and cause irreparable harm and impact to the relevant groups. These are essentially a kind of language violence, which can easily arouse people's resentment and cause visual pollution. The prestige of language is the business card of language, so we should improve our ability to master language and make language positive and soothing through various appropriate and elegant expressions (Zhao & Deng, 2020).

The second aspect is to pay attention to prestige planning for dialects, sign language, braille and foreign languages, and safeguard the language rights of these language groups. In the development of national emergency language capacities, attention should be paid to the establishment of a good image for dialects, sign language, braille and foreign languages, especially by widely promoting their positive role in responding to public emergencies. For example, developing and designing language products can promote the positive effects of these languages, which is helpful to create a favorable atmosphere for their development and participation in emergency language services, enhance their social recognition and strengthen the language identity.

The third aspect is to strengthen the prestige planning of Chinese international communication and set up a good international image for China. Many countries attach great importance to language prestige planning. For example, France depicts French as "the most beautiful language in the world," Britain describes English as "the language necessary for national, social and personal development." (Shen & Xia, 2018) However, our government does not have a clear position for the international image of Chinese, which makes some foreign learners think that "Chinese is the most difficult language to learn." This is not conducive to the international dissemination of Chinese and will have a negative impact on China's image. The government should organize experts and scholars to fully explore the characteristics of Chinese culture and spread the good image of Chinese through literary creations (Shen & Xia, 2018), such as sorting out and publishing China's experience and practices in dealing with major public emergencies. Meanwhile, language product providers should understand and grasp the public's feelings and opinions about language products at the aesthetic and intellectual levels through a variety of means, and make timely improvements to meet the public's needs and improve product recognition. In terms of products for foreign users, the differences in political, economic and cultural aspects should be focused on to enhance the international image of Chinese.

3.5 Discourse planning

The discourse planning for the development of national emergency language capacities mainly involves three aspects: ensuring the safety of national emergency discourse, enhancing the international discourse power in the global public crisis and building a global emergency discourse community. The first is to ensure the safety of national emergency discourse, which is a fundamental task and reflects a bottom-line thinking and crisis awareness in international public security. From the perspective of international discourse, some foreign media and politicians have "stigmatized" the prevention and control of public emergencies in China by means of words and pictures on different occasions, which has seriously damaged China's international image. As China's participation in global governance becomes more and more prominent, the related discourse security issue will become increasingly conspicuous. How to maintain the security of China's emergency discourse is of great significance. Besides, to ensure the safety of emergency discourse, we must dispel rumors related to public emergencies. Objectively speaking, rumors confuse the public and still persist for quite some time despite repeated prohibitions. One of the reasons is that they are closely related to the rapid speed, the wide range, the low cost and the difficult information screening of information dissemination in the Internet era. Practice has proved that the prevention and control of rumors is one of the important tasks to guarantee the safety of emergency discourse. Relevant government departments should improve the public opinion guidance ability related to public emergencies and grasp the direction of public opinion. A favorable atmosphere of public opinion can inspire people and boost morale. On the contrary, a terrible atmosphere of public opinion will seriously hinder the development of relevant work and cause side effects.

The second is to enhance the international discourse power in the global public crisis. In the face of global public crisis, no country can stay on the sidelines. However, in the global discourse field, since the long-established "strong in the West and weak in the East" international discourse system cannot be changed for a moment, the majority of developing countries are in a "silent" state. It will take time to break this situation. China's voice, influence and right to select topic in the international discourse system to deal with public crisis needs to be improved. At present, the key to enhancing China's international discourse power in the global public crisis is to raise Chinese opinions in time, tell the China's stories well, effectively disseminate the Chinese solutions, set international topics, guide the international discourse orientation, obtain the recognition and positive responses of the international community. At the same time, we should focus on improving the ability of emergency discourse communication in key areas, such as foreign affairs and diplomacy, and truly building the discourse of China's participation in global governance.

The third is to build a global community with a shared emergency discourse. The ultimate goal of discourse planning is to build a discourse community (Shen, 2019). The Ebola epidemic in West Africa, Zika virus and other global health threats that human beings have experienced since the 21st century further illustrate that dealing with global public emergencies requires upholding the concept of a community with a shared future for mankind. The international community should actively participate in global governance and build a global community with a shared emergency discourse to form a global emergency discourse ability to cope with major public health emergencies and other "global risks." In response to global public crisis, China has always taken the initiative to strengthen cooperation and contacts with countries around the world, actively engaged in discourse communication, exchange and consultation with the international community, and increasingly attached importance to sharing experience through multilingual forms to jointly deal with the risks caused by public crisis, which is a positive measure to build a global community with a shared emergency discourse. However, it is worth noting that China's ability to use foreign languages, especially English, in emergency topic setting and discourse communication in overseas media communication still needs to be improved (Wang, 2020b). The role of major world languages such as Chinese and English in building a global community with a shared emergency discourse needs to be further explored, too.

3.6 Language usage planning

As for the language use planning, the main content is to further expand the use of different languages in the development of national emergency language capacities and give full play to the resource value of multilingualism.

In the first place, there is a misconception about language diversity, that is, language diversity is one of the challenges hindering the development of national emergency language capacities. This wrong perception needs to be changed for many reasons. One the one hand, with the improvement of China's comprehensive strength and international status, the number of transnational corporations and foreigners in China is increasing day by day. One the other hand, China is a multiethnic country. These two aspects make the development of national emergency language capacities become an irresistible trend.

Secondly, the right of all languages to participate in emergency language services in various fields or industries should be maintained. Although various fields or industries have their own characteristics and even have their own representative languages, this should not be the reason why they refuse to use other languages for emergency language services. On the contrary, multiple languages entering the same field or industry will expand their original business scope and open up new markets.

Finally, the role of language in dealing with public emergencies is mostly limited to language service and language communication, which shows more the instrumental value of language rather than the resource value. Therefore, for one thing, we should fully explore the multiple values of different languages, including foreign languages, minority languages and dialects, in emergency mobilization, rumor prevention and control, language psychological intervention, public opinion monitoring, volunteer recruitment and other specific work, expand the use and functions of different languages and organically integrate language resources with four activities: prevention and preparation, monitoring and early warning, emergency response and rescue, and post-recovery and reconstruction. For another, we should also pay attention to the role of multilingual resources in participating in global governance, and expand the use of language resources in different fields, regions and institutions. For example, we can explore how to improve the efficiency of cooperation between countries and regions along the "Belt and Road" in the field of international public health and enhance international mutual trust through reasonable planning of foreign language choice. We can also satisfy the emergency language needs in public service field, judicial field and security field through the implementation of multilingual planning.

3.7 Translation planning

Translation planning mainly covers three aspects. The first aspect is to strengthen emergency translation research and solve the language communication problems caused by improper translation. At present, the theoretical framework of applied translation studies can be used to explore the oral and written understanding, conversion, expression and strategies of emergency language (Wang et al., 2020), so as to ensure the smooth communication of information in public emergencies.

The second aspect is to increase types of language in translation, improve the practical ability of translation talents and safeguard the language rights of all kinds of people to access information. During the COVID-19 epidemic, many documents, notices and messages were released in English. The ability to release information in minority languages was so weak that the information could not be transmitted through translation in time, which exposed the weakness of China's multilingual translation ability. At the same time, restricted by China's long-term teaching system, curriculum and teaching content, many students majoring in translation are not familiar with some practical and professional materials, such as "contract text," "quality inspection report" and "drug information." Their language ability and practical ability are not up to standard. Therefore, in terms of translation talents cultivation, colleges and universities should pay more attention to the practicability and avoid being divorced from reality.

The third aspect is to deepen the integration of translation and modern information technology, and give full play to the resource value of language diversity. Although there are currently a variety of translation software that can improve the efficiency of translation, the quality problem remains difficult to solve, especially in emergency circumstances, translation errors may bring serious consequences. In the meantime, the translation needs of special groups in public emergencies should also be met. Relevant enterprises and scientific research institutions should accelerate the pace of using modern technology to improve the quality of translation. For example, Voice of Hand Information Technology Co., Ltd. has developed China's first remote video sign language translation service platform for hearing-impaired people (Liu, 2020). In addition, India's language diversity, while bringing difficulties to its domestic clinical trials, has also inspired life science companies to cooperate with experienced language service providers (LSPs) who provide professional medical translation services, allowing India to occupy an important position in global clinical trials.[1] This enlightens us to innovate ideas, introduce market mechanisms and strengthen the research on translation services in different fields.

3.8 Language technology planning

Language technology planning mainly contains three aspects. The first aspect is to employ language technology to solve the communication problems in public emergencies. For example, in 2022, led by the school of foreign languages of Tongji University, "Trans On" (a cloud-based platform for simultaneous interpretation) and International Education Association Shanghai, the school of foreign languages and the graduate institute of interpretation and translation of 17 universities in Shanghai jointly launched the translation volunteer activity, effectively provided contactless multilingual instant emergency translation services for foreigners in Shanghai. Trans On, a cloud-based platform for simultaneous interpretation, offered strong technical support for this activity. Volunteers took orders in the platform and then provided online translation services for those in need (Tongji University, 2022). On the whole, the relevant research and achievements in China are still relatively rare, and there is still a gap with foreign countries. For example, having realized the importance of high technology in crisis, the

---

[1] The Impact of India's Linguistic Diversity on Global Clinical Trial Patterns(印度语言多样性对全球临床试验格局的影响). See: https:// mp. Weixin.qq.com/s/ -xS3IkdUUHHET9yzt1dCCA .

Japanese government developed some language translation programs for residents to use whenever and wherever possible, which reflects the trend towards automatic emergency language services (Teng, 2020). The approaches above in dealing with emergencies are worth learning from.

The second aspect is to promote the deep integration of multilingualism and language technology. Establishing a language technology research and development system led by the government and participated by think tanks, enterprises, colleges and universities, and academic organizations may be a proper exploration. Besides, we should make overall planning for language technology research and development to make sure that all kinds of languages have equal opportunities in the integration of language technology and all kinds of languages can better participate in emergency language services with the help of language technology.

The third aspect is to make full use of the advantages of language technology to expand the fields of language services and improve the quality of services. For example, we can adopt language technologies such as corpus, speech recognition and synthesis, language information processing, intelligent translation and translation blockchain to complete the key tasks such as information statistics and release, public opinion research and judgment, rumor prevention and control, and language rescue, so as to provide customized services. What's more, applying language technology to develop relevant language products is beneficial to enhance the recognition of the Chinese language, international understanding and mutual trust, and increase people's scientific knowledge, so as to realize the intrinsic value of language. However, there is still much room for improvement in this area for China, especially in the use of language technology to promote scientific popularization.

This paper discusses the fundamental content of language planning for the development of national emergency language capacities from the above eight dimensions, pointing out the direction and providing the important focus for dealing with the language problems in major public emergencies. These eight dimensions are not completely independent, but are complementary and closely related to each other. Exploring the path to improve the national emergency language capacities from the perspective of language planning cannot only rely on the power of the government or the linguistic community. Taking a fragmented and palliative approach that only treats the symptoms need to be avoided, either. We should develop a national emergency language capacity system with the participation of the country, society, individuals as soon as possible, carry out scientific and effective language planning, improve the national emergency language capacity, and earnestly solve the language problems in public emergencies.

4. Conclusion

Strong national emergency language capacity is essential to deal with major public emergencies. Developing national emergency language capacities from the perspective of language planning is a protracted battle that requires a comprehensive layout to prevent problems before they occur. Firstly, language planning needs to be powered by discipline construction. At present, the reality of the disconnection between the construction of language discipline in colleges and universities and the actual needs of the society cannot be ignored, so it is urgent to strengthen the discipline construction. Secondly, it is necessary to conduct a scientific investigation on the current situation and needs of the development of national emergency language capacities, set the emergency language standards and scientifically plan the national investment. Thirdly, establishing and improving the system and mechanism for the development of national emergency language capacities and the talent training mechanism for emergency language service are important breakthroughs in enhancing the national emergency language capacities. Scientific and effective system and mechanism is helpful to improve the national emergency language capacity and set the language problems in major public emergencies at rest. Fourthly, improving the international discourse ability to cope with major public emergencies is the key goal of national emergency language capacity development. Improving international discourse ability is not only a necessary condition for safeguarding national discourse security, but also an objective requirement for China to participate in global governance.

Today's world is undergoing momentous changes unseen in a century. Human beings are facing an increasing number of unpredictable public emergencies. Exploring ways to promote the development of national emergency language capacities from the perspective of language planning is the close combination of theory and practice, which is not only the objective demand to deal with the crisis, but also the opportunity to improve the national emergency language capacity. Besides, it also broadens the research field of linguistics. On the basis of language planning theory, this paper analyzes three types of language planning orientations in the development of national emergency language capacities and puts forward the basic content of language planning for the development of national emergency language capacities from eight aspects, looking forward to providing some references for the development of national emergency language capacities.

References

Bao, L.(包联群). Emergency Language Service for 3/11 Great East Japan Earthquake

("3·11"东日本大震灾应急语言服务). *Chinese Journal of Language Policy and Planning*(语言战略研究), 2020,5(3): 62-74.

Cadwell, P. *Translation and Trust: A Case Study of How Translation was Experienced by Foreign Nationals Resident in Japan for the 2011 Great East Japan Earthquake*. Dublin: Dublin City University, 2015.

Choi, S., Lee, J., Kang, M., et al. Large-scale Machine Learning of Media Outlets for Understanding Public Reactions to Nation-wide Viral Infection Outbreaks. *Methods*, 2017,129: 50-59.

Fang, Y.(方寅). Concern for the National Security to Promote the Development of National Language Emergency System and Capacities (关注国家语言安全, 推进国家语言应急体系与能力建设). *Chinese Journal of Language Policy and Planning*(语言战略研究) , 2020, 5(2): 11-12.

Forrester, M. B., Villanacci, J. E. & Valle, N. Use of Interactive Voice Response Technology by Poison Centers during the H1N1 Outbreak. *Prehospital and Disaster Medicine*, 2010, 25(5): 415-418.

Gesser-edelsburg, A., Shir-raz, Y., Bar-lev, O. S., et al. Outbreak or Epidemic? How Obama's Language Choice Transformed the Ebola Outbreak into an Epidemic. *Disaster Medicine and Public Health Preparedness*, 2016, 10(4): 669-673.

Huang, L.(黄立鹤). How to More Effectively Convey Information to the Elderly During the Epidemic (疫情期间, 如何更有效地向老年人传达信息), 2020. Available from: https://www.thepaper.cn/newsDetail_forward_6451515 [Accessed on March 29, 2020] .

Hult, F. M. & Hornberger, N. H. Revisiting Orientations in Language Planning: Problem, Right, and Resource as an Analytical Heuristic. *Bilingual Review*, 2016, 33(3): 30-49.

Li, Y.(李宇明), Rao, G.(饶高琦). On State Emergency Language Competence(应急语言能力建设刍论). *Journal of Tianjin Foreign Studies University*(天津外国语大学学报),2020, 27(3): 2-13.

Li, Y.(李宇明), Wang, C.(王春辉). On Research Productivity and Publishing in Chinese as a Priority(科研生产力与中文首发制度). *Chinese Journal of Language Policy and Planning*(语言战略研究), 2020, 5(2): 10-11.

Li, Y.(李宇明), Zhao, S.(赵世举), He, L.(赫琳). The Practice of and Reflections on "Epidemic Language Service Corps"("战疫语言服务团"的实践与思考). *Chinese Journal of Language Policy and Planning*(语言战略研究), 2020, 5(3): 23-30.

Li, Y.(李宇明). Reflection on Promoting State Language Competence(提升国家语言能力的若干思考). *Nankai Linguistics*(南开语言学刊), 2011 (1): 1-8.

Li, Y.(李宇明). Theories and Practices of China's Language Resources(中国语言资源的理念与实践). *Chinese Journal of Language Policy and Planning*(语言战略研究), 2019, 4(3): 16-28.

Liu, M.(刘梦). A Sociological Case Analysis of Language Practice in Hotline Counseling during the COVID-19 Pandemic(社会学视角下新冠疫情心理咨询的语言使用个案分析). *Chinese Journal of Language Policy and Planning*(语言战略研究), 2020, 5(5): 21-31.

Liu, Q.(刘琼). Chen Bin, An Entrepreneur Born in the 1980s in Zhuzhou, Founded the First Remote Video Sign Language Translation Platform in China, Bringing "Voice of Hand" to the Hearing-impaired Community(株洲80后创业者陈斌: 创立全国首个远程视频手语翻译平台, 为听障人士带来"手之声"),2020. Available from: https://kknews.cc/zh-my/finance/5jrabj6.html [Accessed on September 8, 2020].

Liu, X.(刘晓宇). On Emergency Language Comforting(应急语言抚慰刍议). *Contemporary Foreign Language Studies*(当代外语研究), 2022, 461(5): 110-119.

Nallasamy, U., Black, A. W., Schultz, T., et al. Nine One One: Recognizing and Classifying Speech for Handling Minority Language Emergency Calls. *In Proceedings of the International Conference on Language Resources and Evaluation*. Paris: European Language Resources Assoc-Elra, 2018: 2888-2891.

O'brien, S., Federici, F. M. Crisis Translation: Considering Language Needs in Multilingual Disaster Settings. *Disaster Prevention and Management*, 2020, 29(2): 129-143.

Odlum, M., Yoon, S. What Can We Learn about the Ebola Outbreak from Tweets? *American Journal of Infection Control*, 2015, 43(6): 563-571.

Rudra, K., Sharma, A., Ganguly, N., et al. Classifying and Summarizing Information from Microblogs during Epidemics. *Information Systems Frontiers*, 2018 20(5): 933-948.

Ruiz, R. Reorienting Language-as-resource. In Petrovic, J. *International Perspectives on Biligual Education. Charlotte*, NC: Information Age, 2010: 155-172.

Shen, Q.(沈骑), Kang, M.(康铭浩). A Framework of Language Governance Planning against Public Health Emergency of International Concern(PHEIC) (面向重大突发公共卫生事件的语言治理能力规划). *Journal of Xinjiang Normal University (Edition of Philosophy and Social Sciences)*[新疆师范大学学报(哲学社会科学版)], 2020, 41(5): 64-74.

Shen, Q.(沈骑), Xia, T.(夏天). Fundamental Issues of Language Strategic Planning for "the Belt and Road Initiatives"("一带一路"语言战略规划的基本问题). *Journal of Xinjiang Normal University(Edition of Philosophy and Social Sciences)*

[新疆师范大学学报(哲学社会科学版)], 2018, 39(1): 36-43.

Shen, Q.(沈骑). Discourse Planning of China: A New Task for Language Planningin Building a Community of Shared Future for Mankind(中国话语规划: 人类命运共同体建设中语言规划的新任务). *Applied Linguistics*(语言文字应用), 2019(4): 35-43.

Sousa, L., De Mello, R., Cedrim, D., et al. VazaDengue: An Information System for Preventing and Combating Mosquito-borne Diseases with Social Networks. *Information Systems*, 2018, 75: 26-42.

Squiers, L., Lynch, M., Dolina, S., et al. Zika and Travel in the News: A Content Analysis of US News Stories During the Outbreak in 2016-2017. *Public Health*, 2019, 168: 164-167.

Tao, Y.(陶源) & Zhao, H.(赵浩). On Nomenclatures of SARS-CoV-2 and COVID-19 from the Perspective of Emergency Language Capabilities(论应急语言能力视角下的新型冠状病毒及新型冠状病毒肺炎术语命名). *Journal of Beijing International Studies University*(北京第二外国语学院学报), 2020, 42(1): 45-56.

Teng, Y.(滕延江). On Language Planning for Public Emergency(论应急语言服务规划). *Chinese Journal of Language Policy and Planning*(语言战略研究), 2020, 5(6): 88-96.

Teng, Y.(滕延江). The Construction of Emergency Language Service System in the United States and Its Implications(美国紧急语言服务体系的构建与启示). *Journal of Beijing International Studies University*(北京第二外国语学院学报), 2018,40(3): 31-43.

Tesseur, W. Communication is Aid-But Only if Delivered in the Right Language: An Interview with Translators without Borders on Its Work in Danger Zones. *Journal of War & Culture Studies*, 2019, 2(3): 285-294.

Tongji University(同济大学). "Language doctor" is coming!("语言大白"来了!), 2022. Available from: http://m. cyol. com / gb / articles / 2022 - 05 / 12 / content_gnq6gflqV.html [Accessed on May 12, 2022].

Wang, C. (王春辉). Language Emergency and Social Governance in Public Emergencies(突发公共事件中的语言应急与社会治理), *Social Governance Review*(社会治理), 2020(3): 42-49.

Wang, H.(王辉). The Role of Utilizing Social Emergency Language Competence during Sudden Public Events(发挥社会应急语言能力在突发公共事件中的作用). *Chinese Journal of Language Policy and Planning*(语言战略研究), 2020a, 5(2): 8-10.

Wang, H. (王辉). The Development of Emergency Language Competence: A Perspective from State Governance(国家治理视野下的应急语言能力建设).

Chinese Journal of Language Policy and Planning(语言战略研究), 2020b, 5(5): 13-20.

Wang, J.(王娟) & Qu, Z.(曲志强). "Easy Japanese" in Emergency Relief and Its Implication for China("简易日语"与救灾应急).*Chinese Journal of Language Policy and Planning*(语言战略研究), 2020, 5(5): 57-66.

Wang, L.(王立非) & Sun, J.(孙疆卫). The Nomenclature and English Translation of Emergency Language Services Terminology under COVID-19 Pandemic(疫情引发的应急语言术语称名与英译). *Journal of Tianjin Foreign Studies University*(天津外国语大学学报), 2020, 27(3): 14-23.

Wang, L.(王立非), Wang, M.(王铭玉), Shen, Q.(沈骑), et al. Diverse Views on Issues Concerning Emergency Language ("应急语言问题"多人谈). *Chinese Journal of Language Policy and Planning*(语言战略研究), 2020, 5(3): 75-79.

Wei, Y.(韦钰) & Qian, Y.(钱颖). Modernization of China's Emergency Language Service System and Capacities in the New Era(新时代我国应急语言服务体系与能力现代化建设). *Journal of South-Central Minzu University(Humanities and Social Sciences)*[中南民族大学学报(人文社会科学版)], 2022: 1-9.

Wen, Q. (文秋芳). Defining National Language Capacity and Identifying Its Evaluation Indicatiors(国家语言能力的内涵及其评价指标). *Journal of Yunnan Normal University: Humanities and Social Sciences Edition)*[云南师范大学学报(哲学社会科学版)], 2016, 48(2): 23-31.

Winger, J. Plain Language Emergency Alerts. *Journal of Emergency Nursing*, 2017, 43(5): 451-456.

Xiao, J. (肖俊敏) & Zhang, Y. (张瑜). Two Decades of Emergency Language Research in China: Retrospect and Prospect(中国应急语言研究二十年回顾与展望). *Chinese Journal of Language Policy and Planning*(语言战略研究), 2022, 7 (2): 62-73.

Yang, S.(杨书敏) & Du, M.(杜敏). Study on Language Service of Rail Transit Under COVID-19 Epidemic(新冠肺炎疫情期间轨道交通语言服务研究——以西安市为例). *Journal of Xianyang Normal University*(咸阳师范学院学报), 2021, 36(5): 47-51.

Zhang, T.(张天伟). An Effective Way to Build up U.S. On-Call National Language Capacity: A Case Study of the U.S. National Language Service Corps(美国国家语言服务团案例分析). *Chinese Journal of Language Policy and Planning*(语言战略研究), 2016, 1(5): 88-96.

Zhang, T.(张天伟). Approaches and Methodologies of Emergency Language Studies Abroad(国外应急语言研究的主要路径和方法). *Chinese Journal of Language Policy and Planning*(语言战略研究), 2020, 5(5): 67-78.

Zhao, S.(赵世举) & Deng, B(邓毕娟). In Crisis, the Positive Power of Language is More Desired Than Ever(危难之时更需语言正能量). *Chinese Journal of Language Policy and Planning*(语言战略研究), 2020, 5(2): 13-14.

Zhao, S. (赵世举). Host's Words: Three Perspectives of Emergency Language Research (主持人语: 应急语言研究的三大视域). *Chinese Journal of Language Policy and Planning*(语言战略研究), 2020, 5(5): 11-12.

Zheng, X. (郑璇). Reflections on Language Emergency Services for People with Hearing Loss in Epidemic of COVID-19(新冠肺炎疫情下听障人群语言应急服务的思考). *Chinese Journal of Language Policy and Planning*(语言战略研究), 2020, 5(3): 40-49.

Zheng, Z.(郑泽芝) & Xu, B.(徐铂). Analyzing the Basic Concepts and Elements of Emergency Language Service(应急语言服务的基本概念及要素分析). *Journal of Beijing Union University(Humanities and Social Sciences)*[北京联合大学学报(人文社会科学版)], 2020, 18(3): 43-49.

Zhu, H. Countering COVID-19-related Anti-Chinese Racism with Translanguaged Swearing on Social Media. *Multilingua*, 2020, 39(5): 607-616.

International Language and Culture Promotion Institutions and National Language Capacity Research*

Zhang Tianwei**

Abstract: International Language and Culture Promotion Institutions (ILCPIs), with the main purpose of spreading language and culture, is a major content for national language capacity research. ILCPIs can enhance national language capacity in terms of language education, language culture and language economy. From the perspective of national language capacity, ILCPIs' development can be divided into three stages, characterized by spontaneity, self-awareness, and comprehensive integration. Within the framework of the national language capacity evaluation index, ILCPIs can be evaluated based on a two-level indicator system, covering their management ability, development ability, and communication ability.

Keywords: international Chinese education; international language and culture promotion institutions; national language capacity; national language capacity evaluation index; Confucius Institute

1. Introduction

The study of international language and culture promotion institutions (ILCPIs henceforth) has been one of the hot spots in academia in recent years. In particular, the government clearly stated "to build a Chinese language communication platform, and to build a global communication system for Chinese language and culture as well as an international Chinese language education standards system" in the 14th Five-Year Plan for National Economic and Social Development. The General Office of the State Council issued the "Suggestions on Comprehensively Strengthening Language-related endeavor in

* This article was originally published in *Journal of Shaanxi Normal University (Philosophy and Social Sciences Edition)*, Vol. 52, No.3. Original Title:国际语言文化推广机构与国家语言能力研究.

Translator: Wuyun Saina(乌云赛娜), Associate Professor of School of Chinese Language and Literature, Shaanxi Normal University. Her research focuses on Discourse Analysis, Formal Syntax and Child Language Acquisition.

** Zhang Tianwei(张天伟), Ph.D., Professor of National Research Centre for Foreign Language Education/National Research Centre for State Language Capacity, Beijing Foreign Studies University.

the New Era" in 2021, which also clearly proposed to vigorously enhance the international influence of the Chinese language, strengthen international Chinese education and services, and expand international language exchanges and cooperation.

The major issue that needs to be focused on in regard of national language capacity construction is how to build a global communication system for Chinese language and culture so as to vigorously enhance the international status and influence of Chinese. In this process, the role of ILCPIs needs special attention. A great deal of ILCPIs have been continuously reformed in recent years, via which institutions such as the Chinese International Education Foundation, the Centre for Language Education and Cooperation, and the International Society for Chinese Language Teaching, each finds its own work characteristics and division of labor. Under current circumstance that countries all over the world are exploring new methods and new paths to promote national common language and culture, conducting in-depth academic and strategic analysis and comparative research on the world's major ILCPIs bear more theoretical value and practical significance for improving our national language capacity.

Domestic studies of relevant issues make comparative analyses between foreign language and culture promotion institutions and Confucius Institutes. These studies start from analyzing promotion strategies, operation methods, teaching activities, as well as teacher construction of these institutions in aim of exploring the experience of foreign language communication and the inspiration for the development of related domestic undertakings (Cf. Zhang, 2008; Cao, 2016; Wu, 2013; Dai, 2023; Liu, 2021). Previous studies could be divided into two parts, namely literature review, and comparative analysis. Specifically, the former conducts research based on the *status quo* of foreign language and culture promotion institutions; whereas the latter makes comparative analysis of foreign language and culture promotion institutions and Confucius Institutes, and analyzes language and culture promotion institutions from an interdisciplinary perspective.

Foreign literatures specifically studying language and culture promotion institutions are limited in comparison to domestic studies. Most of the studies involve ILCPIs in the dimensions of language communication, cultural policy, economic benefits, etc. For instance, Adamson (2007) analyzes the achievements and problems of French language promotion by focusing on Alliance Française. Li (2018) introduces and comments on the British Council, Alliance Française and Goethe-Institut by focusing on their institutional management, funding sources, and course settings, teaching staff, and examination methods, etc., and in turn discusses the language policy, language management and language practice of the Confucius Institute. Other researches include "Research for Cult Committee-European Cultural Institutes Abroad" conducted by the European Parliament's

Culture and Education Committee, which involves 29 institutions among EU countries; and Paschalidis's (2009) study on the development history of cultural institutions abroad. Li & Tang (2022) provide a comprehensive overview of related research, which will not be repeated here due to limited space.

Previous studies have mostly focused on a specific institution or a particular aspect of measures, and there has been no research on ILCPIs from the perspective of national language capacity. National language capacity represents the overall *status quo* of national language management and language affairs, which takes international language and culture promotion as an important aspect. Therefore, this study intends to analyze the ILCPIs from the perspective of national language capacity. Via identifying the specific relations between these two aspects, we expect to promote our national language capacity and the construction of Confucius Institute.

2. The Relationship between ILCPIs and National Language Capacity

National language capacity refers to the ability to use language and various means to handle all related matters involving national interests, national security, national needs, national consciousness and other dimensions, including core elements such as management ability, development ability and communication ability, taking into account different internal and external aspects (Zhang, 2021). National language communication ability constituents an important aspect of the external performance of national language capacity, including dimensions such as promotion power, international influence, and power of speech, etc. (Zhang, 2022) The construction of national language communication ability is based on language resources, and the construction of ILCPIs is an important starting point for improving national language communication ability, which is mainly reflected in the three dimensions of language education, language culture, and language economy, among which language education is the basic means to improve the national language capacity, language culture is the specific foothold of the national language capacity construction, and the language economy is the inevitable product of the national language capacity developing to a certain stage.

First of all, the key to improving national language communication ability is language education, which takes ILCPIs as important promoters. The main activity of the ILCPIs is the teaching and promotion of the country's main language in foreign countries or among non-native speakers. Therefore, it is an important part of the country's foreign language education system. Taking Chinese as an example, 82 countries around the world have, by far, incorporated Chinese into their national education systems. Chinese education is widely carried out in more than 180 countries and regions around the world.

There are more than 30 million people learning Chinese outside China, and the cumulative number of people learning and using Chinese is close to 200 million. These achievements are inseparable from the more than 500 Confucius Institutes and Confucius Classrooms around the world. Many countries' exposure to Chinese education began with the establishment of Confucius Institutes. The booming international Chinese education is not only an important manifestation of our country's international communication ability, but also an important symbol of the improvement of national language capacity.

At present, the top priority for language education in support of our country's language communication ability is the cultivation of language teachers. On the one hand, the country urgently needs cultivating multi-lingual Chinese teachers with global vision, sense of identification with the motherland, and professional abilities; on the other hand, the cultivation of local Chinese teachers in the target country who are proficient in our country's common language is also one of the essential tasks, which is one of the purposes of the ILCPIs. ILCPIs such as the Goethe-Institut, Instituto Camões, Instituto Cervantes, the Japan Foundation, and the Russkiy Mir Foundation have made full use of online and offline resources, targeting different countries, adopting different promotion models and organizing various special projects to cultivate local language teachers.

Secondly, the international dissemination of language and cultural soft power and the international power of speech are two important indicators of a country's language capacity; and it is the ILCPIs' responsibility to shoulder such important mission of language and culture dissemination. The promotion of language and culture are closely linked, which constituents an important manifestation of the country's soft power and power of speech. Therefore, the construction of national language capacity must increase the promotion and dissemination of the national common language. For our country, we need to draw nourishment from our traditional culture, modern spirit, humanistic thoughts, and philosophical concepts, etc. in order to increase the international dissemination of Chinese. It is important to adhere to the principle that "what belongs to the nation, belongs to the world," to build cultural confidence when communicating to the outside world based on the country's excellent language and cultural resources, and to tell Chinese stories in a good way, to tell Chinese stories well, and to tell good stories about China.

International Chinese education is an important way of external communication. Persistence in tapping the country's excellent language and cultural resources is the driving force for promoting the reform and development of international Chinese education. An important driver in promoting the international communication of language and culture is ILCPIs. ILCPIs in various countries regard cultural promotion as one of their important tasks both explicitly and implicitly. For instance, the Japan Foundation lists cultural and artistic exchanges, overseas Japanese education, and Japanese language research and knowledge exchange as its three main business areas. It is evident that the characteristics and paths of language and culture promotion in different countries are diversified in the context of globalization and multiculturalism, it is thus necessary to carry out targeted and market-oriented promotion based on regions, fields, countries and other relevant dimensions.

Finally, the economic attributes of language are an important measurement at certain developmental level of a country's language capacity. ILCPIs are closely related to language economy. Li (2022) demonstrates that language capacity is an important component of the labor force, and language plays an important role in technology dissemination and market unification. He emphasizes that attention should be paid to the economic attributes of language and promote national development by giving full play to the economic role of language. The promotion and dissemination of language also need to pay attention to the economic attributes of language and combine planning with market means. This is also an inevitable product of the development of a country's language capacity to a certain stage.

In the early stages of development, ILCPIs in general focus on adopting planned means to promote and disseminate the national common language. At a certain stage of development, the focus is shifted to the economic attributes of language and the development of language market, such as language industry, language education, language testing, etc. ILCPIs in different countries take different promotion strategies and paths based on their own language conditions, regional cultures and economic foundations. For example, after the World Trade Organization and the International Monetary Fund have implemented a series of neoliberal economic policies, Neoliberalism, which promotes the inevitability of competition, is an implicit language policy that packages English as a natural and neutral medium for excellent academics (Piller & Cho, 2013). In view of this, in the context of English becoming an international lingua franca, the British Council focuses on developing the language education industry and language testing market in target countries. However, some ILCPIs in non-English speaking countries often need to use planning means to make proactive promotion, such as the Chinese International Education Foundation, and the King Sejong Institute of South Korea. Only under the circumstances that planning means are the mainstay and the country's language communication ability has developed to a certain extent can it be possible to gradually form a market for language learning and consumption. Therefore, our current task is to vigorously develop the language industry and pay special attention to language-related data.

ILCPIs are an important starting point for improving national language capacity, especially national language communication ability. It is evident that a country's national language capacity is closely related to its political *status quo*, its economic development, and its cultural influence, etc. National language capacity becomes increasingly closely related to the ILCPIs due to the fact that latter play a vital role in the development of the former. In the era of major political changes, economic de-globalization and technological informatization, how to improve the breadth and depth of language and culture promotion and dissemination, and how to refine and differentiate expressions for different regions, fields, countries, cultures and audiences, deserve constantly reflection as key to the reformation of the ILCPIs.

3. Different Stages of Development of ILCPIs

Paschalidis (2009) divides the development of the ILCPIs into four stages, namely the "cultural nationalism" period (before World War I), the "cultural propaganda" period (during the two world wars), the "cultural diplomacy" period (after World War II), and the "cultural capitalism" period (after the Revolutions of 1989). Li & Tang (2022) divide the development into three stages, namely the initial stage, the development stage, and the modern stage. This division is mainly based on the historical development of the ILCPIs. However, from the perspective of the relationship between national language capacity and the ILCPIs, as well as the development of national language capacity over time, this paper proposes that the development of the ILCPIs has gone through three stages, namely the spontaneity stage, the self-awareness stage, and comprehensive integration stage. ILCPIs in different periods, due to their different purposes, missions, and international environments, have promoted national language capacity in different ways.

3.1 The stage of spontaneously promoting national language capacity (from the late 19th century to World War II)

Western capitalism has developed rapidly, and the world has begun to compete for overseas trade and colonial expansion since the Age of Discovery. The languages of the major colonial countries, such as Spanish, Portuguese, French, English, etc., spread around the world along with this process, which result in the widespread use of Indo-European languages in Asia, Africa and Latin America nowadays. However, the spread of language was still in a spontaneous stage and was often linked to the spread of religion during the early days of colonialism. Most of the people who carry out language dissemination are missionaries, who objectively promote the communication and exchange of languages in the world through a series of activities such as learning local languages, teaching native languages, and translating two languages. Nonetheless, the spread and communication of language are mostly individual behaviors at this stage, which have not yet been taken seriously by the state and the political power. For example, in China's modern history, there was a large number of missionaries and sinologists who studied Chinese, notated Chinese phonetics, interpreted Chinese vocabularies, and translated Chinese into their native languages through teaching activities. In this way, the establishment of the earliest ILCPIs did not appear until the 19th century despite the fact that the international spread of languages has a history of several centuries.

In 1883, Alliance Française, the world's first language and culture promotion institution with the purpose of international language promotion, was established. During this period, the ILCPIs actively cooperated with colonial expansion and the competition for the interests of the mother country given the fact that the emergence of Alliance Française was closely related to the disadvantage of France in the competition with Britain and the United States in European and world affairs. With its political and military expansion restrained, France began to focus on cultural conquest. French, as a common language that once dominated European affairs, was valued by the country and used as an important factor in cultural conquest. Therefore, the establishment of Alliance Française marked the beginning of national emphasis on the influence of national language capacity, after which other countries also began to attach importance to the spread of language and culture. The Società Dante Alighieri and the British Council were established during this period, and played a role in the language promotion and national cultural communication strategies of their respective countries.

Nevertheless, the promotion of national language capacity by the ILCPIs is still spontaneous and unconscious at this stage. The purpose of establishing these institutions is not entirely to construct national language capacity but is closely related to the social background and political interests of the time in many cases. For instance, Germany attached great importance to the relationship between the German language and social ideological trends before and after World War I and World War II. It is believed that its defeat in World War I was related to the cultural weakness of the German language relative to English. Therefore, the Deutsche Akademie was established in 1925 in aim of vigorously promoting German and spreading German culture and values around the world, in order to exert political influence on foreign governments and people.

3.2 The stage of consciously promoting national language capacity (from the post−World War II period to the late 1980s)

The national liberation movement surged after World War II, and a large number of countries got rid of colonial rules and achieved national independence. Meanwhile, a large number of international political and economic organizations such as the United Nations and the World Bank have been established, which have greatly increased the international exchanges with countries as the main body. The need for language communication has also been valued by various countries, which shifted the focus of the ILCPIs to language *per se*. Language policy and planning has developed rapidly as an emerging interdisciplinary subject, in which the status planning, ontology planning, and acquisition planning of language have a profound impact on a country and its foreign exchanges. Thus, the influence of the ILCPIs on the national language capacity has shifted from spontaneity to self-awareness at this stage.

For example, the United States' national strength increased significantly and had a profound impact on the world in the fields of culture and values after World War II. During this period, the U.S. attached great importance to the promotion of English and related cultures, and continued to expand the global influence of American culture through national projects, study abroad funding, and language teaching despite the fact that it did not establish a special language promotion institution. The same is the case for Japan, which established the Japan Foundation in 1972 to promote the overseas spread of Japanese. Germany changed the name of the Deutsche Akademie to the Goethe-Institut in 1951, which continued the endeavor of promoting German language and culture around the world.

In addition to the efforts of Western countries to promote language and culture, other developing countries have also realized the importance of language to the country. Taking Chinese as an instance, the Confucius Institute as an ILCPI had not yet been established during this period; nonetheless, teaching Chinese as a foreign language was launched immediately after the founding of the People's Republic of China. In the 1950s, teaching Chinese as a foreign language to Eastern European countries witnessed great achievement, and a specialized university was established for this purpose, i.e., Beijing Language Institute (the predecessor of Beijing Language and Culture University). In the 1980s, four universities in China began to offer undergraduate majors in teaching Chinese as a foreign language to cultivate teachers for teaching Chinese as a foreign language. India and Bangladesh also established the Indian Council for Cultural Relations and the Bangla Academy at the beginning of their founding, attaching great importance to the international promotion of their own language and culture.

3.3 The stage of comprehensive integration between ILCPIs and national language capacity development (since the 1990s)

Brecht & Walton (1993) bring about the concept of national language capacity, which mainly refers to the capacity to meet the country's various language needs, especially the needs of non-universal foreign language capacity, which links language capacity with national strength. This proposal indicates that the concept of national language capacity is being recognized and actively researched as an important part of national soft power. In the 1990s, international relations underwent major changes, which is marked by the end of the Cold War between the United States and the Soviet Union, the weakening of political and military confrontations, and the increasing prominence of cultural conflicts and contradictions.

In 1993, American scholar Samuel Huntington published the book *Clash of Civilization*, and a widespread discussion was aroused concerning its view that conflicts in the future world will mainly come from differences and conflicts between different civilizations. A small number of countries that dominate the world order pursue cultural expansion and cultural hegemony, which are opposed to the cultural sovereignty claims of nationalist. The important role that language plays in this process is increasingly valued. For instance, the key language strategy proposed by the United States elevates language to the level of a national strategy and formulates a series of language plans from the federal to the states. Thus, ILCPIs began to be fully integrated with the theoretical study and practice of national language capacity at this stage, new institutions emerged in large numbers, and old institutions were also adjusted according to the national interests and national strategies of each country.

The discussion on national language capacity continues to deepen, which boosts the constant expansion of the denotation and connotation of national language capacity (Cf. Wen & Zhang, 2018; Wen, 2019; Li, 2021). National language capacity is the language capacity required by the country to handle various international and domestic affairs. As the disseminator of the country's language and culture, the national language and culture promotion institution is an important starting point to promote this capacity. Taking China as an example, the Confucius Institute was established in 2004 with the aim of enhancing understanding of Chinese language and culture among people around the world and strengthening educational and cultural exchanges and cooperation between China and other countries. At the beginning of its establishment, the Confucius Institute mainly targeted countries and regions with close political and economic relations with China, such as the United States, Japan, South Korea, Southeast Asia, Europe, etc. In 2013, the "Belt and Road" initiative was proposed, and the Confucius Institute strengthened its effort on countries along the "Belt and Road" accordingly, which shows that ILCPIs are closely integrated with the development of national language capacity.

The economy of South Korea developed rapidly in the 1970s. As a developed economy in Asia, South Korea attached great importance to enhancing its international image and national popularity through cultural promotion. The popularity of "Korean Wave" and Korean culture around the world is an outstanding result of this cultural strategy. In this process, the King Sejong Institute established in 2007 and the Korean Cultural Center established in 2009 are not only important measures for South Korea to improve its national language capacity, but also the main institutions for the promotion of Korean language and culture. The King Sejong Institute is a special legal person established in accordance with the "Basic Korean Language Law" with the main purpose of promoting Korean in the world, which has received donations from many well-known Korean companies such as Samsung, Hyundai, and Lotte. These institutions enhance the international influence of Korean and in turn serve national language capacity construction through a series of measures such as providing Korean academic education, opening Korean international schools, and attracting foreign researchers to study Korean. In the 2022 National Language Capacity Evaluation Index ranking, the communication ability of South Korea ranks 17th in the world, and its promotion power of related languages and characters ranks 14th, which shows the effectivity of South Korea's language and culture promotion endeavor.

Statistics show that more than 260 ILCPIs have been established in the world since the establishment of Alliance Française in 1883. The purposes and missions of these institutions are highly consistent, i.e., to spread national language and culture (Li & Tang, 2022). In particular, each country has become more aware of the important correlation of language and culture with national competition starting from the third stage, and therefore pays more attention to its own language and cultural sovereignty. A series of ILCPIs have been established to maintain advantages or gain resources in global language competition, promote the improvement of national language capacity, and thereby enhance the country's soft power and international voice. From this perspective, ILCPIs, as the basis for improving the external influence of language, must be emphasized in the study of national language capacity.

National language capacity is the product of the long-term development of language and nation. It has experienced three stages, namely inward cohesion, symbiosis & mutual assistance, and outward development (Zhang, 2008). ILCPIs mainly emerged and boosted in the second and third stages. In the second stage, the ILCPIs promotes the international spread of language on the one hand, and helps the global expansion of national interests on the other; whereas in the third stage, ILCPIs are more characterized by its social, market and economic characteristics. By promoting language testing and expanding the scale of language education, it helps the development of national language capacity not only in terms of soft power but also in terms of hard power.

4. Evaluation of ILCPIs under the National Language Capacity Evaluation Index System

The national language capacity evaluation index refers to a quantitative study of national language capacity on basis of objective data and expert knowledge, through steps such as indicator determination, data collection, and weight assignment. An important manifestation of a country's language capacity is the communication ability of the country's main language, especially the international communication ability of its common language. It is an essential component of the country's cultural soft power and power of speech. In the stage of comprehensive integration between ILCPIs and national language capacity development, relevant indicators and data from the ILCPIs are an important basis for evaluating national language capacity. Previous researches on the national language capacity evaluation index take the following aspects as the criteria for judging the promotion power of secondary indicators: the presence or absence of a national common language international communication institution, the distribution of the international communication institutions, as well as the number of institutions (Zhang, 2008). The top ten most influential countries are France, China, Italy, Portugal, Ireland, Australia, Canada, the United States, South Africa, and Singapore.

Currently, Beijing Language and Culture University has released the National Language Capacity Evaluation Index for two consecutive years, providing a quantitative reference for comparing language capacity in countries around the world. Be that as it may, the evaluation indicator system of the National Language Capacity Evaluation Index is rather complex which involves a wide range of content and needs to consider different dimensions such as academic evaluation, media evaluation, and social evaluation. In-depth research on each of its internal indicators can make the National Language Capacity Evaluation Index system more accurate and complete. Therefore, in order to better evaluate the promotion power of national language capacity, this study intends to compare the promotion effects of different ILCPIs by constructing an evaluation system for the ILCPIs under the national language capacity evaluation index system and better understand the theoretical and practical issues of language communication, in order to promote the development of China's international Chinese education and improve our national language capacity.

The purpose of evaluating ILCPIs is to objectively analyze the effectiveness of the institution in language communication activities and the sustainability of the institution's development. To this end, the construction of the indicator system needs to be carried out from three levels: management abilities based on self-management and development abilities and communication abilities based on external expansion (refer to Table 1). Management ability in this system refers to the protection of communication institutions at the national level and the institution's own management system and measures. Development ability refers to the measures taken by the institution itself to promote its innovation and sustainable development. Communication ability refers to the institution's communication effects and impact on society.

Table 1 Evaluation index system of ILCPIs

Primary indicators	management ability	development ability	communication ability
Secondary indicators	1.whether there are relevant legal protections 2.whether there is social capital participation 3.whether there is a complete organizational structure 4.whether there are complete charters, plans, and regulations 5.whether it has obtained important legal status in the host country or recognition by other international organizations 6.how long it has been established	7.annual funding amount 8.annual operating income 9.teacher development 10.whether there is an intelligent teaching platform 11.whether there is international cooperation 12.whether there is a self-evaluation system	13.the number of countries being covered 14.the number of institutions 15.the number of overseas students 16.whether the language has entered the national education system of the target country 17.the number of language and cultural activities 18.number of people taking language proficiency tests 19.number of social medias

Note: Data of the first indicator comes from the official website of each institution and the relevant laws and regulations of the target country. Data of the fifth and the 19th indicator come from self-inquiry. Data of the remaining indicators come from the official website of each institution and the institution's annual report.

Among these three primary indicators shown in Table 1, management ability is the foundation, which determines the direction of development abilities and the effect of communication abilities. The secondary indicators of management ability include whether there are relevant legal protections; whether there is social capital participation; whether there is a complete organizational structure; whether there are complete charters, plans and regulations; and how long it has been established, etc. Development abilities are the core of the ILCPIs which determine its long-term development. Its secondary indicators include annual funding amount, annual operating income, teacher development, etc. Communication ability refers to the communication effect of the ILCPIs, and its secondary indicators include the number of countries covered by communication, the number of institutions, the number of overseas students, and whether the language has entered the national education system of the target country, and the number of language and cultural activities held by the institution, etc.

The establishment principles of these evaluation indicators are scientificity, feasibility, simplicity and replicability. Scientificity means that the determination of the indicators must be subject to expert argumentation, and the value of the indicators can be objectively evaluated to ensure a tight logical relationship between the evaluation indicators. Feasibility requires that each evaluation indicator is measurable, and the data can be obtained and compared. Simplicity demands simplifying each index as much as possible, retaining the core indicators, and reflecting the purpose of the evaluation as comprehensively as possible. Lastly, replicability means that data collection can be traced and verified. The sources of data can be official websites, annual reports of various institutions, public data of education authorities, etc. The construction of the indicator system is a process of continuous demonstration and improvement, which requires many iterations through subjective judgment and objective statistics before it is finalized. Due to limited space, this paper takes the development ability as it study object and selects several major language communication institutions in the world to conduct its trial collection and data analysis, so as to provide a preliminary verification of the feasibility of this evaluation system (as shown in Table 2).

Table 2　Data on the development ability of five major ILCPIs in 2021

Development ability	British Council	Goethe-In-stitut	King Sejong Institute	Alliance Française	Japan Foundation
Annual funding amount (million grand)	55,583	43.8	3,865	20,490	3,809
Annual operating income (million grand)	111,539	0.3	3,881	14,900	101
Staff size (person)	12,000	4,070	911	8,000	N/A
Intelligent teaching platform	√	√	√	×	√
International cooperation	√	√	√	√	√
Self-evaluation system	√	N/A	N/A	N/A	N/A

Source of data: Official websites and annual operating reports of each institution.

Data shown in Table 2 in general meets the basic requirements. A comparison of data on funding amount, operating income, and staff size indicates that the development potential of the British Council and Alliance Française is higher than that of other institutions. It is further shown that these five major institutions attach great importance to international cooperation and information technology, which reflects the development trend of the ILCPIs. Nonetheless, some indicators of individual institutions may be difficult to obtain, such as the staff size of the Japan Foundation. Therefore, it is necessary to adopt a flexible approach by means of dynamically updating and standardizing the data, expanding data collection channels and the collection scope when it comes to such data, in aim of conducting a comprehensive and dynamic assessment of the indicators. The indicators should be discarded and replaced by other indicators under the circumstances that most of the data for the indicator in question has problems and does not meet the authoritative, reliable, objective and replicable characteristics of indicator selection.

Weighting needs to be carried out according to the specific situation after data collection, i.e., each indicator is given a weight based on the purpose of the evaluation and the characteristics of each graded indicator. In general, indicators with high importance, high variability, and low correlation will be assigned greater weights(Yang, 2021). The weighting methods could be either subjective or objective. The former includes Delphi method, analytical hierarchy process, etc.; whereas the latter includes principal component analysis, entropy value method, factor analysis method, etc. A combined method such as linear synthesis method is also available.

This paper provides a preliminary construction on the evaluation system of ILCPIs. The specific evaluation of the indicator is still in the data collection stage, and the determination of indicators and weights requires multiple expert discussions and repeated demonstrations. Various methods including but not limited to Delphi method, analytical hierarchy process, principal component method, CRITIC method need to be comprehensively considered so as to make the final determination, which will be discussed in another paper.

5. Conclusion

Case studies, comparisons and evaluations of major ILCPIs have important practical and strategic significance for improving China's national language capacities and international communication abilities. In the context of post-epidemic, high technology, and great changes, relevant research needs to be problem- and demand-oriented, focusing on the main business of language teaching and cultural communication so as to answer the questions concerning how to promote and what to promote. Specifically, it is not recommended to blindly believe or follow any existing experience when it comes to learning from foreign countries. Instead, it is important to analyze specific issues in light of our national conditions. In regard of issues such as deepening institutional reform, enriching school resources, improving school quality, and promoting diversified development, practical exploration should be accompanied by a world perspective and a Chinese standpoint. This allows us to summarize operable countermeasures and suggestions that combine planning with the market, align entities with diversity, and promote socialization and localization.

The issues that need to be solved in this process include the following three aspects: First, what is the relationship between the subjectivity and diversification of each ILCPS? The Confucius Institute adheres to the combination of subjectivity and diversification. It is suggested that taking the government as the main body to promote the development of the cause should still be the core principle, on the basis of which lessons should be drawn from the operation methods and communication measures of various research institutions so as to make diversified improvements in practices so as to further enhance the competitiveness and influence of Confucius Institutes. Second, what is the relationship between the explicit measures and implicit strategies of each institution in the process of promotion? Importance should be attached to the excavation of the implicit strategies and explicit measures taken in the process of institutional communication, as well as the analysis of their underlying reasons. This enables us to reveal the national intentions and practical considerations contained in various measures, thereby providing reference for the subsequent development of the Confucius Institute. Based on this, it helps the Confucius Institute better understand international conventions and practices in language communication and in turn take appropriate response measures. Third, are each institution fully market-oriented while integrating social capital? The model of planning and market integration currently adopted by the Confucius Institute does not need to be completely changed. On the basis of adhering to top-level design, long-term planning, and orderly implementation, we should absorb reliable methods of market-oriented operation from various foreign institutions in order to promote the diversification of school running entities and teaching models, the localization of teaching materials, the intelligentization of teaching methods, and the refinement of promotion measures.

To sum up, the study of international language and culture promotion institutions from the perspective of national language capacity needs to combine foreign experience with our national situation. Such combination enables us to constantly explore and enrich new models for the development of international Chinese education, and actively promote the development of Confucius Institutes. Such transformation and development will in turn promote the development of international Chinese education in the direction of endogeneity, embeddedness, localization and marketization, which makes international Chinese education an integral part of the foreign language education in the host country.

Funding Statement

Research for this paper is supported by a grant from the National Social Science Foundation Key Project "The study on the construction of national language capacity evaluation index and China's key foreign language strategy" (国家外语能力指数构建和中国关键外语战略研究)(Project No. 22AYU011).

Reference

Adamson, R. *The Defence of French: A Language in Crisis?* Clevedon: Multilingual

Matters, 2007.

Brecht, R. D., & Walton, A. R. National Strategic Planning in the Less Commonly Taught Languages. *The Annals of the American Academy of Political and Social Science*, 1994(1):190-212.

Cao, D.(曹德明). *Research on Foreign Language and Culture Promotion Institutions* (国外语言文化推广机构研究). Beijing: Shishi Publishing House(北京：时事出版社), 2016.

Dai, D.(戴冬梅). The Operational Strategies and Enlightenments of the Alliance Française (法语联盟的运作策略及启示). In Zhang Tian-wei(张天伟)(ed.) *Language Policy and Planning Studies: Volume 17* (语言政策与规划研究：第17辑). Beijing: Foreign Language Teaching and Research Press(北京：外语教学与研究出版社), 2023: 25-35+178.

Huntington, Samuel P. (塞缪尔·亨延顿) *Clash of Civilization*(文明的冲突). Beijing: Xinhua Publishing House(北京：新华出版社), 2017.

Li, Linda Mingfang. *Language Management and Its Impact: The Policies and Practices of Confucius Institutes*. New York: Routledge, 2018.

Li, Y.(李宇明) & Tang, P.(唐培兰). The History and Development Trend of International Language Promotion Institutions (国际语言传播机构发展历史与趋势). *Chinese Teaching In The World* (世界汉语教学), 2022(1):3-18.

Li, Y. (李宇明). A Brief Discussion on Language Planning Studies (语言规划学说略). *Lexicographical Studies* (辞书研究), 2022(1): 1-17+125.

Li, Y.(李宇明). On Individual Language Ability and National Language Capacity (试论个人语言能力和国家语言能力). *Applied Linguistics* (语言文字应用), 2021(3): 2-16.

Liu, J. (刘晶晶). *Comparative Study on the School Running Status of Major Language Communication Institutions in the World* (世界主要语言传播机构办学状况比较研究). Changchun: Changchun Publishing House(长春：长春出版社), 2021.

Paschalidis, G. Exporting National Culture: Histories of Cultural Institutes Abroad. *International Journal of Cultural Policy*, 2009(3):275-289.

Piller, I., & Cho, J. Neoliberalism as Language Policy. *Language in Society*, 2013(1): 23-44.

Smits, Y., Daubeuf, C., & Kern, P. Research for Cult Committee—European Cultural Institutes Abroad. Available from: European Union. http://www.europarl.europa.eu/RegData/etudes/STUD/2016/563418[Accessed October 20, 2022].

Wen, Q.(文秋芳) & Zhang, T.(张天伟). *Research on the construction of national language proficiency system* (国家语言能力体系构建研究). Beijing: Peking

University Press(北京:北京大学出版社), 2018.

Wen, Q.(文秋芳). Reexamining the Concept of "National Language Capacity"——The Achievements of and Challenges on National Language Capacity Development in China in the Past 70 Years (对"国家语言能力"的再解读——兼述中国国家语言能力 70 年的建设与发展). *Journal of Xinjiang Normal University (Edition of Philosophy and Social Sciences)* [(新疆师范大学学报 (哲学社会科学版)], 2019(5):57-67.

Wu, Y.(吴应辉). *Theories and Methods of Chinese International Communication Research* (汉语国际传播研究理论与方法). Beijing: China Minzu University Press(北京:中央民族大学出版社), 2013.

Yang, D.(杨丹). *Meta Index Research Report 2021*[元指数研究报告 (2021)]. Beijing: Beijing Foreign Studies University(北京:北京外国语大学), 2021.

Zhang, T.(张天伟). Development of National Language Capacity Evaluation Indexes: A Comparative Study (国家语言能力指数体系的发展与比较分析). *Foreign Languages Research* (外语研究), 2022(4): 1-8+112.

Zhang, T.(张天伟). National Language Capacity Evaluation Indexes and Their Applications (国家语言能力指数体系完善与研究实践). *Chinese Journal of Language Policy and Planning* (语言战略研究), 2021(5):12-24.

Zhang, X.(张西平). *Overview of Language Promotion Policies in Major Countries around the World* (世界主要国家语言推广政策概览). Beijing: Foreign Language Teaching and Research Press(北京:外语教学与研究出版社), 2008.

Research on the Language Service System in the Tourism Industry: A Case Study of Emperor Qinshihuang's Mausoleum Site Museum[*]

Li Qiong, Lai Jianling[**]

Abstract: To explore the current state of the language service system and to promote the systematic, standardized, and normalized development of language services in the tourism industry, this paper investigates the language service system at Emperor Qinshihuang's Mausoleum Site Museum as a case study. First, based on field research, it describes the language service system at Emperor Qinshihuang's Mausoleum Site Museum from three subsystems: static composition, dynamic participation, and regular management. Next, the paper evaluates the level, quality, and optimization space of the language service from the perspective of the consumers—tourists at Emperor Qinshihuang's Mausoleum Site Museum and infers the general needs of tourists for language services in the tourism industry. Finally, by comparing the current state of the language service system and the language service needs of tourists at Emperor Qinshihuang's Mausoleum Site Museum, the paper summarizes the characteristics and shortcomings of its language services. It aims to propose feasible suggestions for the construction, governance, and improvement of language services at Emperor Qinshihuang's Mausoleum Site Museum and in the tourism industry at large.

Keywords: language service; tourism industry; Emperor Qinshihuang's Mausoleum Site Museum; language service system construction

1. Introduction

Language services, as a typical representation of the industrialization of spoken and written language, possess both cultural and economic attributes reflecting the important

---

* Date Received: December 21, 2023; Date Revised: March 6, 2024.

** Li Qiong(李琼), Associate Professor of School of Chinese Language and Literature, Shaanxi Normal University. Lai Jianling(赖健玲), Postgraduate of School of Chinese Language and Literature, Shaanxi Normal University.

role of language in economic construction and social development. In today's increasingly advocated cultural tourism in China, language services in the tourism industry not only directly relate to the communication effectiveness between tourists and related practitioners, affecting tourists' travel experiences and the development of regional tourism, but also carry the important mission of bearing and spreading China's excellent historical and cultural heritage.

Currently, the construction of language services in the tourism industry lacks systematic suggestions and presents a significant research gap. There is considerable room for improvement in the language services of tourist attractions, such as insufficient systematic construction, lack of service awareness, room for improvement in service level, and low international compatibility.

The Terracotta Army, hailed as one of the "Eight Wonders of the World," enjoys international fame. Emperor Qinshihuang's Mausoleum Site Museum, based on the Terracotta Army Museum and Emperor Qin Shi Huang's Mausoleum Site Park (Lishan Garden), is a large-scale heritage museum. As one of the first batch of key national cultural relics protection units, the first batch of Chinese World Heritage sites, and the first batch of national AAAAA tourist attractions, the construction of the language service system at Emperor Qinshihuang's Mausoleum Site Museum is of significant importance.

Therefore, this paper takes the actual language service situation at Emperor Qinshihuang's Mausoleum Site Museum as the object of investigation, systematically assesses it in conjunction with tourist needs, and proposes suggestions for adjustment and optimization paths for the language service system at Emperor Qinshihuang's Mausoleum Site Museum based on a supply and demand analysis. It also hopes that this micro-research case can serve as a reference for the construction, adjustment, and optimization of language services in the tourism industry.

The concept of the language service lacks a clear and unified definition both domestically and abroad, but can generally be divided into narrow and broad senses. The narrow sense of the language service mainly refers to language translation services, language teaching and training, language technology tool development, language support services, multilingual information consulting, and specific industry language services (Qu, 2007; Wang, 2014). In the tourism industry, the language service more often refers to its broader concept, which is "the act and activity of providing help to others or society with spoken and written language as the content or means." (Zhao, 2012)

Activities with language elements have always accompanied the development of human society. Abroad, the concept of "language + service" emerged in the 1990s, and the term "language service" began to be widely used by scholars entering the 21st century, although it was still limited to the fields of language translation and language training. With the deepening of globalization, human social life has become increasingly complex, highlighting a variety of language needs, and language service has begun to establish connections with various industries, expanding from translation and training to other sectors such as tourism, business, hotel and other industries, etc.

Domestic academia's attention to the language service has been roughly synchronous with abroad trends. Since the concept of "language service" was proposed by scholars like Qu Shaobing at the International Forum on Language Environment Construction at Shanghai World Expo in 2005, some scholars have defined "language service" from different perspectives and expanded on the concept's extension, such as Qu Shaobing, Li Yuming, Zhao Shiju, Li Xianle, etc. The 2008 Beijing Olympic Games marked a significant turning point for domestic language service research, and especially since the 2010s, with the construction of the "Belt and Road" initiative generating a more diverse range of language service needs, the language service has gradually become a hot research topic in linguistics.

In tourism, "Language Situation in China: 2006" dedicated a section to "Language Service Status in the Tourism Industry." Although, domestic scholars paid less attention to language services in tourism before the 2010s, after then, related research gradually increased, with scholars like Li Xianle, who explored the economic value of language resources from the perspective of linguistic economics to drive regional tourism development; Tian Hailong, who studied the interaction between tourism and discourse from a discourse perspective, proposing discourse-based tourism research theoretically and analyzing discourse with tourism websites, attractions, services, marketing, etc., practically in 2012. Feng Jieyun, who focused on 3,830 foreign tourists' travelogues on the Forbidden City on the Trip Advisor platform, discussing foreigners' perceptions of the Forbidden City's tourism image and suggesting improvements based on issues encountered during visits in 2017. Typical researches on the language landscape in the tourism industry include Chen Lishi, who investigated the current status of language guidance services of the Five Sacred Mountains of China from dimensions such as language code orientation, presentation form, and stylistic features in 2018; Li Xiaotian, who conducted research on the current status of language service construction, language services by staff, and tourists' language service needs in scenic areas of Suzhou Gardens in 2021.

Current linguistic researches on Emperor Qinshihuang's Mausoleum Site Museum mainly fall into two categories: One is the written translation service of Emperor Qinshihuang's Mausoleum Site Museum. For example, Wu Yongzhi summarized the problems in the translation of the names of the major cultural heritage scenic spots in Shaanxi Province on the basis of comprehensive research, including Terracotta Army Museum, and proposed the principles and methods for the translation of cultural heritage scenic spots in 2012. Wei Yu analyzed the problems in the English translation of the cultural relics of Terracotta Army Museum using translation techniques and methods on the basis of translation theory in 2013. The other is the oral interpretation service at Emperor Qinshihuang's Mausoleum Site Museum. For example, Liu Weina compared and analyzed different versions of tour guide scripts in Japanese for the museum's exhibits at Terracotta Army Museum from the context perspective in 2016. Wang Zhanfeng and Shen Lijuan studied the interpretation of the cultural relics of Terracotta Army Museum from an intercultural perspective in 2022.

In summary, previous scholars' research have laid a solid foundation for language service studies. While abroad research generally lack theoretical exploration in the language service but are broad in application fields and diverse in methodologies; domestic researches have a variety of perspectives but lack a unified theoretical concept, and are strongly policy-oriented and closely linked to social needs. Overall, there is a relative lack of in-depth theoretical discussion on the language service and a complete theoretical system has not yet been formed, indicating a gap in research on the application of language services in social practice. Therefore, this paper builds on existing research to further explore the construction and improvement pathways of the language service system in tourism scenic areas, taking the language service at Emperor Qinshihuang's Mausoleum Site Museum as the research subject.

2. Research on the Language Service System at Emperor Qinshihuang's Mausoleum Site Museum

This study focuses on the language service system at Emperor Qinshihuang's Mausoleum Site Museum. The investigation began with on-site research and interviews with staff, yielding 612 photographs and 9 face-to-face interviews in the first half of 2023. This process analyzed the language service system objectively by observing and recording the various language services provided by the museum.

Additionally, through a combination of online and offline survey distribution, 192 valid questionnaires and another 7 face-to-face interviews targeting visitors were collected. The data provide insights into the language service needs of consumers-tourists, including their attitudes, evaluations, and expectations towards language services at the museum, from which the general demands for language services in scenic areas are explored. Finally, by comparing and analyzing language services offered by the museum against tourists' needs, this study identifies the shortcomings of the language service system at Emperor Qinshihuang's Mausoleum Site Museum and proposes targeted and feasible strategies for the improvement.

2.1 Current status of language services at Emperor Qinshihuang's Mausoleum Site Museum

Scholar Qu Shaobing, starting from service management theory, defines the language service system as "the entire system that provides language services, including service providers, media, and content, as well as involving service consumers." (Qu Shaobing, 2016) He believes that the service system is characterized by complexity, openness, and dynamism. The complexity of the language service system is manifested in the multi-level structure of the system and the interrelationships between subsystems as well as between subjects and objects.

Based on this, the paper further details the language service system into three main levels: service providers, service consumers and service media and content. The interaction between these three levels gives rise to three interlocking subsystems: static composition, dynamic participation, and regular management. Firstly, during the development and design phase of language services, service providers, based on the needs of service consumers, form the static composition subsystem using service media and content as the foundation, including the orientation of language codes, presentation methods, and content types. Secondly, in the phase of promoting and practicing language services, the continuous interaction between service providers and consumers creates the dynamic participation subsystem, in which the tour guides/interpreters and general staff play an important role. Lastly, in the phase of ongoing optimization, service providers and consumers together form a regular management subsystem including rules & regulations, supervision mechanism and feedback channel. The details are shown in the following figure.

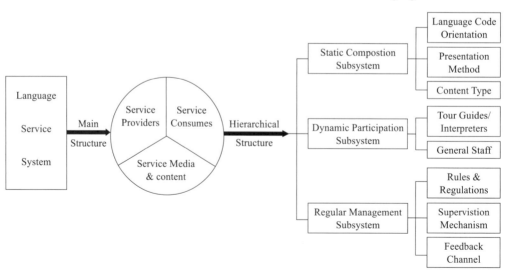

Figure 1   Internal composition of language service system

2.1.1 The static composition subsystem of the language service system

The static composition subsystem of the language service system refers to the decisions made during the design and development phase of the language service system to meet tourists' needs regarding how to provide or present language services. These decisions are primarily reflected in the language landscape including the orientation of language codes, presentation methods, and content types.

Based on the field survey of Emperor Qinshihuang's Mausoleum Site Museum, which recorded 424 language service signs, and the analysis of 7 interviews, the orientation of language codes in the language service system at the museum is mainly in Chinese, supplemented by English, with Japanese and Korean following (as shown in Figure 2). The choice of these languages is firstly based on national regulations that AAAAA scenic areas must provide services in four languages. Secondly, it considers the common languages of the museum's visitors, and lastly, the language resources available to the museum itself. While the inclusion of these four languages generally meets the needs of tourists at home and abroad, the implementation is not consistent across all scenic area signage and cultural relics introduction, with only Chinese and English used.

Figure 2   Four language selection page of vr experience center at
Emperor Qinshihuang's Mausoleum Site Museum

The presentation method of the language service system refers to the carriers and forms through which language services are delivered, including the technological aspects involved in providing language services. The language service system at Emperor Qinshihuang's Mausoleum Site Museum exhibits both diversity and uniformity in the presentation method. The diversity is evident in the different types of carriers used at two of the museum's sites — the Terracotta Army Museum and Lishan Garden. The former primarily uses wood, plastic plates, and stainless-steel plates, with electronic screens as a secondary option, while the latter mainly uses electronic screens, with stainless-steel plates as a supplement. This difference is largely due to the different development and excavation times of the two sites. The trend towards uniformity is demonstrated by the museum's initiative to unify the design style of its language landscapes. In 2020, a unified design was adopted featuring stainless-steel plates as the carriers, with black as the background color and gold for decoration around the edges as shown in Figure 3.

Figure 3   The signage at Emperor Qinshihuang's Mausoleum Site Museum

Regarding content types, the static composition subsystem of the language service system at Emperor Qinshihuang's Mausoleum Site Museum can be divided into seven categories: route guidance, explanatory introduction, cultural promotion, civilization advocacy, commercial promotion, emergency evacuation, and facility guidance.

Table 1 Examples of language service content types at Emperor Qinshihuang's Mausoleum Site Museum

Language Service Content Types	Examples
route guidance	电子导览请到售票大厅右侧 (For electronic guides, please go to the right side of the ticket hall)
explanatory introduction	一号坑概况 (Overview of Pit 1)
cultural promotion	沧海月明珠有泪 蓝田日暖玉生烟——(唐)李商隐 Bright Moon over the Sea Shedding Tears in the Pearls, Jade Made in Lantian Giving Off Steam in the Sunshine — Li Shangyin, Tang Dynasty
civilization advocacy	垃圾不落地 文明在手中 (Garbage never lands, civilization in hands)
commercial promotion	文创冰淇淋 景区热销第一名 (Cultural creative ice cream, the top seller in the scenic area)
emergency evacuation	消防安全三提示 (Three Tips for Fire Safety)
facility guidance	消防器材摆放处 (Location of Fire-fighting Equipment)

Among these, Emperor Qinshihuang's Mausoleum Site Museum primarily focuses on route guidance and explanatory introduction as its main types of language services. However, there is a significant gap in cultural promotion language services.

2.1.2 Dynamic participation subsystem of the language service system

The dynamic participation subsystem refers to the phase of language service practice and promotion, where continuous interaction between service providers and consumers makes language services an immediate and flexible element, thereby invigorating the entire language service system. This subsystem mainly includes the language services provided by general staff and tour guides / interpreters at Emperor Qinshihuang's Mausoleum Site Museum.

According to the 7 interviews, all staff at the museum, including ticket inspectors, security guards, visitor service center employees, gatekeepers, and cleaning staff, are implicitly expected to provide language services. These services provided by all staff can be divided into two aspects: One is the routine checks and feedback on language service-related facilities. If the texts are found to be loose and blurred on the signages, or electronic display screens are damaged, the staff will report it to their respective departments. The information integrated by various departments will be reported to the Exhibition Department of the Museum, which will be responsible to verify and repair them. The other is the passive response services to tourists' inquiries, that is, providing answers when tourists ask in person, mainly for ticket purchase operation guidance and route guidance.

The situation with the museum's tour guides/interpreters is more complex. Firstly, the museum's interpretation services are provided by diverse entities, including the museum's official interpreters, tour guides from Xi'an Tour Guide Industry Association, and guides from Lintong District Tourism Information Center. These three entities operate independently with barriers to information sharing, lacking communication and collaborative mechanisms. Secondly, there are varied interpretation styles and uneven quality levels in different entities. Official museum interpreters offer high-quality, accurate, and timely information, while the performance of other guides varies, with some providing outdated or incorrect information, indicating significant room for improvement. Furthermore, the museum's official interpreters are few in number, making it difficult to meet the tour guide needs of ordinary tourists. They mainly focus on official reception tasks, while the tour guides from Xi'an Tour Guide Industry Association and Lintong District Tourism Information Center are mainly tour group tourists, supplemented by individual tourists. Lastly, unauthorized "illegal guides" operating at the museum's entrance can deceive tourists into paying much higher fees for unofficial tours.

2.1.3 Regular management subsystem of the language service system

In the phase of ongoing optimization, service providers and consumers form a regular management subsystem for the static composition and dynamic participation subsystems, encompassing rules and regulations, supervision mechanisms, and feedback channels. Overall, there is a significant void in the museum's regular management subsystem for the language service system at Emperor Qinshihuang's Mausoleum Site Museum.

Aside from national regulations requiring AAAAA scenic areas to offer services in four languages and standardized emergency signs, the museum lacks explicit rules for its own language services. Although there is no formal regulation, all staff and tourists are assumed to have the authority to supervise and provide feedback.

In practice, both the static composition subsystem and dynamic participation subsystem are provided by various departments based on their operational needs, without a distinct awareness of language service responsibilities. This has led to language services being considered secondary to other services and a lack of dedicated organizational units for language services at the museum. Not only are regulations lacking, but supervision mechanisms and feedback channels are also unstructured and unclear.

Overall, the construction of the language service system at Emperor Qinshihuang's

Mausoleum Site Museum is unbalanced and insufficient. While the static composition subsystem is relatively well-established, needing only minor adjustments, the dynamic participation subsystem is in its early stages but faces issues such as a lack of language service awareness and unclear responsibilities. The regular management subsystem, in particular, is notably absent, indicating a significant gap.

2.2 Tourists' language service needs at Emperor Qinshihuang's Mausoleum Site Museum

Forrester J.W., an American scholar, suggests that the behavior of complex systems depends on internal multiple factors and their feedback structures, where feedback can be positive (enhancing action) or negative (regulating future actions to stabilize the system) (Forrester J. W. 2010:245-246). The language service system, being a complex system with multiple subsystems and feedback functions, relies on the continuous linguistic practices of its service consumers : tourists. The experiences and feedbacks from tourists are crucial for the continuous optimization of the language service system. Therefore, to identify the directions for optimizing the language service system at Emperor Qinshihuang's Mausoleum Site Museum, it is essential to pay attention to the feedback of the tourists' needs.

2.2.1 Static language service needs

Static language service needs refer to the tourists' demands for the static composition subsystem of the language service system, including the orientation of language codes, presentation methods and content types.

(1) Language code orientation

The demand for language code orientation from tourists indicates their expectations for the language codes that should be available in the museum's language services, based on their own needs and their perception of the museum's positioning.

The data reveal a discrepancy between the tourists' demands for language code orientation and the language orientations provided by the Museum, with a slightly higher demand for Russian over Korean. As shown in the above figure, tourists prioritize Mandarin (28.4%), followed by English (22.9%), Japanese (9.9%), and Russian (9.7%). The prominence of Mandarin aligns with national efforts to promote the official language. Some tourists' express ambivalence towards the use of English and suggest that while foreign tourists should adapt to Chinese, reflecting a growing cultural confidence and the role of Chinese in international communication. But the museum's international standing justifies offering services in English. The demand for Japanese, ranking third, likely stems from the volume of tourists from Japan, while Russian demand, closely following

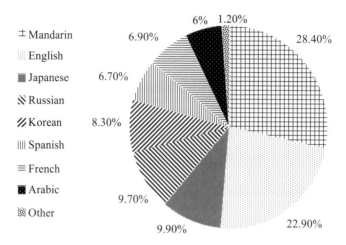

Figure 4   Tourists' demands for language code orientation at
Emperor Qinshihuang's Mausoleum Site Museum

Japanese, is associated with the "Belt and Road" initiative, which has led to an increase in tourists from the Central Asia.

The top four languages requested by tourists are Mandarin, English, Japanese, and Russian, differing from the museum's offerings of Mandarin, English, Japanese, and Korean. Thus, the museum's language settings should be regularly updated based on tourists' demands, rather than remaining unchanged.

(2) Presentation method

The presentation method of language service encompasses the overall design experience for service consumers, including both external carriers and internal language standards. This survey divides the presentation method demands into external appearance (design, placement, style type, quantity) and internal standards (script, language style, creativity), with tourists' satisfaction rated from 1 ("very dissatisfied") to 5 ("very satisfied"). Statistical software SPSS was used to analyze the satisfaction with the museum's presentation methods of language services. Higher values indicate greater satisfaction, with the results presented in the following table.

Table 2   Satisfaction levels of tourists with the presentation method of language service at Emperor Qinshihuang's Mausoleum Site Museum

Category	Presentation Method	Average Value
Carrier Presentation	Appearance Design	4.00
	Placement	4.06
	Style Type	3.90
	Quantity	4.04

continued

Category	Presentation Method	Average Value
Language Standards	Script	4.22
	Language Style	4.30
	Creativity	3.66
Overall		4.03

As shown in Table 2, the overall satisfaction level of tourists with the presentation methods of language services at the Museum is relatively high, leaning towards "4" ("relatively satisfied"). The satisfaction levels for "creativity" and "style type" are average, while all other aspects are more positively viewed. The high satisfaction levels indicate that the recent efforts to renovate and standardize the language and texts on signages at the museum have been successful and meet the needs of tourists. This also reflects the practical mindset of Chinese tourists, with most interviewees' expressing that they are not concerned about the external appearance of language services as long as they are useful. Notably, compared to other aspects, the highest satisfaction was with the "language style" of the museum's language service, while "creativity" received the lowest satisfaction scores. This suggests that while the museum's language services adhere to high standards of linguistic propriety, there is room for improvement in meeting visitors' creative expectations.

(3) Content types

The varying levels of attention paid by language service consumers reflect their differing needs for various content types of language services. This paper categorizes language services at the Museum into seven types: route guidance, explanatory introduction, cultural promotion, civilization advocacy, commercial promotion, emergency evacuation, and facility guidance.

Table 3   Tourists' attention to different content types of language services at Emperor Qinshihuang's Mausoleum Site Museum

Content Type of Language Service	Number of Cases	Percentage
route guidance	115	20.5%
explanatory introduction	116	20.6%
cultural promotion	87	15.5%
civilization advocacy	52	9.3%
commercial promotion	35	6.2%
emergency evacuation	63	11.2%
facility guidance	94	16.7%

The data above indicates that tourists show a higher interest in the content types that are practical and meet the needs of their visiting, while there is a tendency to reject services with a commercial purpose and habitually ignore ubiquitous civil advocacy of language services. In the survey on content types of language services at the Museum, explanatory introduction (20.6%) and route guidance (20.5%) are the most focused on by tourists, followed by facility guidance (16.7%). At the same time, cultural promotion (15.5%) also receives considerable attention; in contrast, commercial promotion (6.2%) and civil advocacy (9.3%) are the least noticed content types of language services. To gain attention, commercial promotion and civil advocacy may need to focus on soft advertising and content innovation to break through the limitations of their commercial purposes and ubiquity.

2.2.2 Dynamic language service needs

In the phase of practicing and promoting language services, continuous interaction between service consumers and providers leads to constant updates and changes in language services. Service consumers' needs direct the improvement and optimization of language services. Direct providers of the language service system at Emperor Qinshihuang's Mausoleum Site Museum include tour guides / interpreters and general staff, while visitors' dynamic language service needs mainly reflected in their evaluations and demands for these two groups.

(1)Tour guides/interpreters

There are three types of explanations available at Emperor Qinshihuang's Mausoleum Site Museum: tour guide / interpreter, electronic guide device, and online language explanations. Despite the museum has an interpretation department with about thirty official tour guides, which cannot meet the needs of tourists, due to high administrative work pressure, frequent official reception tasks, and a large number of visitors. The ordinary tourists receive the manual explanation services that generally come from tour guides associated with Xi'an Tour Guide Industry Association and Lintong District Tourism Information Center, with a small portion even coming from unlicensed "illegal guides" loitering outside the museum entrance.

Table 4   Explanation types chosen by tourists and their satisfaction at Emperor Qinshihuang's Mausoleum Site Museum

Explanation Type	Number of Cases	Percentage	Satisfaction
Tour Guide/Interpreter	66	50.0	4.12
Electronic Guide Device	29	22.0	3.68
Online Voice Explanation	14	10.6	3.95

continued

Explanation Type	Number of Cases	Percentage	Satisfaction
None	23	17.4	—
Total/Average	132	100.0	3.92

As shown in Table 4, among the surveyed tourists, the largest group chose the tour guide/interpreter (50.0%), followed by electronic guide devices (22.0%), which is nearly half of the proportion for the tour guide/interpreter. Only 10.6% of tourists chose online voice explanations, even lower than those who did not choose any explanation service (17.4%). In terms of satisfaction, which is rated on a scale up to 5.0, the tour guide/interpreter receives the highest satisfaction score (4.12), categorized as "relatively satisfied." The satisfaction for online voice explanations (3.95) is higher than for electronic guide devices (3.68), with the former being close to "relatively satisfied" and the latter leaning towards "average."

In terms of the reasons that affect tourists' choice of explanation types, the main reasons for tourists' choosing the tour guides/interpreters are "flexibility in content and approach," "strong interactivity with the ability to answer questions in real-time," "diverse and personalized explanation styles," and "an enhanced emotional experience." Tourists' opting for electronic guide devices or online voice explanations cited "convenience," "a higher degree of freedom during the visit," and "cost-effectiveness" as their main reasons. Those who did not select any explanation service mentioned "distrust in the quality of guide explanations" or "unawareness of other types of explanation services."

Overall, tour guide / interpreter explanations remain the most demanded type of explanation services; however, the least chosen option, online voice explanations, has a higher satisfaction level, indicating it as a promising new type of explanation service that can alleviate the pressure on tour guides/interpreters but is limited by the extent of its promotion. The choice proportion for electronic guide devices falls in the middle among the three types, yet it has the lowest satisfaction score, suggesting a need for improvement in explanation content and device performance.

(2) General staff

The general staff at Emperor Qinshihuang's Mausoleum Site Museum primarily provides language services in a passive manner, answering and assisting tourists upon inquiry. Typically, the frequency of verbal interactions between the general staff and tourists is much lower than between tour guides/interpreters and tourists. Therefore, this paper divides the investigation on tourists' language service needs from general staff into two surveys: language code needs and courtesy language needs.

Table 5　Tourists' demands for language code types from general staff at Emperor Qinshihuang's Mausoleum Site Museum

Language Code	Frequency	Percentage
Mandarin	119	90.2
Shaanxi Dialect	7	5.3
Other Dialects	1	0.8
Minority Languages	1	0.8
English	4	3.0
Total	132	100.0

As shown in Table 5, over ninety percent of tourists express a preference for communication in Mandarin with the staff at Emperor Qinshihuang's Mausoleum Site Museum, reflecting the emphasis on the promotion of National Official Language. A small portion of visitors, either local Shaanxineses or from other provinces, expresses a desire for the inclusion of the Shaanxi dialect in communications, particularly in guided explanations, to add an element of interest.

Using statistical software and solutions like SPSS for mean analysis, the degree of importance tourists place on the use of courtesy language by the staff is categorized into five levels: 1="Do not care at all" indicating very low interest; 2="Do not care much" indicating relatively low interest; 3= "Neutral" indicating moderate interest; 4= "Care somewhat" indicating relatively high interest; and 5= "Care a lot" indicating very high interest. The higher the average value obtained, the greater the degree of concern and demand.

The result of mean analysis is 3.58, which shows that tourists generally care about whether staff use courtesy language, such as "Hello" and "Welcome to Emperor Qinshihuang's Mausoleum Site Museum" leaning towards "Care somewhat." The interviewees indicate that due to the large volume of visitors and heavy workload, the staff seldom use such courtesy languages. Most tourists understand this but still hope for an improvement in service attitudes, with some reporting the encountered staff are expressionless, indifferent, or even rude, which affects their visiting experiences.

2.2.3 Regular management needs for language service

American scholars such as Fremont E. Kast and James E. Rosenzweig distinguish systems as open or closed, with open systems engaging in exchanges of information, energy, and resources with their external environment, leading to dynamic stability through continuous interaction; closed systems do not exchange or interact with their external environment (Fremont E. Kast & James E. Rosenzweig, 1985). Products primarily based on language tend towards closure due to the internal stability of the language system, but language service systems, closely linked to external realities and built on audience-based communicative acts, typically exhibit a mix of openness and closure, as well as stability and dynamism. Effective regular management of language services should bridge the balance between stability and dynamism, maintaining the steady supply of language services while allowing for active engagement.

As previously mentioned, there is a significant gap in the regular management subsystem of language services at Emperor Qinshihuang's Mausoleum Site Museum. Although tourists have some demands for regular management of language services, it is not strong.

Table 6   Suggestions and measures for improvement of language services by tourists at Emperor Qinshihuang's Mausoleum Site Museum

Category	Suggested Measures	Cases	Percentage
Resource Optimization	Enhance tour guides' training, and improve quality and level of explanations	74	63.8%
	Improve performance of electronic guide devices, such as signal stability, clarity of sound, etc.	69	59.5%
	Enrich online explanatory materials, such as videos, audios, and texts	75	64.7%
Content Enhancement	Perfect the language service system, standardize route guidance and emergency services	44	37.9%
	Increase cultural knowledge, enhance cultural content	59	50.9%
	Reduce commercial advertisements, transform hard ads. into soft ads.	50	43.1%
Service Mechanism	Establish and perfect supervision and management mechanisms for language services	36	31.0%
	Pay attention to tourists' language service needs, broaden feedback channels for language services	42	36.2%
	Ensure maintenance and updates of signages and other language service facilities	44	37.9%
Technological Innovation	Innovate in forms and contents of language services, enhance uniqueness and interest	50	43.1%
	Improve integration with modern technology, e.g., adding interactive electronic screens	44	37.9%
Other		2	1.7%

As shown in the table above, when asked about how to improve the level and quality of language services at the Museum, only 31.0% and 36.2% of tourists indicated the need to "establish and perfect language service supervision and management mechanisms" and "pay attention to tourists' language service needs, broadening feedback channels" respectively. Compared to other suggested measures, tourists' responses to "service mechanisms" were not as strong. This reflects a lack of widespread recognition of the language service system in China, where consumers have some demands for regular management but are unfamiliar with establishing mechanisms for the whole language service system.

Overall, the language service system at Emperor Qinshihuang's Mausoleum Site Museum is not fully balanced or sufficient in meeting tourists' needs. While the static composition subsystem of the museum's language services generally meets tourists' demands, there is significant room for improvement in dynamic participation subsystem due to shortages of high-quality guides, poor performance of equipment, and incomplete online resources. However, tourists have a certain demand for the regular management subsystem of language services but lack widespread recognition of establishing mechanisms for the whole language service system.

2.3 The problems and optimization strategies of the language service system at Emperor Qinshihuang's Mausoleum Site Museum

The language service system at Emperor Qinshihuang's Mausoleum Site Museum is not only related to its overall service planning and cultural dissemination mission, but also a microcosm of the current level of systematization and specialization of language services in the domestic tourism industry. Although the language service system at Emperor Qinshihuang's Mausoleum Site Museum has initially taken shape in practical application, there is still significant room for optimization in resource optimization, content improvement, service mechanism, and technological innovation. Based on the results of this survey, the language service system construction in the tourism industry, represented by Emperor Qinshihuang's Mausoleum Site Museum, can be optimized from the following aspects.

2.3.1 Optimize language service resources and improve service quality

At present, the language service system at Emperor Qinshihuang's Mausoleum Site Museum can basically meet the needs of tourists in the static composition subsystem, but in dynamic participation subsystem language, there are problems such as insufficient high-quality tour guides, poor equipment performance, and incomplete online resource sharing.

Firstly, it is necessary to strengthen the construction of the tour guide team by collaborating with the universities, enhancing targeted and precise training related to tourism management based on local attractions, building a talent pool, expanding the size of guides, and improving visitor reception capabilities. Secondly, raise the entry threshold for tour guides, establish a comprehensive assessment mechanism for guide levels and visitor services, strictly combat unlicensed guiding, and regulate the tourism market. Lastly, improve the training and support services for tour guides, eliminate professional discrimination, enhance remuneration, regularly organize training and exchanges to standardize the interpretation process, share information, and improve the quality and level of guide explanations. Additionally, enhance the infrastructure for language services, such as standardizing language service signs and improving the performance of electronic guide devices. Finally, build online platforms for sharing and co-creating resources to enrich online explanatory materials and improve various visiting modes, such as online exhibitions and virtual exhibitions, and further democratize access to cultural heritage.

2.3.2 Enhance language service system and enrich the cultural content

The language service system at Emperor Qinshihuang's Mausoleum Site Museum already has a preliminary framework in place in terms of content types. However, there are still imbalances and insufficiencies, such as frequent promotion of civility, insufficient cultural promotion, excessive commercial promotion, and lack of distinctive features in explanations and introductions. Therefore, it is necessary to improve the systematic construction of the language service system to elevate its level of systematization.

Firstly, there should be a rational planning and layout, standardizing route guidance and effectively integrating specific locations with human line-of-sight inertia to set route and facility guides. Secondly, delve deeper into the historical and cultural connotations of the cultural landscape, highlighting the key points and features of cultural relics introductions, avoiding monotonous shape and specification descriptions. Thirdly, appropriately reduce the frequency of civility promotion slogans, and add historical and cultural knowledge such as poetry, songs, and historical stories to enhance the cultural atmosphere and increase cultural connotation. Lastly, reduce commercial promotions, innovate advertising forms, and transform hard advertisements into soft advertisements.

2.3.3 Establish a normalized management mechanism to systematize language services

As mentioned earlier, there is a significant gap in the normalized management mechanism of the language service system at Emperor Qinshihuang's Mausoleum Site Museum. The language service system is marginalized, independent, and unclear in the overall construction, lacking sufficient attention in the construction of regulations, supervision mechanisms, and feedback channels.

Therefore, it is crucial to establish a scientific concept of language services, build the superstructure of language services, and improve the normalized supervision and management mechanism of the language service system. This includes clarifying language service regulations, establishing a dedicated language service department, defining responsibilities of multiple entities, ensuring the maintenance and update of language service facilities, valuing tourists' language service needs, expanding feedback channels for tourists' language service opinions, and promoting the standardization, regularization, institutionalization, and systematization of language services.

2.3.4 Enhance the Integration of modern technology and innovate language service forms

The Terracotta Army Museum, as an earlier planned part of Emperor Qinshihuang's Mausoleum Site Museum, has a relatively traditional form of language service with the lower technological integration and a flat form of exhibit introduction. In contrast, the language service at the newly built Lishan Garden has seen a significant improvement in both technological integration and innovative forms. However, compared to domestic museums with mature technology applications, there is still much room for improvement.

To further enhance the language service system at Emperor Qinshihuang's Mausoleum Site Museum, it is necessary to increase the technological investment in language services, improve the integration of excellent cultural relics with modern technology, not just limited to the simple addition of electronic display screens and other devices. Instead, modern science and technology should be used to drive innovation in the form and content of language services, enhancing interaction, distinctive displays, and integration of production, education, and research to increase uniqueness and fun.

3. Conclusion

2023 is a year of comprehensive recovery for China's tourism industry, with domestic travel reaching new highs. According to data from Ministry of Culture and Tourism of the People's Republic of China, the total number of domestic trips in the first three quarters of 2023 reached 3.674 billion, an increase of 1.58 billion compared to the same period last year, with a year-on-year growth of 75.5%. China Tourism News points out that the United Nations has designated February 17th as "Global Day for Tourism Resilience" each year, aiming to promote and develop a resilient tourism industry, building sustainable tourism that "fully considers current and future economic, social, and environmental impacts, meeting the needs of tourists, the industry, the environment, and local communities." (Jiang & Guo, 2023)

"Spoken and written language are foundational factors that aid the development and revival of nationhood. The modernization of language governance is an important part of the modernization of the national governance system and governance capacity." (Wang, 2020) Language service is an important component of the industrialization and modernization of language governance, playing a significant role in promoting economic development, strengthening cultural construction, and improving governance levels. To promote high-quality, sustainable development of the tourism industry, it is necessary to comprehensively construct the tourism service system with a forward-looking service consciousness. The construction and improvement of the language service system, an important component with both explicit economic value and implicit cultural value, require the participation of the whole industry and multiple entities.

Through the investigation and analysis of the language service system at Emperor Qinshihuang's Mausoleum Site Museum, the construction of the language service system in the tourism industry represented by this can be optimized in the following aspects: 1.Standardizing the use of bilingual or multilingual in both the static composition subsystem and dynamic participation subsystem; 2. Exploring and excavating diversified language service resources represented by talent teams, infrastructure and shared platforms; 3. Establishing and perfecting language service-related regulations, supervision mechanisms and feedback channels; 4. Developing innovative forms and content of modernized and technological language services; 5. Enriching and balancing the content of the language service system with the goal of meeting the needs of tourists, the industry and society.

The language service system is a complex structure with multiple entities and levels, presenting a semi-open and semi-closed nature, possessing both stability and dynamism. Its construction not only requires the coordination and support of the static composition subsystem, dynamic participation subsystem, and normalized management subsystem but also needs to pay attention to the language service needs of tourists. The construction and improvement of the language service system represented by Emperor Qinshihuang's Mausoleum Site Museum not only concern the improvement of its own tourism industry and governance levels but also are active attempts at the standardized, regularized, institutionalized, and systematized construction of language services for the entire tourism industry, and even the whole society.

Acknowledgements

We would like to express our gratitude to all those who have helped us in writing this paper. During the writing process of the paper, we received valuable suggestions from many experts and scholars. The smooth completion of this paper was inseparable from the support of the tourists who filled out the questionnaire and the staff who participated in the interview. We would like to express our gratitude to all of them.

Reference

Chen, L.(陈丽诗). Research on the Language Landscape of the Five Sacred Mountains of China(中国五岳语言景观调查研究). Unpublished Master Dissertation, Guangzhou University(广州大学硕士学位论文), 2018.

Dai, Q.(戴庆夏). *Language Investigation Tutorial*(语言调查教程). Beijing: The Commercial Press(北京:商务印书馆), 2013.

Davies, J. A Study of Language Skills in the Leisure and Tourism Industry. *The Language Learning Journal*, 2007 (1): 66-71.

Drozdzewski, D. & Geile, A. Language Tourism in Poland. *Tourism Geographies*, 2011(13): 165-186.

Feng, J.(冯捷蕴) & Huangfu, J.(皇甫俊凯). A New Media Study of Forbidden City's Tourism Image: Based on Discourse Analysis of Online Travelogues on TripAdvisor(故宫旅游形象的新媒体研究——基于TripAdvisor在线游记的话语分析). *Modern Communication (Journal of Communication University of China)* [现代传播(中国传媒大学学报)], 2017, 39(5): 137-143.

Forrester J. W. System Dynamics, Systems Thinking, and Soft OR. *System Dynamics Review*, 2010(10): 245-256.

Goethals, P. Multilingualism and International Tourism: A Content and Discourse-Based Approach to Language-Related Judgments in Web 2.0 Hotel Reviews. *Language & Intercultural Communication*, 2015 (11): 1-19.

Guo, X.(郭晓勇). Development Status, Problems, and Countermeasures of China's Language Service Industry - Keynote Speech at 2010 China International Language Service Industry Conference(中国语言服务行业发展状况、问题及对策——在2010中国国际语言服务行业大会上的主旨发言). *Chinese Translators Journal*(中国翻译), 2010, 31(6): 34-37.

Jiang, Y.(蒋依依) & Guo, J.(郭佳明). Enhancing Sustainable Development Capacity to Support the Global Tourism Industry's Recovery and Revitalization(提升可持续发展能力 助力全球旅游业复苏振兴). *China Tourism News*(中国旅游报), 2023-02-21(3).

Kast, F. E. & Rosenzweig, J. E. (Author). Fu, Y.(傅严), Li, Z.(李柱流)(Trans.) et al. *Organization and Management: A System and Contingency Approach*(组织与管理: 系统方法与权变方法). Beijing: China Social Sciences Press(北京:中国社会科学出版社), 1985.

Li, L.(李龙梅), Wang, X.(王晓峰) & Wang, J.(王俊霞). Tourist Satisfaction Assessment of Terra Cotta Warriors Based on Network Comments(基于网络评论的兵马俑景区游客满意度评价). *Journal of Ningxia Teachers University (Natural Science)* [宁夏师范学院学报(自然科学版)], 2011, 32(6): 70-73, 81.

Li, X.(李现乐). Language Service and Service Language: A Study of Language Application from the Perspective of the Language Econom*y*(语言服务与服务语言——语言经济视角下的语言应用研究). Unpublished Ph.D. Dissertation, Nanjing University(南京大学博士学位论文), 2011.

Li, X.(李现乐). Reflections on the Problems of Language Service Research(语言服务研究的若干问题思考). *Journal of Yunnan Normal University (Humanities and Social Sciences Edition)*[(云南师范大学学报(哲学社会科学版)], 2018, 50(2): 51-57.

Li, X.(李啸天). Investigation and Research on the Language Service Status in Suzhou Gardens(苏州园林语言服务现状调查研究). Unpublished Master Dissertation, Xinjiang Normal University(新疆师范大学硕士学位论文), 2021.

Lin, D., Ishida, T. & Murakami, Y. *Language Service Design Based on User-Centered QoS*. Springer Singapore, 2018.

Liu, W.(刘维娜). Comparative Analysis of Different Japanese Versions of Guide Words in the Terracotta Warriors from a Contextual Perspective(语境视角下秦始皇陵兵马俑异版本日语导游词的对比分析). Unpublished Master Dissertation, Xi'an International Studies University(西安外国语大学硕士学位论文), 2016.

Qu, S.(屈哨兵)(Editor). *Introduction to Language Service*(语言服务引论). Beijing: The Commercial Press(北京：商务印书馆), 2016.

Qu, S.(屈哨兵)(Editor). *Language Service Development in China: 2020*(中国语言服务发展报告：2020). Beijing: The Commercial Press(北京：商务印书馆), 2020.

Qu, S.(屈哨兵). An Outline of Language Service Research(语言服务研究论纲). *Journal of Jianghan University (Humanities Sciences)*[江汉大学学报(人文科学版)], 2007, 26(6): 56-62.

State Language Committee(国家语言文字工作委员会)(ed). *Language Situation in China: 2020*(中国语言生活状况报告：2020). Beijing: The Commercial Press(北京：商务印书馆), 2020.

Tian, H.(田海龙) et al. *Discourse Approach to Tourism: Theory and Practice*(旅游话语研究：理论与实践). Beijing: Foreign Languages Press(北京：外文出版社), 2012.

Wang, C.(王传英). Development and Enlightenment of Language Service Industry(语言服务业发展与启示). *Chinese Translators Journal*(中国翻译), 2014(2): 78-82.

Wang, C.(王春辉). Language Governance Aids National Governance(语言治理助力国家治理). *Guangming Daily*(光明日报), 2020-08-22(12).

Wang, H.(王会寨) & Lu, S.(卢石). Language Services for Beijing Olympic Games(北京奥运会语言服务刍议). *Journal of Shandong Institute of Physical Education* and Sports(山东体育学院学报), 2008, 24(2): 22-24.

Wang, Z.(王战锋) & Shen, L.(沈丽娟). A Study on the Influencing Factors of the Translation of Cultural Heritage Interpretation Boards from a Cross-cultural Perspective: Take the Terracotta Warriors and Horses Museum of Qin Dynasty as an Example(跨文化视角下文物解说牌翻译影响因素研究——以秦兵马俑博物馆为例). *Sculpture*(雕塑), 2022, 149(3): 76-77.

Wei, Y.(魏羽). Analysis of English Translation Versions of the Introduction to Relics in Museum of Terra-cotta Warriors and Horses(秦兵马俑博物馆文物简介英文译文问题评析). *Technology and Innovation Management*(技术与创新管理), 2013, 34(6).

Wu, Y.(乌永志). Study on the Standard of Chinese-English Translation of Cultural Heritage Tourist Attraction Names(文化遗产类旅游景点名称汉英翻译规范研究). *Foreign Language Education*(外语教学), 2012, 33(2): 615-617, 624.

Zhao, S.(赵世举). Definition and Types Language Service from the Angle of Its Contents(从服务内容看语言服务的界定和类型). *Journal of Beihua University (Social Sciences)*[北华大学学报(社会科学版)], 2012, 13(3): 4-6.

The Consideration on One–hundred–years Major Achievements of Chinese Archaeology Giving Impetus to the Study on Chinese Ancient Capitals[*]

Zhu Shiguang[**]

Abstract: Over the past century, modern archaeology of China has achieved brilliant results through the arduous efforts of several generations of archaeologists. Among them, the archaeological research of ancient capitals is the most prominent achievement. Under the guidance of the National Cultural Relics Bureau, Chinese Archaeological Association and the China Cultural Relics Newspaper have co-sponsored the "100 Major Archaeological Discoveries of the Century" activity of selection and promotion. Through two rounds of selection, 100 major archaeological discovery projects have been selected. Among them, 23 projects were directly marked as ancient capital sites, and another 17 projects were related to ancient capitals. They combined for 40 projects, accounting for 40% of the total. This fully demonstrates the important role played by ancient Chinese capitals and urban sites in history, and also indicates the important position of their excavation and research in the development of Chinese archaeology. It also indicates that the academia of Ancient Chinese Capitals should strengthen cooperation with the academia of Chinese archaeology based on the previous research results of Chinese archaeology which promoted the formation, establishment and development of ancient Chinese capital study. We should further strengthen in-depth, traceable and pioneering research on the themes like: the capitals of the main dynasties throughout history; the Neolithic capital-like settlements before the Three Dynasties; and the capitals built by various ethnic groups in the border regions around the Central Plain in ancient times. We should also conduct in-depth research and interpretation on the patterns and principles of urban plannings of Chinese ancient capital cities and the academic theories of Chinese

---

    * This article was originally published in *Journal of Shaanxi Normal University (Philosophy and Social Sciences Edition)*, Vol. 52, No.1. Original Title: 中国百年考古学成就与中国古都学研究之思考.

      Translator: Zhao Chao(赵潮), Associate Professor of School History and Civilization, Shaanxi Normal University. His research focuses on Prehistoric Chinese Archaeology, Lithic Analysis and Comparative Analysis.
    ** Zhu Shiguang(朱 士 光), Professor, Northwest Institute of Historical Environment and Socio-Economic Development, Shaanxi Normal University.

Ancient Capital Studies.

Keywords: Chinese archaeology; Chinese ancient capitals study; ancient capital; ancient city

1. Research on Archaeological Excavations of Ancient Capitals: The Highlight of China's Archaeological Achievements in the Past Hundred Years

Modern Chinese archaeology was born a hundred years ago, from October 2 to December 1, 1921, when the Swedish geologist Andersson, then working at the Geological Survey Institute of the Ministry of Agriculture and Commerce of the Beiyang Government, and the Chinese geologist Fuli Yuan carried out archaeological excavations in Yangshao Village in Mianchi County, Henan Province, naming it the Yangshao Culture as an iconic archaeological culture of the Neolithic Age in China. As of October 2021, Chinese archaeology has gone through 100 years of arduous and painstaking work. Under the guidance of the State Administration of Cultural Heritage (SACH), the Chinese Archaeological Society (CAAS) and the China Cultural Relics Newspaper (CCRN) jointly hosted the selection and promotion activity of the "Hundred Years of Archaeological Discoveries" on the occasion of commemorating the brilliant achievements made by Chinese archaeology in the past 100 years in order to pay tribute to the past and encourage the future generations. In this activity, 100 important archaeological projects have been selected after two rounds of selection from the 321 projects recommended by the cultural relics management departments and archaeological research institutions in all provinces, municipalities and autonomous regions. The selection results have been published on *China Cultural Relics Newspaper* (the 5th to 16th edition; November 5, 2021), which is very pleasantly surprised. As a quasi-beginner of Chinese archaeology, after carefully reading the brief introduction and comments of the 100 selected projects, I found that among the 100 major archaeological discoveries, there are 23 projects related to the archaeology of ancient Chinese capitals, and 17 projects related to the archaeology of ancient capitals, which add up to 40 projects (see Table 1), accounting for two-fifths of China's century-long 100 major archaeological discoveries. This is certainly the most influential of the thousands of archaeological discoveries in China over the past hundred years, and if we add the fact that many of the unlisted archaeological discoveries involve ancient capitals and metropolitan sites, the number of discoveries would be even greater and the list would be even longer.

Table 1　Archaeological projects of ancient Chinese capitals and center cities mentioned in China's Hundred-year Archaeological Projects

Period	Nature and number of the sites	Archaeological Project	Period	Nature and number of the sites	Archaeological Project
Neolithic	Ancient center city (5)	Taosi site in Xiangfen, Shanxi	West and East Zhou	Ancient center city (3)	Tomb of the King of Zhongshan state in Pingshan, Hebei
		Niuheliang site in Chaoyang, Liaoning			Jinsha site in Chengdu, Sichuan
		Liangzhu site in Yuhang, Zhejiang			Zhouyuan site in Baoji, Shaanxi
		Shuanghuaishu site in Gongyi, Henan	Qin-Han	Ancient capital (3)	Xianyang city of Qin in Shaanxi
		Shimao site in Shenmu, Shaanxi			Chang'an city of Han in Shaanxi
Xia-Shang	Ancient capital (2)	Shangcheng site in Zhengzhou, Henan			Goguryeo King city, King's mausoleum and site, burials in Ji'an, Jilin
		Anyang Yinxu		Ancient center city (5)	Tomb group of Chu Kings of Han Dynasty in Xuzhou, Jiangsu
	Ancient center city (4)	Erlitou site in Yanshi, Henan			Marquis Haihun's tomb of the Western Han Dynasty in Jiangxi.
		Shangcheng site in Yanshi, Henan			Ruins of the offices and King's tomb of the Nanyue State in Guangzhou, Guangdong
		Panlongcheng site in Huangpi, Hubei			Niya site in Minfeng, Xinjiang
		Sanxingdui site in Guanghan, Sichuan			Shizhaishan tomb groups in Jinning, Yunnan

continued

Period	Nature and number of the sites	Archaeological Project
West and East Zhou	Ancient capital (9)	Liulihe site in Beijing
		Yanxiadu site in Yixian, Hebei
		The cemetery of the Marquis of Jin and Qucun-Tianma site in Linfen, Shanxi
		Jin Sate site in Houma, Shanxi
		Qi old city in Linzi, Shandong
		Lu old city in Qufu, Shandong
		King site of East Zhou in Luoyang, Henan
		Fenghao site in Xi'an, Shaanxi
		Yongcheng site in Fengxiang, Shaanxi
Three Kingdoms to Sui and Tang	Ancient center city (5)	Yecheng site in Linzhang, Hebei and Northern Dynasty tomb groups in Cixian, Hebei
		Longquan Prefecture of Shangjing of Bohai state in Heilongjiang
		Luoyang city site of the Han and Wei Dynasties in Henan
		Luoyang city site of the Sui and Tang Dynasties in Henan
		Daming Palace site in Shaanxi
Song, Liao, Jin and Yuan Dynasties	Ancient capitals (4)	Shangjing site of Liao Dynasty, Inner Mongolia
		Xanadu site of Yuan Dynasty, Inner Mongolia
		Huining Prefecture of Shangjing of Jin Dynasty in Heilongjiang
		Lin'an Prefecture site and official kilns of South Song Dynasty in Hangzhou, Zhejiang

In terms of the 40 selected projects of the top 100 archaeological discoveries in China over the past century, as listed in Table 1, they fully demonstrate the significant role played by the ancient capitals and cities with important strategic significance in the historical development, as well as the importance of their excavation and research in the development of Chinese archaeology. It can also be said that the excavation and research on the ancient capitals and cities is an indispensable part of the excavation and research process of Chinese archaeology, and at the same time highlight that the archaeological excavation and research on ancient capitals are indeed the dazzling highlights of China's century of archaeological achievements!

2. The Excavation and Research Results of the Ancient Chinese Capitals and the Chinese Ancient Capital Cities Study

China has a long history of statehood. Over the course of its extensive 5,000-year development, dynasties have frequently changed and political powers have repeatedly risen and fallen. As a result, numerous political centers of various dynasties and regimes—known as capitals—have emerged across the vast expanse of the Chinese territory. Nianhai Shi, a renowned scholar of ancient Chinese capitals and one of the founders of the China Ancient Capital Society, meticulously sorted and counted the various types of ancient capitals in China in his article "An overview of ancient Chinese Capitals." According to his definition, in a broad sense, there have been as many as 217 ancient capitals since the Three Dynasties (Shi, 1998). Later scholars, including the author of this paper, have continued to add to this list. Facing hundreds of ancient capitals in China, scholars of past dynasties have recorded and discussed them. Famous historical texts such as "*Historical Records* (史记)" and "*Hanshu* (汉书)" contain relevant accounts, and there are even specialized works dedicated to discussing ancient capitals, such as "*Annals of Chang'an* (长安志)," "*Research on the City Layout of the Two Capitals of the Tang Dynasty* (唐两京城防考)," "*Maps and Illustrations of the Three Assistant Prefectures* (三辅黄图)" "*Records of the Buddhist Temples in Luoyang* (洛阳伽蓝记)" "*Dreams of Splendor in the Eastern Capital* (东都梦华录)" "*Records of the Ruins of Bianjing* (汴京遗迹志)" and "*A Chronicle of Capital Cities Throughout the Ages* (历代宅京记)". These historical materials are extremely rich and indeed contain many records of ancient capital ruins from previous dynasties.

In fact, since the birth of modern Chinese archaeology in 1921, many archaeologists have conducted research on the archaeological excavations of some ancient capitals in China, publishing a series of works that have significantly advanced the study of ancient

Chinese capitals. This prompted Nianhai Shi to propose the establishment of the Ancient Chinese Capitals Study at the Third Academic Annual Meeting of the China Ancient Capital Society held in Luoyang in the autumn of 1985. He highly praised the rapid progress and outstanding achievements of Chinese archaeology, with some ancient capitals occupying a prominent position among the archaeological achievements. These excavations and studies have gradually revealed the scale of many ancient capitals in their heyday, which is indeed invaluable. Thus, the excavation and research achievements of Chinese archaeology have long played a promotional role in the establishment and development of the ancient Chinese capitals study, and this role has been recognized by the academic community. Moreover, after a century of development in Chinese archaeology, this role has become even more prominent. Specifically, the excavation and research achievements of Chinese archaeology over the past century have promoted the establishment and development of the ancient Chinese capitals study mainly in the following three ways.

(1) It provides a large number of accurate and precise material data and evidence for the ancient capitals that have relatively specific records in the historical books and are familiar to people. All the archaeological excavation and research reports involving ancient capitals accurately indicate the location and characteristics of the capitals and their forms, structures, and scales based on the excavation results. These reports are mostly equipped with plane maps. Some plane maps of capitals not only indicate the location and shape of each component of the capital, but also indicate the scale size, so that readers can clearly understand the overall layout of the capital and the specific situation of each building. It is more visual and intuitive than the historical records, providing the first-hand and accurate material data and evidence for people to carry out further in-depth research.

(2) For a number of ancient capitals that have a lack of historical records or incomplete descriptions in the period of Xia, Shang Dynasties, and even earlier times, the relevant archaeological excavations and research results have made significant contributions to filling the gaps. There are many examples of this, and the Erlitou site and Shangcheng site in Yanshi, Henan (河南偃师二里头遗址、商城遗址), the Panlongcheng site in Huangpi, Hubei (湖北黄陂盘龙城遗址), the Sanxingdui site in Guanghan, Sichuan (四川广汉三星堆遗址), as well as the Neolithic sites like Taosi site in Xiangfen, Shanxi (山西襄汾陶寺遗址), the Niuheliang site in Chaoyang, Liaoning (辽宁朝阳牛河梁遗址), the Liangzhu site in Yuhang, Zhejiang (浙江余杭良渚遗址), the Shuanghuaishu site in Gongyi, Henan (河南巩义双槐树遗址), and the Shimao site in Shenmu, Shaanxi (陕西神木石峁遗址), have all been selected as the top 100 archaeological discoveries of the century. There are also many other archaeological sites that have not been selected as part of the top 100 archaeological discoveries of the century, especially for capitals of fedual

states and border regions of various ethnic groups during the Xia, Shang, Western and
Eastern Zhou, Spring and Autumn, and Warring States periods. In recent years, some of
these capitals have also been discovered through archaeological excavations. As far as I
know, there is the Xue State ancient city site in Tengzhou City, Shandong Province (山东
滕州薛国古城遗址) that has existed for more than 1500 years through the Xia, Shang,
and Zhou periods (Liu, 2021). There is also the discovery of a Dian King's tomb in Muyi
Village, Guangnan County, Yunnan Province (云南省广南县牧宜村滇王墓) that reveals
the mysterious veil of the ancient state of Quting (句町古国) and its capital in the
southwestern region of Guizhou and Yunnan during the Han Dynasty. There is also the
ancient capital of the Julan State in Jiuzhou Town, Huangping County, Guizhou Province
(贵州省黄平县旧州镇且兰古国都邑). The capital of the ancient state of Guge in Zanda
County, Xizang Autonomous Region (西藏自治区札达县古格王国都邑) from the mid-
9th century to the mid-17th century spanning over 800 years has also been discovered
(Zhang, 2019). The academic community knows very little about these ancient capitals of
feudal states and border regions of various ethnic groups because they were either built
long times ago, or because they were located in remote areas, or were got little or
incomplete historical recordings. It is because of archaeological excavations and research
that revealed the identifies and values of these ancient capitals.

(3) A large number of archaeological excavations and research results on ancient
capitals have revealed new clues for exploring ancient capitals. Among the top 100
archaeological discoveries selected to celebrate the significant achievements of the past
century of Chinese archaeology, in addition to the 40 project names listed in Table 1, there
are also some projects that contain the content of ancient capitals. For example, the sites at
Chengziya in Zhangqiu, Shandong Province (山东章丘城子崖遗址), Qujialing and
Shijiahe in Jingmen and Tianmen, Hubei Province (湖北荆门屈家岭与天门石家河遗址),
and Chengtoushan in Lixian, Hunan Province (湖南澧县城头山遗址), all have quite
large ancient city sites. The Chengziya site has been proved to be "a center of power,
economy, and culture, with the characteristics of early states"; the Qujialing site has been
inferred to be "highly hierarchical, with a large scale, complete structure, strong cultural
continuity, and profound influence"; the Shijiahe site has been determined to be "the
longest-lasting, largest-scale, and highest-level prehistoric urban settlement group in the
middle reaches of the Yangtze River"; and the Chengtoutuan site has been determined to
be "the earliest and most well-preserved ancient city site with extremely rich content
found so far in China. As the earliest city in China, Chengtoushan is the initial coordinate
of the origin of Chinese civilization" (Chinese Cultural Relics Newspaper, 2021). From
the authoritative content of the above-mentioned arguments, these Neolithic ancient city
sites actually had the nature and function of political centers in a certain region at that

time, and they have the characteristics of the emergence of ancient Chinese capitals. They should also be studied as research objects of Ancient Chinese Capitals, so that the origin and complete development process of ancient Chinese capitals can be explored.

It should also be pointed out that among the top 100 archaeological discoveries in the past century of Chinese archaeology, there is another type of sites, such as the Tombs of the Guo State in Sanmenxia, Henan Province (河南三门峡虢国墓地) during the West and East Zhou period and the Tomb group of the Marquis Zeng in Suizhou, Hubei Province (湖北随州曾侯墓群). Although these sites are only the "large duke state-level cemetery" of the Guo State and the "marquis state-level burial site" of the Zeng State, their excavation and research results have also provided clues for exploring the capitals of the Guo and Zeng states and other feudal states. It is possible to find their political centers through ground survey and focused excavation in the nearby areas.

3. Enlightenments of the Major Achievements of Chinese Archeology in the Past Century to the Development of Chinese Ancient Capitals Study

In the development process of Chinese archeology in the past century, the archeological excavation and research of the capitals of all times in more than 5000 years and the previous Neolithic sites with urban characteristics occupy a very important position, and have achieved convincing academic achievements. Therefore, Wei Wang, the director of the Chinese Archaeological Society, wrote in the article "100 major archeological discoveries in 100 years to show the brilliant Chinese civilization" to commemorate the 100th anniversary of the birth of modern Chinese archeology, explained that the century-old archeology has played a major role in exploring the origin and formation of Chinese civilization, demonstrating the civilization of the Three Dynasties, revealing the formation and development of a unified multi-ethnic country, and these three aspects are mainly exemplified by some ancient urban settlements, cities and capitals that have been listed in this article (Wang, 2021). Therefore, it highlights the academic value and practical significance of Chinese Ancient Capitals study. It is also a great encouragement and inspiration to the academia of Chinese ancient capitals researches! This inspired and enlightened me to put forward some opinions on the further development of Chinese Ancient Capitals Study for academic colleagues to consider and practice.

(1) More fully and extensively combine archeologists' excavation and research results, we should focus on conducting in-depth and comprehensive research from the following three aspects. Firstly, we should conduct further research on the capitals of the

main Chinese dynasties from the Xia, Shang, and Zhou dynasties, through the Qin, Han, Sui, Tang dynasties, to the Song, Yuan, Ming, and Qing dynasties. Secondly, we should conduct traceability research on a number of Neolithic settlements and cities with urban characteristics before the Three Dynasties. Thirdly, we should conduct pioneering research on the capitals built by various ethnic groups in the border regions around the Central Plain in ancient times, and comprehensively promote in-depth research on large numbers of ancient capitals in Chinese history. When conducting in-depth and comprehensive research on ancient capitals and settlements and cities with urban characteristics, it is best for the scholars of Chinese Ancient Capitals Study and archaeologists to cooperate and collaborate with each other for research.

(2) Carry out further in-depth research on the patterns and principles for the planning and layout of ancient Chinese capitals. Although many Chinese and foreign scholars have conducted certain investigation and research in this field, more in-depth research is still needed. Future efforts can be carried out in two aspects: On the one hand, we can learn from the research ideas of archaeologists. For example, Weichao Yu once divided the ancient Chinese capitals into several stages in his article "The staged development of the planning of ancient Chinese capitals - for the Fifth Annual Meeting of the Chinese Archaeological Society". These stages include: Shang and West Zhou; East Zhou to West and East Han; North City of capital Ye in Cao-Wei period to dual capitals of Sui and Tang; Bianliang in North Song to Beijing in Ming and Qing. He discussed the planning characteristics and formation reasons of ancient Chinese capitals in each stage, as well as their process of change (Yu, 1985). This clearly provides us with valuable reference for further in-depth discussion of the planning of ancient Chinese capitals. On the other hand, in this field of research, we can also consider cooperating with archaeologists and ancient architects to explore how to restore the representative buildings of some important ancient capitals, making the research on the planning and construction of ancient Chinese capitals more stereoscopic and intuitive.

(3) Continue to build deep-level interpretations of the theoretical framework of the discipline of Chinese Ancient Capitals Studies. According to the consensus in the academic community, the formation and development of a discipline must be guided by the theoretical foundation of that discipline. At the same time, as the discipline continues to develop, it will also make positive contributions to enriching and deepening the theoretical construction of the discipline itself. Since the establishment of Chinese Ancient Capitals Studies advocated by Nianhai Shi at the Third Academic Annual Meeting of the Chinese Ancient Capitals Society in Luoyang in autumn 1985, I have enthusiastically engaged in this emerging discipline due to opportunities. During this period, I have also done some exploratory work on the theoretical construction of the discipline. For

example, in my article "Proposals for the Theoretical Construction of Chinese Ancient Capitals Studies" published in 2005, I put forward some insights on strengthening the theoretical construction of Chinese Ancient Capitals Studies, including paying attention to the nature and tasks of Chinese Ancient Capitals Studies, deeply grasping the disciplinary characteristics of Chinese Ancient Capitals Studies, appropriately focusing on the hierarchical nature of the disciplinary composition of Chinese Ancient Capitals Studies and the corresponding hierarchy of the theoretical systems, etc. (Zhu, 2005); I also proposed in several other related papers that to carry out theoretical construction of Chinese Ancient Capitals Studies, we should start with the macro-geographical situation of the regions where ancient capitals are located and the micro-geographical characteristics inside and outside ancient capital cities, and combine them with regional culture, architectural culture of ancient capitals, and institutional culture involving the development and evolution of ancient capitals. We should conduct comprehensive research, sublimate and condense ancient capital culture, so as to promote more profound and fruitful achievements in theoretical construction of Chinese ancient capitals studies (Zhu, 2004; Zhu, 1990).

Retelling the past is, of course, to plan for the future. Although the theoretical construction of Chinese Ancient Capitals Studies has made considerable progress with the joint efforts of scholars in the academic community, further development is still needed in the future. Therefore, we should fully rely on the rich research results of the excavation of ancient capitals and ancient capitals provided by the development of one hundred years of archaeology. We should conduct in-depth discussions on the location characteristics of these ancient capitals and capital cities, as well as their geographical characteristics inside and outside the city walls, their planning, layout characteristics, and architectural styles, from the theoretical perspective of the discipline. This will undoubtedly add new connotations to the theoretical construction of Chinese Ancient Capitals Studies and enhance its theoretical level.

Reference

Liu, L (刘丽). Elements Reflecting the Fusion of Yi and Xia in Bronze Wares Discovered in the Capital City of Xue State (薛国故城出土青铜器中的夷夏融合元素). *China Cultural Relics Newspaper* (中国文物报), 2021-08-17(6).

Shi, N (史念海). Introduction to China's Ancient Capitals (中国古都概论). *Ancient Capitals and Culture of China* (中国古都和文化). Beijing: Zhonghua Book Company (北京：中华书局), 1998.

Top 100 Archaeological Discoveries of the Century (百年百大考古发现). *China*

Cultural Relics Newspaper (中国文物报), 2021-11-05(8-9).

Wang, W (王巍). Top 100 Archaeological Discoveries of the Century, Showcasing the Brilliance of Chinese Civilization (百年百大考古发现 展示辉煌中华文明). *China Cultural Relics Newspaper* (中国文物报), 2021-11-05(5-6).

Yu, W (俞伟超). The Staged Development of the Planning of Ancient Chinese capitals : for the Fifth Annual Meeting of the Chinese Archaeological Society (中国古代都城规划的发展阶段性——为中国考古学会第五次年会而作). *Cultural Relics* (文物), 1985(2): 52-60.

Zhang, J (张建林). *The Secret Land: in Search of the Vanished Guge Civilization* (秘境之国——寻找消失的古格文明). Xi'an: Northwest University Press (西安:西北大学出版社), 2019.

Zhu, S (朱士光). A View of the Relationship between China's Ancient Capitals and Chinese Culture (论中国古都学与中华文化研究之关系). *Journal of Shaanxi Normal University: Philosophy and Social Sciences Edition* [陕西师范大学学报(哲学社会科学版)], 2004 (1): 26-31.

Zhu, S (朱士光). Commentary on the Theory Construction of the Science of Ancient Capital in China (中国古都学理论建设刍议). *Journal of Chinese Historical Geography* (中国历史地理论丛), 2005(1): 133-135.

Zhu, S (朱士光). The Current Situation and Prospect of Chinese Ancient Capital Studies (中国古都学研究的现状与展望). *Journal of Chinese Historical Geography* (中国历史地理论丛), 1990(1): 1-8 .